APPROACHES TO EXCHANGE RATE POLICY
Choices for Developing and
Transition Economies

Approaches to Exchange Rate Policy
Choices for Developing and
Transition Economies

Editors

Richard C. Barth
Chorng-Huey Wong

HG
3877
.A67
1994

Papers presented at the seminar on
exchange rate policies in developing and transition economies
December 3–11, 1992

IMF Institute
International Monetary Fund
Washington, D.C.

© 1994 International Monetary Fund

Library of Congress Cataloging-in-Publication Data

Approaches to exchange rate policy : choices for developing and transition economies / IMF institute: Richard C. Barth and Chorng-Huey Wong, editors.
    p. cm.
    "Papers presented at the seminar on exchange rate policies in developing and transition economies. Dec. 3–11, 1992."
    Includes bibliographical references.
    ISBN 1-55775-364-4
    1. Foreign exchange—Government policy—Developing countries—Congresses.   2. Foreign exchange—Government policy—Europe, Eastern—Congresses.   3. Foreign exchange—Government policy—Europe, Eastern—Congress.   4. Foreign exchange rates—Developing countries—Congresses.   5. Foreign exchange rates—Central Europe—Congresses.   6. Foreign exchange rates—Europe Eastern—Congresses.   I. IMF Institute.   II. Barth, Richard C.   III. Wong, Chorng-Huey.
HG3877 .A67 1994   94-3937
332.4'562'091724—dc20   CIP

The cover, charts, and interior of this publication were designed and produced by the IMF Graphics Section

Price: US$22.00
(US$20.00 to full-time faculty members and sstudents at universities and colleges)

Please send orders to:
International Monetary Fund, Publication Services
700 19th Street, N.W., Washington, D.C. 20431, U.S.A.
Tel.: (202) 623-7430   Telefax: (202) 623-7201

Preface

This volume is the first published set of proceedings from one of the IMF Institute's seminars. The seminars are designed to provide a forum where high-level officials from member countries can discuss issues of current interest with IMF staff and outside lecturers, and also among themselves. The Institute tries to include in the seminar program leading theoreticians and researchers, as well as practitioners who can present individual case studies, in order to ensure that each subject is approached from both the conceptual and the practical sides. General discussions serve the purpose of associating the participants more closely with the seminar by giving them an opportunity to relate the presentations to their own countries' experiences.

The seminar on Exchange Rate Policy in Developing and Transition Economies was presented in Washington on December 3–11, 1992 for senior officials from 35 countries. Events themselves pressed the Institute to choose this important topic. External sector policies in general, and exchange rate policy in particular, are central both to a country's economic performance and to IMF surveillance functions. In recent years, a number of developing countries have attempted to liberalize their external sector policies and adapt their exchange rate systems to a rapidly changing international environment, in part by adopting measures designed to achieve currency convertibility. At the same time, countries in Eastern and Central Europe, the Baltics, and the former Soviet Union have begun entering into new monetary and exchange arrangements, often as a part of IMF-supported macroeconomic adjustment and structural reform programs. The seminar covered both types of policy initiatives, with the purpose of highlighting common themes and problems.

Like the seminar itself, the sections in this volume include presentations on specific topics, followed by commentaries and discussion, and proceed from theoretical issues to actual country experiences. The papers are the best evidence of the variety of topics discussed in the seminar and the diversity of views expressed there. In the final session, however, there was general agreement with two principles spelled out by Michael Mussa, Director of the IMF Research Department, namely (1) that it is impossible to maintain an exchange rate policy independent of other key elements of economic policy, in particular monetary policy, but also fiscal and trade policies; and (2) that "one size does not fit all," because exchange rate policy must take into account not only the nature of a country's economy, but also any existing constraints on domestic economic policy. In the subsequent discussion, participants agreed on a third principle—that transparency is key to an effective exchange rate policy in the long term. This principle argues, among other things, for the adoption of a single exchange rate.

One caveat is in order here: in the time that has elapsed between the seminar and the publication of this book, many institutional changes have taken place that are not reflected in the papers. Czechoslovakia is now two separate entities. Many countries have their own national currencies, and the European Community has become the European Union. For the most part, references in these papers to monies and political units are current as of the end of 1992, unless otherwise noted.

As in many of its regular activities, the IMF Institute relies heavily on other departments of the IMF for its seminar program. A glance at the table of contents of this volume shows that this seminar was no exception. Special thanks is also due to Chorng-Huey Wong of the Institute, who organized the seminar and served as moderator. It is important to remember, however, that neither the seminar nor the book would have been possible without the interest and cooperation of all the participants.

Patrick de Fontenay, *Director*
IMF Institute

Acknowledgments

Many people contributed to the success of the seminar on Exchange Rate Policy in Developing and Transition Economies and to the ensuing book. Much of the credit belongs to our colleagues in the IMF and World Bank who participated in the seminar. In addition, Liam Ebrill, Thomas Reichman, and Tessa van der Willigen helped review some of the case studies. Pat Bielaski transcribed the tapes of the seminar, and Evelyn McClung typed the manuscripts. Emily Chalmers provided editorial assistance and saw the volume through production. And finally, the authors gave generously of their time in revising the material presented at the seminar.

Guillermo Calvo and Carlos Végh's "Inflation Stablization and Nominal Anchors" was originally published in *Contemporary Economic Policy* (formerly *Contemporary Policy Issues*) in April 1994. W. Max Corden's "Exchange Rate Policy in Developing Countries" first appeared in *Trade Theory and Economic Reform: North, South, and East*, edited by Jaime DeMelo and Andre Sapier (Oxford: Basil Blackwell, 1991). And Sebastian Edwards' "Exchange Rate Misalignment in Developing Countries" appeared in *The World Bank Research Observer* (January 1989). These articles are reprinted by kind permission of the publishers.

Richard C. Barth
Chorng-Huey Wong
IMF Institute

Table of Contents

PART III
Experiences with Alternative Exchange Rate Systems

PART I

Opening Address and Introduction

Opening Address

Michel Camdessus

This seminar is particularly timely in view of the fact that countries in Eastern Europe and the former Soviet Union are in the process of establishing or securing new monetary and exchange arrangements, while many developing countries are actively pursuing external sector liberalization and moving toward currency convertibility.

What guidelines should these countries be using in the design of their monetary and exchange arrangements and their exchange rate policies? This is among the questions you will be considering over the next week or so. I am sure you would agree that good monetary and exchange arrangements are those that help secure the two objectives of macroeconomic stability—domestic price stability together with sustainable internal and external imbalances—and the efficient allocation of financial and real resources. Thus there should be workable arrangements for the effective conduct of monetary policy in pursuit of its paramount objective, price stability. But monetary and exchange arrangements should also facilitate the economy's adjustment to internal and external shocks and promote allocative efficiency. In the context of allocative efficiency, it is natural to stress the importance of an open, multilateral system of payments, together with a liberal trade regime, because the promotion of such a system is one of the most important purposes of the IMF. Openness will help to ensure that the domestic economy is subject to the discipline of international competition and that domestic prices are in line with world prices.

Let me now say a few words about the particular problems faced by transition economies, particularly those in Eastern Europe and the former Soviet Union. While embarking on the transformation process, these countries have been encumbered with their inheritance from the previous system, which includes, among other things, distortions and restrictions in international payments and trade; widespread domestic price controls, with prices distorted and insensitive to market forces; large macroeconomic imbalances; low official foreign exchange reserves; and large excess money balances that represent repressed inflation. When introducing new monetary and exchange arrangements in pursuit of the objectives to which I have referred, the authorities in these countries have had to make delicate strategic choices.

One set of strategic choices concerns the adoption of currency convertibility and the resolution of problems with payments arrangements among the former centrally planned economies. I am glad to say that in the countries of Eastern Europe, a substantial degree of currency convertibility has been established. In the former Soviet Union, a substantial degree of convertibility has been established in the Baltic states, and current account convertibility is a policy objective of the Russian authorities recognized in Russia's current arrangement with the IMF. However, I would emphasize that substantial problems remain to be resolved in payments arrangements between the states; I shall return to these in a moment, in the context of the ruble area.

Another set of issues relates to the choice of an exchange rate regime, the conduct of monetary policy, and the connection between the two. As we have all observed, the initial stage of the transformation process brings especially virulent inflationary pressures, the result of price liberalization against a background of monetary overhang. In order to fight inflation effectively, monetary policy needs to be tight and supported by fiscal policy. It is also helpful if there is an intermediate target on which to focus.

For transition economies that have a strong fiscal position, adequate foreign exchange reserves, and a credible central bank, I believe there is something to be said for pegging the exchange rate to a hard international currency in the early stage of the transition. But if these conditions are not met, premature attempts to peg may, when they fail, actually diminish the credibility of the authorities' policy intentions. Thus, it is not surprising that the former centrally planned economies have adopted a variety of exchange rate regimes, depending upon what is feasible in individual country circumstances.

For countries without an exchange rate peg, a nominal anchor must be sought elsewhere, primarily in targets for monetary growth, and supported by appropriate fiscal targets and incomes policy. But even in a flexible exchange rate system, the exchange rate itself should play a role, because it will be an important indicator of domestic monetary conditions (such an arrangement is specified in our agreement with Russia, for example). Let me emphasize here that official intervention in the foreign exchange market is likely to have only limited usefulness in countering exchange market pressure unless that intervention is accompanied by changes in monetary conditions. As monetary authorities in the established market economies have found, intervention can help to stabilize disorderly market conditions and to signal the stance of monetary and fiscal policies but is unlikely, on its own, to have a sustained effect on the exchange rate. It is amazing to see how leaders and commentators are frequently mistaken on this point and how they believe in the magic of intervention—that good intervention can do a lot. So I hope you will not be disappointed if I tell you that at the end of this seminar you will not be able to go back to your countries with the magic trick of intervention in your pockets.

A word about the ruble area. The recent agreement at the Bishkek Heads of State meeting was a welcome step forward, but a clarification of policies is still urgently needed. It is essential for those staying in the ruble area that effective and workable arrangements for the coordination of monetary and exchange policies be established. The lack of monetary cooperation inside the area has led to extensive trade restrictions and a major shrinkage of interstate trade that has been a primary factor in the decline in output. Moreover, without improved monetary cooperation inside the area, it will be difficult, if not impossible, to reduce inflation and stabilize the ruble. I would also emphasize that countries choosing to exercise their legitimate right to withdraw from the area must recognize that a decision to adopt a separate currency does not reduce the need for fiscal and monetary discipline or for cooperation with the countries staying in the area. Countries that choose to leave the area must also do so in a way that minimizes the disruption of trade and payments arrangements: it is in the interests of all that the common economic space be preserved.

Let me turn now to some of the more general issues on exchange rate policy in developing countries. Two decades have passed since the breakdown of the Bretton Woods system. Over this period, we have witnessed economic disturbances that have made economic adjustment in developing countries most complex and challenging. At the same time, countries have gained experience in formulating adjustment programs under different circumstances. In the area of exchange rate policy, it is clear from the experience of many developing countries that exchange rate flexibility can help in maintaining international competitiveness and thus ensure a viable balance of payments position. In cases where imbalances are large, exchange rate changes can play a role in correcting the underlying cost-price distortions and limiting the cost of adjustment in terms of forgone output. To be effective, an exchange rate action in such a situation must be supported by restrictive monetary and fiscal policy and by appropriate structural measures. The IMF has been giving increasing attention to structural problems, because more and more we have discovered that good monetary and fiscal policies cannot do the job if the structural rigidities are not addressed.

The role of the exchange rate seems to be more problematic in the case of countries seeking to stabilize after a protracted history of inflation and financial imbalances. In such cases, a fixed or stable nominal exchange rate can serve a useful role as an anchor for price stability, both by providing a benchmark for price level expectations and by serving as a highly visible signal of the authorities' commitment to financial discipline. However, as in the transition economies, such a strategy requires not only a firm resolve to maintain sound financial policies but also the availability of the means to defend the exchange rate, in the form of exchange reserves or access to external funds.

Developing countries have also learned some lessons in using exchange rate rules. In particular, it has been found that rigid adherence to a real exchange rate target may prove destabilizing, not only because of the usual problems associated with indexation, but also because of the difficulties inherent in identifying the equilibrium real exchange rate and the fact that this rate moves over time in response to domestic and external shocks.

I have not spoken about exchange rate policy in major industrialized countries and the IMF's systemic responsibilities, because these are beyond the scope of the seminar. But I have alluded to exchange rate issues in the industrial countries, and I hope I have convinced you that their problems and the susceptibility of their officials to mistakes in this area are basically the same as yours. As you know, the subject of exchange rates is at the core of the IMF's responsibilities. It is important for us to ensure that the IMF is helping its members in an appropriate way to deal with the problems confronting them in changing circumstances.

Introduction

Patrick de Fontenay

Let me again welcome all of you and thank you for your participation in this seminar. Every year the IMF Institute holds a seminar for high-level officials that offers them, among other things, an opportunity to discuss important issues. Experience has shown that this exchange of views is probably one of the most valuable aspects of the seminar. As participants, you will learn as much from talking to one another and discussing common problems and experiences as you will from listening to the lecturers, good as they may be. And this year, this exchange of views will be even more stimulating than it has been in the past, since in the last year the IMF has become a truly universal institution: nearly all the world's countries are now members.

As our Managing Director has pointed out, this year's topic is one that lies at the core of the IMF's responsibilities. Wide swings have taken place in both the theory and practice of exchange rate policy. After the breakdown of the Bretton Woods system, floating not only became respectable but was recommended by many academics, and a number of countries adopted floating regimes. But after some years, disillusion set in about the effects of floating, leading to a return to more stable exchange rates. This trend was particularly strong in Europe, which was making great progress toward a fixed exchange rate system and common currency until the turmoil of the last month. Now the mood is changing again. It is interesting that the Nordic countries (except Denmark), which had for a long time followed a flexible exchange rate policy and then decided to peg their currencies to the European currency unit (ECU) or another strong currency, have in the past few weeks abandoned pegging and gone back to floating. It was also interesting to hear Bundesbank President Helmut Schlesinger observe that the European Monetary System (EMS) is encouraging speculation. This is almost an echo of the German criticism of the Bretton Woods system as an engine of inflation. Maybe Wolf-Dieter Donecker can tell us more about the German position on the EMS and exchange rate arrangements.

It is not surprising that in this confusion, developing and transition economies have adopted various exchange rate regimes and policies. You will have ample opportunity to discuss their experiences during the seminar.

Is there an IMF doctrine on exchange rate policy? Under Bretton Woods, there was a very clear one: exchange rates were fixed but adjustable—in fact, they had to be adjusted if there was a structural disequilibrium—and in theory they could not be changed without the IMF's agreement. Since the breakdown of Bretton Woods and the adoption of the Second Amendment to the Articles of Agreement, however, the IMF has followed Article IV, which sets out the general obligations of members. According to the Article, members shall

(i) endeavor to direct economic and financial policies toward the objective of fostering orderly economic growth with reasonable price stability;

(ii) seek to promote stability by fostering orderly underlying economic and financial conditions and a monetary system that does not tend to produce erratic disruptions;

(iii) avoid manipulating exchange rates or the international monetary system in order to prevent effective balance of payments adjustments or to gain an unfair comparative advantage over other members; and

(iv) follow exchange policies compatible with the undertakings under this Section.

The second section of Article IV states that all IMF members are free to choose their own exchange rate system: their only obligation is to notify the IMF. Section 3 concerns IMF surveillance over exchange rate policies. The Executive Board of the IMF elaborated on Section 3 through a decision made in 1977 that adopted "Principles for the Guidance of Members' Exchange Rate Policies" (Guidelines for Surveillance).

Both the Articles and the Guidelines are couched in fairly broad terms that are open to interpretation. One example is the reference in the Guidelines to the obligation to intervene in the exchange market to counter "disorderly conditions." Shortly after the Guidelines were adopted, "disorderly conditions" was interpreted as meaning a change in the effective exchange rate of more than 1 percent in one day. Today, 1 percent is a fairly small change; it is not infrequent to see exchange rates change 2–3 percent in one day. Theory follows the practice and realities of the market.

The IMF puts perhaps greater emphasis on another aspect of exchange rate policy: the convertibility and maintenance of a multilateral exchange rate and payments system. You probably know that surveillance and consultation missions with the membership derive from the old Article VIII under the original Articles of Agreement. Initially, the purpose of the annual consultations—which continue to this day under Article IV—was to make sure that members were in a position to maintain the convertibility of their currencies. Convertibility has always been a concern because it is the basis of a multilateral payments system. IMF surveillance has in part been aimed at ensuring that conditions conducive to maintaining convertibility are present and at encouraging countries to remove any remaining restrictions on current payments. It is interesting that neither the original Articles nor the subsequent revision says very much about capital transactions. Members are under no formal obligation to remove restrictions on capital movements. At the same time—and again, practice and theory have moved together—the IMF has supported recent efforts by a number of countries to liberalize and remove restrictions on capital movements.

PART II

Exchange Rate Policy and Economic Adjustment

The Choice of an Exchange Rate Regime 1

Manuel Guitián

I. Introduction

Exchange rate management, which is among the most discussed economic policy subjects, is one on which a consensus is hard to gather. To a large extent, this state of affairs reflects the complex interrelationship between exchange rate management and domestic economic policy, as well as the importance of these two policy areas for economic performance.

Some contentious points come to mind in the context of the seminar. Its very title, *Exchange Rate Policies in Developing and Transition Economies*, provides a good illustration of the absence of consensus that I have just mentioned. The title conveys, at least by implication, the idea that exchange rate policy varies or can vary depending on the type of economy. I, for one, do not think such a proposition is valid. Certainly, the workings of a particular exchange rate policy or regime depend on (and will differ with) the characteristics of the economy in which it is being pursued or established. But the fundamental tenets of exchange rate policy itself apply to any and all types of economy. Yet the notion that there are exchange rate policies that apply to or are more appropriate for only one type of economy is fairly widespread.[1] My own impression is that there is a unity, a *oneness*, to exchange rate policy which can get lost in arguments that describe this important policy area as if it acted differently in different economies. Therefore, although the seminar focuses on developing and reforming economies, the major issues I will raise and the main points I will make in my remarks have wider applicability.

Exchange rate management has numerous dimensions and can be viewed from many perspectives. Most, if not all, of them can be classified into two broad categories: the *macroeconomic aspect*, which

Note: In preparing these remarks, I have relied extensively on a large amount of research and policy work in the exchange rate management area conducted by the IMF over a long period of time. And with regard to various specific sections in this paper, I have drawn on a previous lecture given last October at the Joint Vienna Institute; see Guitián (1992a).

[1]For example, this is the case in much of the work published by the International Monetary Fund: see, among others, Aghevli, Khan, and Montiel (1991); Frenkel, Goldstein, and Masson (1991); Corden (1990); and Balassa (1987).

is concerned with issues of domestic financial stability; and the *microeconomic aspect*, which focuses instead on the question of the international competitiveness of the economy. Much of the absence of consensus that I noted at the outset reflects the prevalence of intellectual or analytical positions that stress one or the other of these two aspects. Those who focus on the macroeconomic dimensions of exchange rate policy emphasize the importance of establishing a clear and credible anchor as one element of a policy strategy aimed at domestic price level stability, a nominal variable. Although the argument is nowadays phrased in terms of the role of the exchange rate as a nominal anchor, it nevertheless addresses an age-old concern. The reasoning underlying the usefulness of this type of nominal anchor—or of the pursuit of hard currency options—closely parallels the case made in earlier periods for the exchange rate's important role in ensuring discipline in domestic financial management.[2]

In contrast, those who focus on the microeconomic dimensions of exchange rate policy stress the importance of maintaining international competitiveness in any economy. The argument points accurately to the need in open economies to keep a viable, sound balance of payments position, a need that requires those economies to be and remain competitive or, in other words, to pursue an exchange rate policy geared to a real variable. This line of reasoning can also be traced far back in the literature on exchange rates.

Indeed, these two different perspectives or angles are modern versions of the relative weight given in the classical potential conflict between domestic and foreign conditions or exigencies to the attainment of *internal balance* (price level stability with sustainable employment and growth rates) as opposed to *external balance* (balance of payments viability).[3] An important difference between current and previous analyses, though, is the international setting in which they take place. A prominent feature of present discussions of exchange rate management, and more generally, of domestic economic policies, is the presence of a closely interdependent world economic

---

[2]For an enlightening discussion of this subject, see Friedman (1953). In presenting what is generally acknowledged as a classical statement of the case for flexible exchange rates, Friedman lists arguments that view the exchange rate as an indicator of inflation and that consider this variable a constraint on a government's ability to undertake inflationary actions. Friedman, of course, proceeds to present a case against this type of reasoning, but there can be no doubt that the logic of such lines of thought is equivalent to what lies behind modern discussions of exchange rate anchors and hard currency policy options: see also, in this general context, Johnson (1973, chapter 8).

[3]For an excellent analysis of this subject, see Mundell (1968, chapter 11).

space. Trade and current account flows, which have been increasingly liberalized over the past four decades, have linked national economies, but perhaps more importantly, the growing international capital movements that have been progressively freed during the last ten years have strengthened and consolidated those links. As a result, the permeability of national boundaries has increased markedly, to the detriment of their ability to keep national economic domains separate.[4] Consequently, although conflicts between internal and external balance or stability can and do continue to arise, their potential duration is becoming increasingly limited—a feature of the current world economic setting that warrants attention from the standpoint of economic policy formulation in general and from the perspective of the choice of an exchange rate regime in particular.

The plan of my remarks will be the following: Section II focuses on the nature of and the main considerations involved in the choice of an exchange rate regime. Section III examines the implications of this choice for the design and implementation of domestic economic policy; in turn, this examination provides the basis for a discussion of the dilemmas that must be confronted when selecting an exchange rate system (Section IV). The linkage of exchange rate management with other domestic policies and the consequent dilemmas are considered from the standpoint of currency convertibility, a concept that has acquired renewed interest with the prospective integration into the international system of the previously centrally planned economies (Section V). Finally, the central points and their relevance for developing and reforming economies are laid out as concluding remarks in Section VI. Table 1 outlines schematically various types of existing exchange rate arrangements.

II. Making the Choice

The choice of an exchange rate regime revolves around two crucial issues: the relationship of national economies to the global system and the degree of activism envisaged for domestic economic policies. With regard to the first issue, the choice of an exchange rate regime amounts to the expression of a national preference for either an open

---

[4]For a recent discussion of the consequences for economic policy of the predominance of capital flows, see Guitián (1992b) and Corden (1990). And a discussion of the relevance of porous national boundaries for the design and implementation of economic policy can be found in Guitián (1992c, section II).

Table 1: Types of Exchange Rate Regimes

Basically Fixed Regimes: Pegged Exchange Rates

- Vis-à-vis a single currency: economies that peg to major international currencies with no or rare parity adjustments; economies that announce a prearranged schedule of exchange rate adjustments against the currency of the peg (the exchange rate changes, but at a fixed pace).

- Vis-à-vis a currency basket: economies that peg to a basket of currencies of their main trading partners or to standardized currency composites such as the European currency unit (ECU) or the SDR.

- Within pre-established margins: economies that peg to a single currency or a currency basket within certain (typically narrow) margins.

- Fixed but adjustable peg: the arrangement that prevailed under the Bretton Woods par value system.

Basically Flexible Regimes: Adjustable and Flexible Exchange Rates

- Indicators: economies that adjust their currencies automatically to changes in selected indicators, such as developments in the real effective exchange rate.

- Managed float: economies that adjust their exchange rates frequently on the basis of judgments made following developments in variables such as reserves and the payments position.

- Independent float: economies that let markets and market forces determine the exchange rates for their currencies.

or a closed system. The interaction of national economies can be described as consisting of two basic elements: the *point of intersection*, represented by the balance of payments; and the *terms of intersection*, represented by the existing exchange arrangements, in particular the exchange rate regime. Both elements are, of course, interdependent, as any economic relationship between a quantity variable (balance of payments flows) and a price variable (exchange rate, exchange regime) must be.

The available choices for exchange rate systems lean either toward a fixed exchange rate and/or a flexible exchange rate. The connection I make between this choice and the preference for an open or closed system is based on the following considerations. Selecting a *fixed exchange rate arrangement* is equivalent to accepting a constraint on national economic policies. Of all the combinations of domestic economic policy stances and mixes that a country, taken in isolation, can in principle adopt, a fixed exchange rate most effectively limits the range of possibilities. The country will be able to adopt only those policy combinations consistent with maintaining the fixed exchange rate; domestic policy formulation thus becomes endogenous and subject to the exchange rate commitment. In a nutshell, this option is tantamount to placing an *international constraint on national economic policies*. In this generic sense, the choice of a fixed exchange rate regime is equivalent to a preference for an open system, in that no insulation is sought from the interactions between the national component and the world system.

In contrast, a *flexible exchange rate arrangement*, in principle, indicates a desire to accept no constraint on the pursuit of any particular domestic economic policy package. Whatever the effects of the policies undertaken may be, exchange rate fluctuations will keep them within the domestic domain. And correspondingly, whatever the consequences for the national economy of policies elsewhere, exchange rate adjustments will keep them outside the domestic domain. In fact, this option is tantamount to keeping *national economic policy free from international constraints*. In this broad sense, the preference for a flexible exchange regime reveals a corresponding preference for a closed system, in that the exchange rate arrangement that has been chosen will insulate the national economy from the international environment.

Therefore, the issue at stake in the choice of an exchange rate regime goes well beyond the technical aspects of exchange rate management. In effect, it entails a preference for internationally or nationally based systems and reflects the relative importance given to international and national considerations and objectives. The types of interaction between the part and the whole that will develop under a fixed or a flexible exchange rate are quite different. Under the former, the effects of internal and external policy impacts and shocks will be disseminated across the system at large. Under the latter, in contrast, each component of the international system remains insulated so that policy impacts and shocks do not carry across national boundaries.

Let me now discuss the issue of the degree of activism envisaged or sought for domestic economic policies. The differences on this score are quite marked. A fixed exchange rate, because it represents a commitment that sets a constraint (as already noted) on national policies means that domestic economic policies cannot be pursued independently. This is a feature typical of open systems, which, because of the inevitability of leakages, cannot but discourage independent action. A flexible exchange rate, in contrast, is a policy instrument that can be used to keep the scope of domestic policy action unconstrained by the economy's participation in the international system. Accordingly, national policies can be pursued actively without concern for the outside world, and this arrangement is therefore akin, in its basic features, to a closed system.[5]

So far, I have described the nature of and the considerations involved in the choice of an exchange rate regime in the broadest of senses, because I believe it is in that context that relevant issues must be considered. There are, however, other criteria to guide the choice, and I now turn to these.

The criteria in question are technical in character and focus on the following three issues: the types of disturbance to which economies are exposed, the structural characteristics of those economies, and the commonality of the risks to which they are subject and the objectives that they pursue.[6] Conventional wisdom relates the comparative advantage of the two exchange rate regimes to the *types of disturbances* to which the economy is most likely to be subject. Formal analyses conducted on the basis of a downwardly rigid cost-price model of output determination exhibit the insulating properties of a market-determined flexible exchange rate when an economy experiences *external nominal shocks*. Whatever effects these shocks could have had on the foreign price level have been countered by compensating changes in the exchange rate, shielding the domestic economy from the disturbance.[7]

As for *domestic disturbances*, the traditional line of reasoning distinguishes them as either real or nominal in nature, on the grounds that this is the relevant distinction for purposes of choosing an exchange rate regime. *Domestic nominal shocks*, such as those originating from money market imbalances, are best handled under a fixed exchange rate system. For example, a disturbance that creates an

[5]The analogy carries in the following sense: a possible definition of a closed economy is one in which national income and expenditure, *ex post*, must coincide. A flexible exchange rate, if not tampered with and in the absence of capital flows, will ensure that balance obtains in the current account of the balance of payments, rendering national expenditure and income equal; see Guitián (1973).

[6]For fuller discussions, see Aghevli, Khan, and Montiel (1991); Flood and Marion (1991); and Frankel (1992). A collection of interesting articles discussing technical and empirical aspects of the choice of exchange rate regime will be found in Argy and De Grauwe (1990).

[7]See Friedman (1953) for an incisive analysis of these issues. I will point out here that the justification for using a downwardly rigid model of prices is that, to quote Friedman, if "internal prices were as flexible as exchange rates, it would make little economic difference whether adjustments were brought about by changes in exchange rates or by equivalent changes in internal prices. But this condition is clearly not fulfilled" (p. 165).

excess supply of domestic currency will lead to a balance of payments deficit that will restore balance to the money market through international reserve losses; the disturbance, in these circumstances, does not spill over to the real economy, which is protected by the fixed exchange rate regime. In contrast, *domestic real shocks*, such as those from imbalances in the goods market, are best coped with under a flexible exchange rate arrangement, because shocks to domestic demand will lead to changes in the exchange rate that will bring about offsetting movements in foreign demand, so that domestic output is not severely affected.

Interesting though these analytical findings are likely to be, the reality is that all economies confront both nominal and real shocks. Yet a shift in exchange rate regime in response to the nature of shocks is clearly an unworkable proposition. Apart from the uncertainty such a variable course of action would entail, there is the pragmatic issue of determining the nature of the disturbance affecting the economy, not always an easy task. In purely practical terms, selecting an exchange rate regime on this basis is far less suitable, despite the conceptual validity of this distinction.[8]

A second set of considerations to guide the choice between exchange rate regimes focuses on the *structural characteristics of the economies* in question. These considerations, developed in an effort to ascertain the scope of an optimum currency area, focus on the degree of mobility of labor (and more generally, of factors of production) among the various economies in the system—that is, on a measure of *economic openness* in terms of the markets for production inputs. The established conclusion is that a high degree of mobility of factors of production advocates in favor of the use of a fixed exchange rate. The reasoning has been extended to openness in terms of (and to the diversity of product mix in) the market for goods and services to lead to the same conclusion: open economies with these characteristics are better off fixing the rate of exchange.[9]

A third set of considerations with a bearing on the choice of exchange rate regime stresses the extent to which national economies

---

[8]It has been argued that since both nominal and real shocks afflict all economies, the best choice is an exchange rate regime that exhibits an intermediate degree of flexibility (see Flood and Marion (1991)). I am not persuaded by this reasoning, which implies that *average* suboptimal responses to both types of shocks are preferable to optimal responses to one type of disturbance combined with subpar suboptimal responses to the other type of shock. This is, of course, an empirical question.

[9]The classic article on the subject of optimum currency area is by Mundell (1961), and the analysis was subsequently extended by McKinnon (1963) and Kenen (1969); see, for a brief summary of the various intellectual strands, Guitián (1988).

either share *common policy aims*, exhibit *similar policy attitudes*, or both. The reasoning in this context leads of course to the inference that the more (less) common the policy objectives and the more (less) similar the policy attitudes, the more efficient a fixed (flexible) exchange rate regime will be.

In contrast, those systems based on the structural (openness) or attitudinal (commonality of objectives and policies) characteristics of economies are more operational. It is indeed possible to determine the openness of an economy, just as it is to ascertain how widespread and widely shared are its policy instruments and objectives. And consequently, criteria such as these can be (and have been) used to select an exchange rate arrangement.[10]

Fundamentally, all these various sets of criteria (including, to a certain extent, those based on the nature of shocks) can be subsumed in the more general considerations of the choice between open and closed systems. International mobility, openness, and common aims, all of which advocate for fixed exchange rates, are typical features of an open system. In contrast, their absence, which favors flexible exchange rates, is representative of closed systems.

III. Ramifications for Economic Policy

In order to illustrate the differences between the two types of exchange regimes, this section traces the relationship between exchange rate management and other domestic economic policies in the context of the correction of imbalances. In the domain of economic policy, establishing and maintaining appropriate economic incentives in general and price incentives in particular are of great relevance, if at times controversial. Their relevance, and also their contentiousness, reflect the complexities and difficulties involved in designing and implementing policy actions that affect key variables in the economy, such as the exchange rate or the structure of interest rates. They also reflect the critical role these variables play in allocating resources among economic sectors and agents.

At times, caveats are voiced concerning the dangers of undue reliance on price signals as the main instrument to guide resource allocation and use. These caveats typically stress the notion that price incentives place too much emphasis on the role of market forces and

---

[10]For example, goods, factors of production, market openness, and commonality of aims—as well as policy—are behind the establishment of the exchange rate mechanism (ERM) of the European Monetary System (EMS). Absence of factors of production—in particular, labor mobility—and different policies and aims are behind the independent float among Europe, Japan, and the United States.

private enterprises. Yet the issue to be confronted is the need to ensure that economic decision making is based on the accurately measured opportunity cost of scarce resources. For this purpose, prices are relevant to all economies and to all decision makers. The acknowledgment that the pricing system serves a central function based on the interplay of market forces has become increasingly accepted over the last decade, as more and more countries have come to realize that keeping an appropriate structure of relative prices and costs in the economy contributes directly to its productive capacity and efficiency.

Generally, domestic imbalances can be traced to the pursuit of macroeconomic policies that are not compatible with the economy's potential level and rate of growth of production. Such imbalances, unless corrected promptly, result in movements of domestic prices and costs that diverge from those occurring abroad. As a consequence, the economy's ability to compete internationally is put at risk, and the efficiency of domestic resource allocation is impaired by the emergence of distortions in the structure of relative prices. When circumstances such as these are allowed to persist, inflation and balance of payments pressures build up, and the rate of growth soon falters.

Among the possible means of correcting situations of this nature is the well-known option of an exchange rate adjustment, be it policy induced (as would be the case in a fixed exchange rate regime) or market determined (as would be the case under a flexible exchange rate arrangement). Exchange rate adjustments are highly visible events, and as such they can lead to controversy and resistance. The typical conceptual rationalization of such resistance is the argument that an imbalance created by inadequate domestic macroeconomic management should be rectified by correcting macroeconomic policy. In the abstract, this reasoning is correct. But whether or not a policy strategy that excludes exchange rate adjustments is superior from an efficiency and welfare standpoint to one that includes them is a question that cannot be settled a priori.[11] A theoretical proposition of great importance in this context warrants stressing: there is no lasting trade-off between exchange rate adjustments and appropriate domestic financial policies. In the context of a flexible exchange rate, what this means is that exchange rate depreciations are no substitute for and cannot replace adequate policies. And in the context of a fixed exchange rate, the implication is that devaluation does not eliminate the need for domestic financial restraint. Exchange rate

---

[11] A point worth noting here is that the economic consequences of corrective policy packages that exclude exchange rate adjustments are not likely to coincide with those that include them. There is, of course, an empirical question involved here, which has already been discussed earlier (see the quotation from Milton Friedman in note 7 above).

adjustments, though, have a bearing on the degree of strictness in domestic policy.

As briefly noted earlier, when domestic prices and costs (or their rates of increase) are rigid in the downward direction, relying exclusively on domestic demand management to restore balance to the economy may be unnecessarily costly in terms of employment and output. The adjustment will require a decline in the level or rate of increase of domestic prices and costs relative to those prevailing abroad, and, with the postulated downward rigidity, such a decline will place the brunt of the adjustment on output and employment. In these circumstances, it has been argued, it would be more appropriate to accompany demand policy with an exchange rate adjustment.[12] This course of action does not require a decline in the domestic cost-price structure; relative price balance (i.e., competitiveness) is restored by raising the domestic currency price of internationally traded goods rather than by lowering the domestic price of nontraded goods.

These considerations illustrate the extent to which exchange rate management and macroeconomic policy are interrelated. But the association is closest between exchange rate and monetary management. This association will now be examined not only to bring out the limitations of each of these policies, but also to highlight their potential for mutual reinforcement. In the process, the appropriate variable for monetary management will be identified, an issue for which the presence or absence of an external constraint is of relevance, as is the type of exchange rate regime in effect.

From the perspective of the money market, there are two main sources of liquidity in an open economy: the credit extended by the central bank and, more broadly, by the banking system to the rest of the economy through purchases of domestic assets; and the supply of money that the banking system provides through purchases of international reserves and foreign assets.

For purposes of stabilization, balance is required in the money market, calling for the monetary expansions that actually take place to be commensurate with the growth in the demand for money. This is the flow equilibrium dimension of the money market, which has as a broad counterpart the prevalence of balance between expenditure

[12]Correction of an imbalance with no exchange rate adjustment requires, other things being equal, a relatively more stringent domestic policy stance than is called for when the strategy includes such an adjustment. How durable this trade-off is, though, depends on how often it is used. Acceptance of frequent devaluations to relax the degree of policy restrictiveness will erode the credibility of the strategy, tending to eliminate the trade-off or render it less favorable; see Guitián (1976).

and income in the economy. In addition to flow equilibrium, stabilization requires balance in the stocks in the system—that is, the actual and the desired stocks of money and international reserves must be equal. In the absence of such stock-flow balance, adjustments will take place that may call for policy action.

Absence of external constraint

In a hypothetical closed economy, there is only one source of liquidity: purchases of domestic assets by the central bank or the banking system at large. In this setting, an excess expansion of credit, or the existence of credit flows that surpass the rate at which the economy is willing to increase its money holdings, tend to raise expenditure over income. Prices and, temporarily, output increase as a result. The demand for cash balances rises with them, helping to restore balance to the money market and contribute to stability in the economy at large. This, of course, is the sequence of events only if the excess supply in the money market does not persist. Otherwise, prices continue rising (inflation takes off), and output stops growing as resources are fully employed. As a consequence, the persistent money market imbalance perpetuates inflation; if the degree of imbalance remains unchanged, so does inflation, because the value of the excess nominal money holdings is precisely eroded by given, constant price increases, and actual and real cash balances will once again coincide.

Conceptually, the closed economy can be compared with an open economy that operates under a freely fluctuating exchange rate regime, where the sources of liquidity are domestic *and* foreign asset purchases by the central bank or banking system. If the exchange rate is allowed to fluctuate freely on the basis of market forces, the central bank will not intervene in the foreign exchange market, and the link between foreign exchange flows and the money supply process will be severed. A money market imbalance in this setting, besides fueling inflation, creates excess demand for foreign exchange and pressure for an exchange rate depreciation. Price increases, rising output, and devaluations may correct the imbalance, but only if the causes do not persist. If they do, inflation will continue and depreciation will follow. In this scenario, the respective rates and the variability in both prices and the exchange rate are determined by the degree and variation of the imbalance in the money market.

In these two situations, the monetary authorities determine the nominal quantity of money, while the rest of the economy determines its real value. Any incipient or persistent differences between the two are eliminated either by a change in the price levels and exchange rate or by ongoing inflation and depreciation.

Presence of external constraint

In open economies with a fixed rate of exchange or with limited exchange rate flexibility, a link is established between the money supply and the balance of payments that must be taken into account in the formulation of monetary policy. In this setting, both the monetary authorities and the economy as a whole influence the nominal supply of money in the system through balance of payments outcomes that result from the interaction of policy with economic performance.

Achieving stability in open economies requires coincidence between domestic credit expansion and money demand growth, together with equilibrium in the balance of payments. These two factors are important because a given rate of growth in the demand for money is compatible with different balance of payments results, and therefore money market equilibrium need not coincide with external balance.

Transmission of monetary impulses

The channels through which monetary policy operates reflect the behavior of the different sectors in the economy. In general, as the latter grow, so does the demand for money, reflecting a decision by the community to devote part of its growing income and wealth to increasing its money balances. Resources are thus provided to the banking system, which channels them to finance activities where, for a time, outlays exceed income. In this way, saving and investment flows are brought together by bank intermediation. Whenever the banks expand credit in amounts that differ from those the holders of cash balances make available, prices, output, and the balance of payments adjust. Thus, in designing monetary policy, it is possible to render the monetary authorities' international reserve objectives compatible with the evolution of the demand for money in the economy. In this context, it has been argued that monetary policy in the open economy constitutes a powerful tool for aggregate demand and balance of payments management. This said, however, it should be pointed out that deviations of monetary policy from economic fundamentals cannot be sustained and that the effectiveness of monetary policy in this regard has often been overstressed.

Capital movements

The analysis so far has proceeded without considering capital account transactions, the introduction of which adds a market for domestic and foreign securities to the economy. The presence of capital flows, however, does not alter the relationships already discussed. If anything, it strengthens the link between domestic credit, the balance of payments, and the international reserve position. With capital mobility, for example, excessive domestic credit expansion relative to the growth in the demand for money will induce a current account deficit, a net capital outflow, and hence a decrease in net international reserves. The balance of payments thus continues to be one of the channels through which the supply of money is adjusted to demand. An important consequence of capital movements that warrants early mention is the intimate link they create between monetary and exchange rate policies. Any inconsistency between these two types of policy will be rapidly eliminated by the free flow of capital.

IV. Policy Interactions and Dilemmas

An important issue in the implementation of monetary policy in the context of any exchange rate regime is the type of instrument variable that should be used. A well-established tenet in this regard is that domestic credit expansion is the appropriate variable to monitor, as in open economies the money supply is outside the monetary authorities' control. The logic behind this tenet is that the rate of domestic credit expansion is closely linked to aggregate expenditure and demand. The demand for money, on the other hand, is related to income and wealth. Therefore, choosing domestic credit expansion as the monetary policy instrument is simply recognizing that the counterpart to an imbalance between credit and money increases is a discrepancy between expenditure and income flows.

Instances of excessive money growth due to external (foreign exchange) surpluses have stimulated arguments in favor of using the money supply as the policy instrument, a view also supported by the direct relationship between money and prices (a relationship, it must be noted, that keeps implicit the links between money and spending and between spending and prices). Clearly important in this context is determining whether the balance of payments surpluses are the result of an increase in the demand for money (in which case the resulting monetary growth could not be deemed excessive) or whether they are due to other factors (in which case policy dilemmas could arise, such as the need to choose between controlling inflation and maintaining competitiveness). The outcome of external surpluses or of unanticipated net capital inflows will, of course, depend on the exchange rate regime in existence, providing yet another illustration of the closeness between money and exchange rates.

A foreign exchange surplus develops following a sequence of events that depend on the nature of exchange arrangements. With a *fixed exchange rate*, both net international reserves and the money supply rise at a higher-than-anticipated rate. As already noted, no inflationary pressure need arise if the surplus is caused by money demand developments. In similar circumstances, but with a *flexible exchange rate*, there is no monetary expansion owing to the incipient balance of payments surplus. Instead, the exchange rate appreciates, and downward pressure is exerted on inflation or the price level. Credit and money developments coincide in these circumstances, but credit expansion is still the policy instrument used to keep expenditures under control. With a *partially flexible exchange rate*, a combination of the two above sequences of events takes place: some monetary expansion, a measure of exchange rate appreciation, and downward price pressure occur; net international reserves increase, but not at the same rate as the balance of payments surplus. Other things being equal, once the unexpected external outcome works itself throughout the economy, real cash balances will be the same in all situations. Nominal money balances, however, will differ: they will be highest in the economy with a fixed exchange rate and lowest in the economy with a freely fluctuating exchange rate.

When the external surplus is not the result of money demand developments, a different sequence of events unfolds. With a *fixed exchange rate*, the resulting monetary expansion is voluntarily held, expenditures rise (so that the surplus diminishes with a growing current account deficit), and prices tend to increase. With a *flexible exchange rate*, the exchange rate appreciation tends to eliminate the surplus. With *incomplete exchange rate flexibility*, some monetary expansion and upward price pressure take place, together with a measure of exchange rate appreciation.

The adjustment is not open ended, however. In the first (fixed exchange rate) case, pressure on aggregate demand and prices deflects more and more spending abroad, eliminating the impact of the foreign exchange surplus on the domestic money market. In the second (flexible exchange rate) case, exchange rate appreciation initiates diversion toward the rest of the world. In the third (intermediate) case, higher domestic prices and lower foreign prices (in domestic currency terms) divert outlays abroad. In all three cases, the various adjustments in the economy eliminate the foreign exchange surplus.

One conceivable by-product of unanticipated foreign exchange surpluses is that in the process of reacting to the disturbance, the exchange rate may become unrealistic and require direct adjustment, supporting adaptations of other economic policies, or both. An exchange rate appreciation is most likely to occur whenever the foreign exchange inflows do not respond to developments in fundamental economic factors but rather are a manifestation of inflation abroad.

When the initial situation is one of external and internal equilibrium, exchange rate appreciation caused by unexpected foreign exchange accumulation can pose a dilemma in terms of maintaining the competitiveness of the economy. When the magnitude and duration of the external inflow are limited, the extent of real exchange rate appreciation may be small or even negligible, requiring no specific policy reaction. However, should the inflows become significant or persist for a relatively long period, domestic policy adjustments will be required either to prevent an erosion of or to restore competitiveness. Preventive action to safeguard the economy's competitiveness in such circumstances requires early identification of disturbances (such as the foreign exchange inflow just described) so that they can be sterilized. In this case, low rates of domestic credit expansion relative to the growth in the demand for domestic cash balances can help to avert the erosion in competitiveness from the outset.

Such timely identification of a disturbance and its characteristics is unlikely, however, and in most instances the task of economic management will be to restore a lost margin of competitiveness. The goal of restoring competitiveness also calls for a policy of restraint in domestic credit expansion in relation to the growth in money demand in order to offset the price and exchange rate effects that the unanticipated external inflow has caused. As already discussed, the degree of actual restraint in domestic credit expansion will depend, among other things, on whether or not the policy mix includes an adjustment in the nominal exchange rate. While domestic credit and fiscal restraint are usually required in the presence of unanticipated capital inflows, they provide primarily short-run solutions. More fundamental changes in the economy are required, if the capital flows persist, to reestablish global balance. These changes must include some means of enhancing the economy's adaptability, mainly through flexibility in the markets for and prices of factors of production, particularly those for labor.

Related areas where adverse consequences from unexpected foreign exchange surpluses may arise are output and production. The sequence of events that unfolds in an economy experiencing an unanticipated foreign exchange surplus varies, depending on the nature of the surplus as well as on the prevailing exchange rate regime. To the extent that the foreign exchange surplus influences domestic expenditure levels, domestic prices and the exchange rate will be affected, and with them output and activity. Conceptually, it is possible to eliminate effects on output by postulating the existence of symmetry in the behavior of domestic prices and costs—that is, symmetry in the sense that such prices and costs can rise or fall with the same ease or, in other words, that supply price elasticities are the same when prices are rising and when they are falling. This presumption of symmetrical behavior in prices and costs permits the argument to overlook impacts on production, because, under these conditions, although output varies with movements in prices and costs in one direction, such a variation is virtually offset by equivalent price and cost movements in the opposite direction, so that the equilibrium level of output is not affected. As noted earlier, however, such a presumption does not always hold, and there is evidence that downward price and cost rigidities prevail in most economies. Under those circumstances, a process that restores balance to the economy through reductions in the level or the rate of increase of prices and costs is likely to entail output losses. This fact has led some authors to advocate exchange rate flexibility.

In essence, the dilemmas discussed in this section are but reflections of the two basic perspectives from which exchange rate policy is typically analyzed, its macroeconomic or its microeconomic aspects. Views on exchange rate management that reflect concerns over maintaining competitiveness or over output developments are based on the belief that exchange rate policy (supported, to be sure, by other domestic economic policies) can and should be used actively to attain real objectives. The implication here is that *real economic objectives* can be attained and maintained using *nominal policy instruments*. In addition, these views imply that nominal exchange rate adjustments have real effects durable enough to make them worth pursuing. It is worth recalling that this line of reasoning is based on the assumption that domestic prices and costs are rigid in the downward direction.

The alternative view of exchange rate policy, though equally concerned with competitiveness and output developments, is based on the proposition that nominal exchange rate adjustments do not lead to *sustained* real economic changes. This is an extension to the exchange rate domain of a disbelief in the existence of *money illusion*.[13] In other words, this view postulates that in circumstances requiring real economic adjustment (typically, a variation in output, employment, or real income), economic behavior that varies depending on the nominal policy instruments used cannot prevail for long. Consequently, proponents of this view argue that the best role for the exchange rate is to provide a nominal anchor for the economy as a means of attaining price stability or, more generally, keeping domestic price performance in line with the evolution of prices abroad. A development that gives credence to this view is the prevalence of wage indexing in inflationary settings. The potential for exchange

---

[13] This point has been insightfully and compactly made by Mundell in his "Monetary Dynamics of International Adjustment under Fixed and Flexible Exchange Rates" (1968, Chapter 11), as follows: "The argument is based on money illusion: the community is unwilling to accept variations in real income through changes in money prices, but it will accept the same changes in real income through adjustments in the exchange rate" (p. 152).

rate adjustments to influence real variables is rapidly eroded in the presence of indexed wages, because the resulting real wage rigidity severs any link between exchange rate changes and competitiveness.[14]

V. The Issue of Convertibility

The subjects of foreign exchange management and exchange rate policy that I have been discussing so far are fundamental components of any strategy aimed at economic stabilization, adjustment, or reform. Their importance is, of course, even larger in the context of strategies aimed at all three. In the process, it has become clear that besides playing a critical role in economic policy in general, foreign exchange management and exchange rate policy are inextricably linked to monetary management, both conceptually and in practice.

Now I will turn to a related subject, currency convertibility, which bears heavily on issues of foreign exchange management and has significant implications for exchange rate policy[15]. I will discuss the subject from three perspectives: that of the formerly socialist economies, that of the market-based economies, and that of the International Monetary Fund, for which exchange rate policy and exchange arrangements are a central part of its mandate and responsibilities.

At the time of the IMF's inception in the years just after World War II, full currency convertibility, important though it was, was not considered an urgent or immediate goal of economic policy. For well-known reasons, it was not until the late 1950s that the currencies of most industrial countries were given the status of convertibility. The reasons for the lengthy transition included the understandable focus on the immediate and urgent task of reconstruction, which took precedence over that of economic opening; the prevalence of extensive controls on and interference with international transactions, which required dismantling; and a belief in the importance and effectiveness of government policy, which tended to override the relevance of price signals as guides for economic behavior.

The first consideration, reconstruction, was clearly an urgent matter that had priority; economic policy, therefore, was aimed at and became subordinate to its attainment. The second consideration,

---

· [14]The consequences of wage indexation for the effectiveness of exchange rate changes have been amply discussed by Corden (1990).

[15]Currency convertibility is a subject that has recently regained widespread interest, particularly in the context of reforming economies. Analyses of convertibility will be found in Gilman (1990), Greene and Isard (1991), and Williamson (1991); but see also Polak (1991).

lifting controls and restrictions on international transactions, was not only an endeavor that contributed to the task of reconstruction (in that it helped increase the efficiency of economies) but an important ingredient of exchange rate policy and a step toward currency convertibility. This was the period of the Bretton Woods par value system, when exchange rates, though adjustable, were fixed; therefore, the elimination of controls on exchange transactions was equivalent to the introduction of currency convertibility. The third consideration, belief in the effectiveness of government policy, may also have influenced the speed and scope of convertibility. It was clearly behind the decision to confine convertibility to a limited set of transactions (those on current accounts).

The IMF actively sought the elimination of trade and other current account restrictions, a goal enshrined in its Articles of Agreement. The focus on current transactions was appropriate at the time, if only because of their predominance in the balance of payments. The era of dominant capital flows had yet to arrive, and member obligations under the Articles of Agreement extended only to current account convertibility.

At present, it is clear that the reforming economies place a higher priority on the introduction of currency convertibility as an economic policy aim than did the industrial countries of the postwar period, in at least two respects: timing (most of the transitional economies plan to make their currencies convertible in a relatively short time); and scope (they make less of a distinction between, and an implicit or explicit sequence of, current and capital transactions). In addition, capital movements have been increasingly liberalized in industrial and developing countries, so that the scope of de facto convertibility has broadened significantly.[16] In today's global economic environment, the notion of establishing currency convertibility promptly and with respect to all transactions seems eminently reasonable, particularly for those economies in the throes of reform, for several reasons. First, the previously centrally planned economies are engaged in a process of deep economic, political, and social transformation with two underlying themes or aims. One is the curtailment of the dominant role of the state or the government; the other, related aim is the move toward a free market and away from the controls and restrictions characteristic of central planning. From the standpoint of these aims, the case for establishing full convertibility during the early stages of reform is certainly strong. A convertible currency takes away much of the scope for discretionary government action

---

[16]For an extensive discussion of developments in international capital flows and their consequences for economic policies, see Guitián (1992b); see also Corden (1990).

on exchange rate policy and the exchange regime. It also implies the removal of exchange restrictions and controls over the international transactions required to integrate these economies with the international system.

This said, however, the adoption of convertibility does carry with it a number of important prerequisites that link it to the other areas of reform. Typical preconditions for the establishment of a convertible currency, besides the adoption of an appropriate exchange rate level or regime, include sound macroeconomic policies—that is, a set of domestic financial policies which, by keeping the level and growth rate of demand in the economy in line with developments in its productive capacity, ensure a sustainable balance of payments position and help maintain domestic price stability. These are aims of the reform process itself, and, if attained, they will pave the way for currency convertibility. Thus, effective reform is important to convertibility, and convertibility is also important to reform, because an appropriate exchange rate and a sound currency constitute the flip side of a sustainable balance of payments position. In addition, the proper environment for convertibility allows market incentives to guide economic behavior. Creating such an environment entails liberalizing prices and opening the economy—actions that are also essential components of the reform process. A third important prerequisite for convertibility is the availability of an adequate stock of international reserves. These reserves not only will allow the economy to withstand policy or exogenous shocks that could threaten convertibility but will buttress confidence in the exchange regime in general and the permanence of convertibility in particular.

Generally speaking, convertibility is best contemplated after an economy has been stabilized, liberalized, and opened up, and after it has accumulated a healthy stock of international reserves. This, of course, is a tall order—so tall, in fact, that waiting for these conditions to materialize may be the best prescription for never introducing convertibility. But an argument can also be made that there is no need to wait for such stringent conditions to be met. Currency convertibility at an early stage may help induce, or may even force, the adoption of sound macroeconomic policies, the liberalization of prices, and the opening of the economy. Under such circumstances, it is also likely that international reserve earnings will accumulate to further support the convertibility action.

At stake here is an age-old controversy on how to approach the presence of a constraint: one view contends that a constraint should not be imposed or accepted until conditions are right. An alternative view asserts that, on the contrary, it should be imposed and accepted before appropriate conditions develop, if only because its mere presence will bring about those conditions. The matter is one of balance, of course; the right approach is neither to wait for all conditions to be completely right nor to move ahead when they are clearly impossible. With subjects such as convertibility, the controversy can be seen in a variety of lights. To accept convertibility early on is to remove exchange rates and monetary policy from the realm of politics; to wait for the right conditions, in contrast, is to opt for discretion in policymaking and risk making policy a prey to politics. On the other hand, haste may impair sustainability—hence the need for balance in this matter.

Convertibility is typically understood to mean freedom to use or exchange a currency at a given exchange rate. And indeed, this is the clearest concept. But the notion of convertibility has further dimensions that can render it compatible with other than fixed exchange rate regimes. The most comprehensive concept of convertibility involves several criteria. A currency's convertibility implies that its holder may use it without restrictions for any purpose; it also implies that the currency can be exchanged freely for any other currency and that this exchange, as already noted, can always be made at a given exchange rate. Full convertibility obtains when these three criteria are met, but partial convertibility is also possible. In particular, different exchange rate regimes can be compatible with convertibility, although the broadest concept of convertibility operates with a fixed exchange rate.

In general, convertibility, interpreted as the ability of residents and nonresidents of a country to freely exchange domestic for foreign currency without limit, is consistent with any exchange regime that has exchange restrictions. This interpretation specifically includes a flexible exchange rate regime, which should, in principle, ease the introduction of convertibility, since conceptually such a regime needs no restrictions to support the exchange rate. In practice, however, few governments have been willing to give their currencies total freedom or to eschew the use of restrictions on international transactions. As is the case with the argument contending that exchange rate flexibility renders international reserves redundant—accurate in principle but unrealistic in practice—flexible exchange rates did not lead to convertibility because restrictions remained and did not become redundant.

VI. Conclusions

A variety of criteria can be used to justify the choice of a particular exchange rate regime. In this paper, I have argued that the process of making the decision is best served by following fundamental criteria that go beyond the purely technical characteristics of different exchange rate regimes. In this vein, my argument has been that the essence of the choice of a particular exchange arrangement lies in the national preferences it reflects.

One of these preferences corresponds to the decision to form part of an open system and the other to the perception that national economies, though interacting in an international system, derive more advantages by keeping themselves relatively closed. With a fixed exchange rate, an economy expresses its willingness to withstand the consequences of external shocks and disturbances and, correspondingly, to disseminate across the system at large the effects of its own domestic economic management. Under a fixed exchange rate regime, domestic policies become endogenous, and their effects are subject to leakages that substantially reduce the scope for divergence between national and international policies and objectives, if they do not eliminate it altogether. The large measure of economic interaction typical of open systems offers the prospect of enhancing individual component welfare, if on balance most governments pursue appropriate policies—that is, policies consistent with the constraints of interdependence. In such a setting, the costs of individual country policy errors are shared, as are the benefits of individual country policy efficiency. But these policies also raise the possibility of malfunction if countries do not focus sufficiently on the costs of their own policy shortcomings (because their dissemination across the system will tend to lower the incentive to avoid incurring such costs), concentrating instead on the benefits that can be derived from other countries' adept management. Such moral hazard and free rider syndromes plague open systems constantly.

The other course of action corresponds to deciding whether there are advantages to organizing national economic behavior on the basis of pre-established norms, or *rules*, which exceed the benefits that can be derived from the primary use of *discretion*. Here again, preference for a rules-based system leads toward fixed exchange rate regimes. Indeed, a fixed exchange rate is in itself a rule that exacts a measure of domestic policy consistent with the policies prevailing elsewhere. Such consistency is both a feature and a requirement of open systems, in that it implies giving precedence to maintenance of the rule over those national interests that would conflict with it.

The choice of flexible exchange rate arrangements exhibits the opposite preferences. This choice goes in the direction of keeping national economies relatively contained, closed, and insulated within the system as a whole. Rather than being based on the willingness to share, flexible exchange rates are based on the general philosophy that exchange rate flexibility will provide a shield against outer disturbances and a boundary to contain the effects of domestic policies, which typically are perceived to exceed in quality those abroad. This particular choice also indicates a preference for a system based on discretion rather than on rules. Each economy is seen as free to pursue its own national objectives rather than as obligated to constrain them to the exigencies of interdependence. The essence of this choice, in contrast to that involving fixed exchange rates, is the belief that it leaves each economy independent to handle its own affairs. The belief, of course, presupposes that linkages are limited and that vulnerability to external shocks can be contained.

These considerations bring to the forefront the difference between the two types of regimes that is perhaps most often mentioned: domestic economy policy dependence (fixed exchange rate) versus domestic economic policy independence (flexible exchange rate). There is, of course, a measure of validity in arguments that link flexible exchange rates with policy independence and the ability to pursue national objectives separate or different from those pursued in the system as a whole. It is less clear, though, that such independence can endure.

Clearly a country that, on balance, adopts and implements better policies than its neighbors most of the time will be well advised to opt for a flexible exchange rate, which permits a relatively closed economic attitude or discretion in economic policy. But just as clearly, there will be an incentive for those countries that generally pursue less appropriate policies to opt for a fixed exchange rate and establish a direct link to the well-managed economy, based on a well-defined and transparent rule. Thus, even if economies that exhibit good policy performance strive for independence, their method of attaining it may not be straightforward.

If, on the contrary, the economy opting for discretion and independence generally pursues less appropriate policies than its peers (and the key question here is why it would choose this course of action, which reins in the consequences of policy errors), limits to such independence and discretion are likely to arise rapidly, created by resource flows from the mismanaged to more stable economies. In such circumstances, using a flexible exchange rate regime to attain policy independence is likely to prove more successful in theory than in reality.

What this line of reasoning hints at is that limits to independence and national discretion exist, and that, in general, the possibilities for closing off a national economy within an integrated environment like that of the global economy are quite narrow. The choice of a flexible exchange regime gives an economy scope to diverge from the rest of the system only up to a point, and by not too large a margin. Floating exchange rates do not give full independence, and total dependence does not characterize a fixed exchange rate regime.

An issue that often crops up in this connection is the size of the economy. It is generally argued that relatively small countries can hardly benefit from a flexible rate, since developments in their economy are typically dominated by events in large countries. There is some truth in this reasoning, and to that extent it could be contended that flexible exchange rates provide little, if any, advantage to many developing and reforming economies. Of course, this line of reasoning presumes that, in general, the large economies display a relatively stable policy environment. This said, size, like the nature of the shocks, is a technical criterion unlikely to suffice as the basis for choosing an exchange rate regime. Rather, such technical criteria need to be accompanied by broader factors, such as the quality of economic management and the prevailing attitude toward open systems, in order to ensure an efficient choice.

References

Aghevli, Bijan B., Moshin S. Khan, and Peter J. Montiel. 1991. *Exchange Rate Policy in Developing Countries: Some Analytical Issues*. IMF Occasional Paper No. 78. Washington, D.C.: International Monetary Fund.

Argy, Victor, and Paul De Grauwe, eds. 1990. *Choosing an Exchange Rate Regime: The Challenge for Smaller Industrial Countries*. Washington, D.C.: International Monetary Fund.

Balassa, Bela. 1987. "Effects of Exchange Rate Changes in Developing Countries." *The Indian Journal of Economics* 68 (October): 203–21.

Corden, W. Max. 1990. "Exchange Rate Policy in Developing Countries." World Bank Working Paper WPS 412. Washington, D.C.: The World Bank.

Flood, Robert P., and Nancy P. Marion. 1991. "Exchange Rate Regime Choice." IMF Working Paper 91/90. Washington, D.C.: International Monetary Fund.

Frankel, Jeffrey A. 1992. "Monetary Regime Choices for a Semi-Open Economy." Paper presented to a conference on *Monetary Policy in Semi-Open Economies* in Seoul, Korea, November 6–7, 1992.

Frenkel, Jacob A., Morris Goldstein, and Paul R. Masson. 1991. *Characteristics of a Successful Exchange Rate System*. IMF Occasional Paper No. 82. Washington, D.C.: International Monetary Fund.

Friedman, Milton. 1953. *Essays in Positive Economics*. Chicago: University of Chicago Press.

Gilman, Martin G. 1990. "Heading for Currency Convertibility." *Finance and Development* 27 (September): 32–34.

Greene, Joshua E., and Peter Isard. 1991. *Currency Convertibility and the Transformation of Centrally Planned Economies*. IMF Occasional Paper 81. Washington, D.C.: International Monetary Fund.

Guitián, Manuel. 1973. "Credit Versus Money as an Instrument of Control." *IMF Staff Papers* 20 (November): 785–800.

——.1976. "The Effects of Changes in the Exchange Rate on Output, Prices, and the Balance of Payments." *Journal of International Economics* 6 (February): 65–74.

———.1988. "The European Monetary System: A Balance between Rules and Discretion." In *Policy Coordination in the European Monetary System*, IMF Occasional Paper No. 61. Washington, D.C.: International Monetary Fund.

———.1992a. "Monetary and Exchange Rate Policies for Stabilization and Reform." Paper presented to a seminar on *Transition and Adjustment* at the Joint Vienna Institute, October 5–8, 1992.

———.1992b. "Capital Account Liberalization: Bringing Policy in Line with Reality." Paper presented to a conference on *Monetary Policy in Semi-Open Economies* in Seoul, Korea, November 6–7, 1992.

———.1992c. *Rules and Discretion in International Economic Policy*. IMF Occasional Paper No. 97. Washington, D.C.: International Monetary Fund.

International Monetary Fund. 1992. *Developments in International Exchange and Payments Systems*. World Economic and Financial Surveys. Washington, D.C.

Johnson, Harry G. 1973. *Further Essays in Monetary Economics*. Cambridge, Mass.: Harvard University Press.

Kenen, Peter B. 1969. "The Theory of Optimal Currency Areas: An Eclectic View." In *Monetary Problems of the International Economy*, edited by Robert A. Mundell and Alexander K. Svoboda. Chicago: University of Chicago Press.

McKinnon, Ronald I. 1963. "Optimum Currency Areas." *American Economic Review* 51 (September): 717–25.

Mundell, Robert A. 1961. "A Theory of Optimal Currency Areas." *American Economic Review* 51 (September): 657–64.

———.1968. *International Economics*. New York: MacMillan Company.

Polak, Jacques J. 1991. "Convertibility: An Indispensable Element in the Transition Process in Eastern Europe." In *Currency Convertibility in Eastern Europe*, edited by John Williamson. Washington, D.C.: Institute for International Economics.

Williamson, John, ed. 1991. *Currency Convertibility in Eastern Europe*. Washington, D.C.: Institute for International Economics.

Comments

Anthony Lanyi

Manuel Guitián's paper reminded me of the opening sentences of Tolstoy's novel *Anna Karenina*, which begins this way: "All happy families are alike. Each unhappy family is unhappy in its own way." For indeed, Mr. Guitián's message is that there are two kinds of countries: the happy ones, which have fixed exchange rates and convertibility, open economies, and stable macroeconomic policies; and the unhappy ones, which have flexible exchange rates, are insulated from the international economy, and choose their own paths—more likely than not, those of financial ill-discipline and restriction.

Hindsight has taught me, however, that there may be just as many similarities between unhappy families as there are between happy families. In this sense, I have doubts about the linkage Mr. Guitián suggests between fixed exchange rates and openness and between flexible exchange rates and "closedness." I am not sure whether positing such a linkage is a normative or empirical statement. Yet it is interesting to consider what sort of correspondence exists between exchange arrangements and a measure of openness and "closedness."

Included in my discussion are all the IMF member countries, both developed and developing. My table shows the member countries (except for the 15 new members from the former Soviet Union) grouped by types of exchange rate regimes, as classified by the IMF. "Fixed" or "pegged" exchange rates are linked to either a single currency, the SDR, or a composite basket of currencies. "Limited flexibility" refers either to countries that participate in the European exchange rate mechanism (ERM) or to some states in the Middle East that peg their currencies to the U.S. dollar but allow for a wider range of flexibility. The "more flexible" group includes those countries with a managed float and those that adjust the value of their currency according to a set of indicators. And finally, there is the group of so-called "independently floating" countries.

In the left-hand column are two categories. One includes the countries that have accepted Sections 2, 3, and 4 of Article VIII of the IMF Articles of Agreement—that is, the commitments to maintain a current account regime free of restrictions, to avoid multiple currency practices, and to ensure "convertibility" in the sense the Articles

Exchange Rate Arrangements[1]

	FIXED RATES			LIMITED FLEXIBILITY[2]			MORE FLEXIBLE[3]			INDEPENDENT FLOAT			Total
	Countries	In percent of total	In percent of all members	Countries	In percent of total	In percent of all members	Countries	In percent of total	In percent of all members	Countries	In percent of total	In percent of all members	
Article XIV	52	63.4	32.7	0	0.0	0.0	18	66.7	11.3	16	45.7	10.1	86
Article VIII	30	36.6	18.9	15	100.0	9.4	9	33.3	5.7	19	54.3	11.9	73
Total	82	100.0	52.0	15	100.0	9.4	27	100.0	17.0	35	100.0	22.0	159

Sources: IMF, *International Financial Statistics* (September 1992), and IMF Secretary's Department
[1]Excluding Cambodia, for which no current information is available
[2]ERM, flexible single-currency peg
[3]Managed float; adjusted to indicators

suggest, which really means convertibility for current account trans-actions. However, I agree entirely with Mr. Guitián that the distinc-tion between current account convertibility and capital account con-vertibility, which may have been meaningful in the world of 1946, is not very meaningful in today's world of computers and interna-tionally integrated markets.

The other category of countries, the Article XIV countries, com-prises those that have not yet dared make the commitment to Sec-tions 2, 3, and 4 of Article VIII. They are not sure whether they want to keep their hands off various kinds of controls over current transac-tions or to commit themselves to never indulging in multiple ex-change rates.

The table shows that there is not necessarily a clear relationship between fixed rates and open economies. There are many economies—and have been for many years—that use current ac-count restrictions and import controls and that nevertheless find it convenient or useful to have fixed exchange rates. They do not dare open up their economies to convertible regimes. At the same time, many countries (and not just developed countries) have flexible rates and are nevertheless open economies in a meaningful sense: they have convertibility and do not restrict current or, in many cases, capital transactions. There are no apparent reasons why these coun-tries prefer to have flexible exchange rates. (Milton Friedman's argu-ment for flexible exchange rates, written back in the early 1950s, includes the thought that flexible exchange rates preclude the need for import controls and restrictions. Perhaps this argument is some-what dated in terms of liberalizing current and capital accounts, but it is still an interesting consideration.)

There is, of course, another factor at work in exchange rate sys-tems. The major players in the system are floating their currencies against each other, and it is very hard to imagine a world in which Germany, Japan, and the United States would commit themselves to rates fixed against each other. Such a world existed, of course, before 1971, but in today's circumstances, such a world would imply a kind of coordination of the economic policies of different countries that would be difficult to define (in terms of achieving an optimal result) and also, for political reasons, to implement.

My table suggests that most of the countries with fixed rates are, in fact, Article XIV, not Article VIII countries. Why have most Article XIV countries chosen fixed rates? Part of the reason, perhaps, lies in the conflict between different criteria. Mr. Guitián has mentioned two criteria: first, the need to achieve internal and external balance, and second, the desire to encourage international trade and investment through a stable exchange rate. Over the last three decades, a num-ber of the former colonial countries in Africa and South Asia that had heavily controlled trade and exchange regimes have chosen to fix their rates against the currency of either the former mother country, another large country, or a basket of currencies to assure stability in foreign trade and encourage the participation of investors from industrial countries. Another reason for the fixed rates may lie in the need to adapt to an international environment within which major currencies float against each other, world economic conditions are changeable, and countries want the freedom to adjust the value of their currencies when an unexpected shock occurs. If its currency is pegged to a composite, countries may prefer to describe themselves as "managed floaters" in order not to tie themselves down vis-à-vis the IMF or vis-à-vis its own residents, but the exchange regime may, in fact, be relatively stable.

In terms of the "technical" aspects of the choice of an exchange rate regime, there is, of course, a spectrum of regimes to choose from, ranging from fixed to completely market-determined floats. Countries may have a very clear idea where in the spectrum they would like to be, but even within each part of the spectrum important choices have to be made—for instance, between pegging and following some kind of managed flexibility with a rule. Some countries have considered these choices fairly important, for reasons particular to their economies or foreign trade situations.

Peter Wickham

Manuel Guitián's paper on the choice of an exchange rate regime provides much food for thought. My remarks will focus on parts of the paper that carry the arguments somewhat further than I would like.

Mr. Guitián's theme concerns two elements affecting the nature of the choice involved. The first is the relationship of national economies to the global system, the second the degree of activism envisaged for domestic economic policies. The paper characterizes a fixed exchange rate arrangement as reflecting a decision to be *open* to the global system by accepting an international constraint on national economic policies. This regime is seen as limiting the range or mix of domestic economic policies a country can adopt. On the other hand, the choice of a flexible exchange rate regime, at least in principle, reflects the desire for a more closed economic system with no international constraints on the adoption of domestic economic policies.

This argument has deep roots in the literature on the merits of fixed versus flexible exchange rates. In 1953, Milton Friedman argued strongly in favor of flexible exchange rates, which he said would allow each country to achieve "unrestricted free trade and the freedom . . . to pursue internal stability after its own lights."[1] An outgrowth of this argument was that flexible exchange rates had insulating capabilities, whereas (as Mr. Guitián argues) fixed rates implied that the effects of internal and external policy impacts and shocks would be disseminated across national boundaries. The question I wish to pose asks how far this characterization can be pushed. Countries as diverse as Canada, Bolivia, and The Gambia have floating exchange rates. Austria, Botswana, and Malaysia operate under pegged exchange rate arrangements. To what extent do these choices reflect the desire to remain an open or a closed system, to follow independent policies, or to insulate an economy from certain shocks?

I would agree with Mr. Guitián that the choice of an exchange rate regime must go beyond purely technical criteria to issues of a more normative nature, such as a government's reputation, credibility, and commitment. I am less comfortable with the characterization of the choice of regime as one involving preferences for openness and policy activism and would argue, as Mr. Guitián in fact does in his closing remarks, that the scope to indulge in insular preferences has narrowed over time and may be rather restricted in today's international environment. It has not, however, disappeared altogether.

Another way of viewing the difference between a floating and fixed exchange rate regime is to note that in the former, the money market clears through the float with an exogenous money supply, while in the latter, the market clears through an exogenous exchange rate with a fluctuating money supply. So in one sense we can view the choice of a floating rate as a vote for monetary "independence." But what does monetary or, more generally, financial policy independence and exchange rate flexibility buy, and does it also involve costs?

As I have already indicated, much of the early debate on this issue was based on the idea that floating rates could insulate an economy from certain outside disturbances, so that monetary policy could be directed toward short-run stabilization. However, subsequent analysis, which embraced the idea of closely integrated markets for financial capital, tended to undermine this idea. Over time, a standard classification emerged on the comparative advantage of fixed and floating exchange rates in dealing with various types of disturbances, but as Mr. Guitián suggests in his paper, it is difficult to apply the analysis operationally. For optimal exchange rate intervention, the authorities would need to have some idea of the size and frequency of various shocks (including covariance properties) and

[1]Milton Friedman, "The Case for Flexible Exchange Rates," in *Essays in Positive Economics* (Chicago: University of Chicago Press, 1953), pp. 157–203.

would have to extract information from movements in observable variables. But phenomena such as exchange rate overshooting and the poor track record of models in explaining exchange rate movements during the post-Bretton Woods period make the possibility of acquiring such information unlikely.

If the picture with regard to short-run stabilization remains controversial, other ramifications of exchange rate regimes are clearer. A floating or flexible exchange rate does provide for longer-run monetary autonomy and domestic price management. In a country with a floating rate, inflation is determined by domestic monetary policy. In a country with a fixed rate, however, inflation depends on the monetary policies of those countries sharing the common standard. In other words, a floating rate is arguably compatible with complete monetary autonomy, but a fixed exchange rate is not, since it depends on some form of explicit or implicit monetary harmonization with, or subordination to, foreign constraints on economic policy. In this limited sense, I am in agreement with Mr. Guitián's characterization of the nature of the two types of regimes.

But how can, and how should, the monetary autonomy a floating rate offers be exercised? In some cases, such autonomy has been exercised in ways that can be considered only as less than optimal or economically rational. At least one explanation of why the Bretton Woods system broke down and the major industrial countries began to float is that the United States, a key player in the cooperative game, began in the 1960s to pursue an expansionary monetary policy. This policy, which spilled over internationally, was at odds with the inflationary preferences of other important players. The float allowed Germany, for example, to close itself off and reassert its monetary sovereignty and control over the domestic inflation rate. On the other hand, Latin America provides numerous instances of governments adopting monetary policies (often closely linked to fiscal inadequacies) and generating rates of inflation totally inconsistent with any degree of stability in their exchange rates.

In light of the above, can it be argued that some countries would be better off subordinating control of a major policy instrument to external discipline by pegging their exchange rates? One problem with this solution is that a government too weak to follow a monetary policy capable of achieving a reasonable rate of inflation is likely to find it very difficult to submit itself to the monetary and fiscal discipline needed to maintain a fixed peg. Thus, even if the benefits of adopting a fixed peg are clear, the authorities may not be able to commit themselves credibly to it. This factor has led to difficulties in a number of countries that have attempted to bring down their inflation rates after inflationary episodes by pegging their exchange rates, a move that in effect sets up the exchange rate as a nominal anchor in stabilization programs. In such cases, the central bank lacks credibility, and it is often very difficult to convince the public that the authorities will not renege on their commitment to the new peg. This lack of trust is often reflected in high nominal (and hence real) interest rates, which can then depress investment and make fiscal adjustment more difficult. A further complicating factor is that inflationary inertia and the difficulties of changing inflationary expectations may make convergence of the domestic inflation rate with one consistent with the peg a somewhat protracted affair. The tendency for the real exchange rate to appreciate in such circumstances tends to further threaten the peg's credibility. A number of transition economies have faced similar dilemmas during stabilization episodes in the aftermath of price liberalization. Poland, for example, was able (aided by a stabilization fund and a significant devaluation) to use the exchange rate as a nominal anchor in the first stages of its stabilization and reform program. When inflation convergence remained elusive, the authorities moved to a crawling peg. Romania and Bulgaria, on the other hand, had neither high levels of foreign reserves nor a stabilization fund. Given the difficulties of establishing financial discipline in a reform environment, the governments did not view a fixed exchange rate peg as a viable option and so instituted floats instead.

A considerable number of countries continue to opt for some form of flexible exchange rate arrangement, suggesting that the requirements of inflation convergence and the loss of monetary sovereignty associated with a fixed peg are politically very difficult to accept. But how the issues I have been discussing interact with and are affected by the exchange regime is an area worthy of further analysis, particularly in light of the recent turmoil in currency markets.

Summary of Discussion

The discussion of Manuel Guitián's presentation centered on three main issues: the choice between a fixed nominal exchange rate regime and a regime that allows the nominal rate to be adjusted for inflation in order to maintain an unchanged real rate; considerations that would favor a flexible rate system; and the impact of destabilizing capital flows on the exchange rate. Opinion was divided on the choice between maintaining a fixed nominal or real rate. Since the equilibrium real rate is generally unknown, and since a number of participants were reluctant to endorse a policy of using the nominal exchange rate to obtain a real exchange rate objective, there was substantial support for a fixed nominal rate. On the other hand, it was thought likely that in the presence of large internal imbalances and minimal foreign exchange reserves, a fixed nominal rate would have to be changed soon after the initial peg, touching off expectations of further changes. In these circumstances, several speakers favored a fixed real rate.

Some viewed the exchange rate as a price that, like any other price, should be free to adjust to shifts in supply and demand. Proponents of this view regarded a fixed rate as interference with the market's rationing function. Opinion was again divided on when to use a floating arrangement: some felt it was best suited to situations in which domestic imbalances were large, but others thought a flexible rate without appropriate supporting domestic policies would lead to accelerating inflation and a vicious circle.

A related issue was the choice of a hard currency peg in a fixed rate arrangement. The consensus was that the appropriate choice would be the major currency most widely used in trade by the pegging country. It was also pointed out that two escape valves were available to countries choosing fixed nominal rates: temporary restrictions on current payments and the possibility of using IMF resources. Even if the fixed rate was not set at the equilibrium value, a country could, under some circumstances, avoid a devaluation.

Discussing the problem of destabilizing capital flows, participants noted that a country would probably not be able to defend a fixed parity in the presence of speculative capital flows without some assistance from other countries. The exchange rate mechanism (ERM) of the European Monetary System was cited as providing a good example of coordinated action (in this case, by France and Germany) to defend a currency (the franc) against a speculative attack by private capital. The central banks of France and Germany were able to handle the volume of private capital flows and maintain the currency alignment, despite the fact that monetary policies diverged among the ERM countries. Regarding the liberalization of the capital account in developing and transition economies, it was generally agreed that if opening the capital account would lead to a large outflow, it would be advisable to liberalize the capital account gradually.

Exchange Rate Misalignment in Developing Countries 2

Sebastian Edwards

In the past few years, exchange rates have attained great prominence in economic and policy discussion in developing countries. For example, it has been argued that the inappropriate exchange rate policies pursued by some countries in the late 1970s contributed to the international debt crisis of the early 1980s. According to the World Bank (1984), overvalued exchange rates in many African countries have resulted in a dramatic deterioration in agriculture and external accounts. Others have argued that exchange rate policy triggered the disappointing outcome of the Southern Cone (Argentina, Chile, and Uruguay) economic reforms and free market policies during the late 1970s.

One important exchange rate issue is whether a country's real exchange rate is out of line with respect to its long-run equilibrium level. There is general agreement that maintaining the real exchange rate at the "wrong" level results in significant welfare costs. It generates incorrect signals to economic agents and results in greater economic instability (Willet (1986)). If an exchange rate is indeed misaligned, there are alternative ways of correcting it. This raises the issue of effectiveness of *nominal* devaluations in restoring equilibrium in the *real* exchange rate.

The distinction between nominal and real exchange rates has become increasingly important. While the nominal exchange rate is a monetary concept that measures the relative price of two moneys, the real exchange rate measures the relative price of two goods. More specifically, the real exchange rate (RER), is defined as the relative price of tradables with respect to nontradables:[1]

Note: This article is a considerably shortened and revised version of chapters 1 and 2 of my book, *Exchange Rate Misalignment in Developing Countries*, (Baltimore: Johns Hopkins University Press for the World Bank, 1988). Both the article and book originated in a project on exchange rate policy in developing countries undertaken by the Country Policy Department of the World Bank in 1985–86. Armeane Choksi provided strong support for that project. Marcelo Selowsky read every draft of this paper and was relentless with his comments. Comments by Edgardo Barandiaran, Kathy Krumm, Alejandra Cox-Edwards, Farruq Iqbal, Miguel Savastano, Giacomo Luciani, Ruben Lamdany, and Man Walters are gratefully acknowledged.

[1] Although this definition is the most common one, there is still some confusion on what exactly people mean by the real exchange rate. See Edwards (1988 and 1989) on this subject.

$$\text{RER} = \frac{\text{Price of tradable goods}}{\text{Price of nontradable goods}} \tag{1}$$

The most important property of the RER is that it is a good proxy of a country's international competitiveness. A decline in the RER, or a *real exchange rate appreciation*, reflects an increase in the domestic cost of producing tradable goods. If there are no changes in relative prices in the rest of the world, this RER decline represents a deterioration of the country's international competitiveness: the country now produces tradable goods in a way that is less efficient than before, relative to the rest of the world. Symmetrically, an increase in the relative price of tradables represents an improvement in international competitiveness.[2]

Changes in competitiveness are sometimes "justified" by real events in the economy, such as technological progress, movements in external terms of trade, changes in taxation, and so on. These justified changes are an equilibrium phenomenon and do not require policy intervention. In some circumstances, however, there are "unjustified" departures of the actual RER from its equilibrium value, or disequilibrium changes, which have come to be known as RER *misalignments*. Distinguishing equilibrium movements from misalignments has become one of the greatest challenges for macroeconomic analysts. The sections that follow analyze in detail different aspects of equilibrium and disequilibrium real exchange rates.

I. Determinants of the Equilibrium Real Exchange Rate

The equilibrium RER is defined as the relative price of tradables to nontradables that results in the simultaneous attainment of equilibrium in the external sector and in the domestic (that is, nontradables) sector of the economy. This means that when the RER is in equilibrium, the economy is accumulating (or running down) assets at the "desired" rate and the demand for domestic goods equates its supply.

Although the definition of RER given in equation 1 is analytically useful, it is difficult to calculate in practice. A more operational definition of the real exchange rate is the following:

---

[2]In theory, there are better indexes of a country's international degree of competitiveness, such as unit labor costs. Unfortunately, these indexes are unreliable in the case of developing countries.

$$\text{RER: } = \frac{EP_{T^*}}{P_N} \tag{2}$$

where E is the nominal exchange rate defined as units of domestic currency per unit of foreign currency, P_{T^*} is the world price of tradables, and P_N is the domestic price of nontradables. In measuring equation 2, economists have to define proxies for P_{T^*} and P_N. These proxies are usually some foreign price level (wholesale price index, for example) and the domestic consumer price index (CPI). Edwards (1988) discusses measurement problems in detail.

The bare bones of this equation can now be fleshed out. The equilibrium RER is the relative price of tradables to nontradables that, for given (equilibrium or sustainable) values of other relevant variables such as trade taxes, international prices, capital and aid flows, and technology, results in the simultaneous attainment of *internal* and *external* equilibrium. Internal equilibrium means that the nontradable goods market clears in the current period and is expected to be in equilibrium in the future.[3] External equilibrium is attained when the sum of the present current account and the expected current account in the future satisfies the intertemporal budget constraint that states that the discounted value of current account balances must equal zero. In other words, external equilibrium means that the current account balances (current and future) are compatible with long-run sustainable capital flows.[4]

Various implications follow from this definition. First, the equilibrium RER is not immutable. When there are changes in any of the other variables that affect the country's internal and external equilibriums, the equilibrium RER will also change. For example, the RER "required" to attain equilibrium will vary according to whether the world price of the country's main export is low or high. It will also be affected by import tariffs, export taxes, real interest rates, capital controls, and so on. These immediate determinants of the equilibrium RER are called *real exchange rate fundamentals*. Second, there is

---

[3] Implicit in this definition is the requirement that there are no deviations from the natural rate of unemployment. In fact, internal equilibrium—defined as a nontradables market that clears—can take place at different levels of employment. In our definition of equilibrium RER it is implicit that this equilibrium takes place with no unemployment above its natural level.

[4] This intertemporal budget constraint can be written in the following way: $\Sigma_{i=0}^{\infty} (1 + r)^{-i} C_i = 0$ and states that this country cannot be a net lender or net borrower forever. Eventually it must pay its debts. For a formal and technical discussion of the equilibrium real exchange rate, see Edwards (1986c), which defines an intertemporal general equilibrium model. See also the discussion in Williamson (1983).

not "one" equilibrium RER, but rather a path of equilibrium RER through time. Third, the path will be affected not only by the current values of the fundamental determinants, but also by their expected future evolution. If there are possibilities for intertemporal substitution of consumption through foreign borrowing and lending, and in production through investment, expected future events—an expected change in the terms of trade, for example—will affect the current value of the equilibrium RER.

The fundamental determinants of the equilibrium RER are those *real* variables that, in addition to the RER, play a large role in determining the country's internal and external equilibrium. The *external RER fundamentals* include (a) international prices (that is, international terms of trade); (b) international transfers, including foreign aid flows; and (c) world real interest rates. The *domestic RER fundamentals* can be divided into those variables that are policy related and those that are independent of policy decisions. The policy-related RER fundamentals include (a) import tariffs, import quotas, and export taxes; (b) exchange and capital controls; (c) other taxes and subsidies; and (d) the composition of government expenditure. Among nonpolicy fundamentals, technological progress is the most important.[5]

Changes in taxes or subsidies on trade will have significant effects on the equilibrium RER. For example, a (permanent) import tariff will increase the domestic price of importables, which in turn will reduce demand for importables. The increase in the domestic price of importables will also induce a higher demand for nontradable goods, boosting their prices. Thus, under the most plausible conditions, the import tariff will result in a new equilibrium characterized by a lower price of exportables relative to nontradables and a higher price of importables relative to exportables.[6]

Changes in the international terms of trade will also affect the equilibrium RER. From an analytical perspective, a deterioration in

[5]Naturally, these variables are not the only ones affecting the equilibrium RER, but in many cases the relation will go both ways, with changes in the RER also affecting some of the fundamentals. Perhaps the clearest example of this two-way relation has to do with RER movements and tariffs. Real exchange rate overvaluation is usually met by an increase in exchange controls and tariffs.

[6]The "plausible conditions" are that the substitution effect dominate the income effect and that all goods be gross substitutes in consumption (see Edwards (1986c)). Notice that since a tariff affects the relative price of importables to exportables, it is useful to concentrate on the relative prices of both exportables and importables. Depending on the relative weights of importables and exportables in the price index for tradables, the equilibrium RER will appreciate or depreciate when an import tariff is imposed. What is clear, however, is that the relative price of importables has gone up relative to both nontradables and exportables, while the relative price of exportables will fall relative to the other two goods.

the terms of trade and the imposition of a tariff have somewhat similar effects. Both imply a higher domestic price of importables and less demand for them. However, a worsening in the international terms of trade has a bigger negative income effect than a tariff rise. The empirical evidence suggests that terms of trade deteriorations usually lead to an equilibrium real depreciation (that is, to a higher equilibrium RER; see Edwards (1989)).

Capital controls will affect intertemporal consumption and thus the path of equilibrium relative prices and real exchange rates. For example, if these controls are relaxed to allow an increase in capital inflows and foreign borrowing, the result will be higher current expenditure on all goods, including nontradables. As a result, there will be an increase in the price of nontradables or equilibrium real appreciation.

International transfers are another example of how a fundamental variable affects the equilibrium path of the RER. If a country has to make a transfer to the rest of the world, current and future domestic real income and expenditure will fall, generating a fall in the relative price of nontradables or a real depreciation in the current and future periods. In a way, in order to make a transfer to the rest of the world, the equilibrium RER has to depreciate. This is particularly relevant today: in stark contrast to the 1970s, many developing countries now make significant transfers to the rest of the world.

For those countries receiving foreign aid, the analysis is symmetrical. Aid is a transfer from the rest of the world, and as such it will generate an equilibrium real appreciation. Perhaps paradoxically, it therefore reduces the international competitiveness of the recipient country, making the country's exports less competitive internationally.

The fact that the equilibrium RER moves when its fundamental determinants change has significant consequences for policy. Some policymakers still think that the equilibrium RER is a constant or immutable number. According to this approach, which is derived from the simplest notions of purchasing power parity, any deviation of the real exchange rate from its value in some past period (usually called "the equilibrium year") represents a disequilibrium and is cause for concern. On the contrary, actual changes in an RER do not necessarily reflect a disequilibrium. They can reflect changes in equilibrium conditions generated by changes in fundamentals.

II. Macroeconomic Policy and Misalignment

Although the equilibrium RER is a function of real variables only, the actual real exchange rate responds to both real and monetary variables. The existence of an equilibrium value of the real exchange rate does not mean that the actual real rate has to be *permanently* equal to this equilibrium value. In fact, the actual RER will normally differ from its equilibrium level, at least in the short run. However, other types of deviations can become persistent and can generate large RER misalignments.

At any time, the actual RER will depend on the values of the fundamentals (tariffs, international prices, real interest rates, and so on) and also on aggregate macroeconomic pressures, such as an excess supply of money and the fiscal deficit. In this analysis, it is useful to distinguish between three different exchange rate regimes: (a) fixed nominal exchange rates (and variants, including managed and crawling rates); (b) floating rates; and (c) nonunified exchange rates, including dual rates and black market rates for foreign exchange.

Predetermined nominal exchange rates

A fundamental principle of open economy macroeconomics is that in order to have a sustainable macroeconomic equilibrium, it is necessary for monetary and fiscal policies to be consistent with the chosen nominal exchange rate regime. This means that the selection of an exchange rate system imposes limitations on macropolicies. If this consistency is violated, severe disequilibrium, usually concentrated on RER misalignment, will follow.

The case of a large fiscal deficit under fixed nominal rates is the clearest example of inconsistencies between macroeconomic and exchange rate policies. In most developing countries, fiscal imbalances are partially or wholly financed by money creation. If the required inflation tax is as high as the international rate of inflation, there will generally be an inconsistency between the fiscal deficit and the maintenance of a fixed nominal exchange rate. Since the domestic price of nontradables increases at a rate approximately equal to the rate of inflation, and the domestic price of tradables grows at approximately the rate of world inflation, a real appreciation will take place in every period.[7]

Monetary policy is another potential source of macroeconomic inconsistencies. Under predetermined nominal exchange rates, increases in domestic credit at rates exceeding the demand for domestic money will be translated into an excess demand for tradable goods, nontradable goods, and financial assets.[8] The excess demand

---

[7] The domestic price of tradables is equal to $P_T = E P_{T*} \tau$, where P_{T*} is the international price of tradables, E is the nominal exchange rate, and τ is one plus the tax on tradables. If the exchange rate is fixed and there are no changes in τ, P_T will increase at approximately the rate of world inflation.

[8] Notice that here we are considering monetary policy as different from the fiscal problem discussed above. In reality, however, these problems can be considered as related, because in the vast majority of the developing countries, government deficits are financed by money creation.

for tradables will be reflected in a large trade deficit (or lower surplus), a loss of international reserves, and an increase in (net) foreign borrowing above its long-run sustainable level. The excess demand for nontradables will be translated into higher prices for those goods and consequently into an RER appreciation. If there are no changes in the fundamental real determinants of the equilibrium RER, this real appreciation will be a misalignment.

Consistency between monetary and exchange rate policies is needed not only under fixed rates, but also under systems such as passive crawling pegs. Argentina in the late 1970s exemplifies the problem. Its government used a preannounced rate of devaluation, or *tablita*, as a means of reducing inflation. However, the preannounced rate was clearly inconsistent with the inflation tax required to finance the fiscal deficit (Calvo (1986)). This inconsistency generated not only a real appreciation but also substantial speculative bets on when the *tablita* would be abandoned.

Floating nominal exchange rates

Under a floating system, the nominal exchange rate fluctuates freely, responding to changes in macroeconomic policies. However, domestic prices and nominal exchange rates adjust to shocks at different speeds. A crucial difference between nominal exchange rates and the prices of goods is that the exchange rate behaves like an asset price; it is extremely sensitive to changes in expectations and to new information. In contrast, goods prices usually react much more slowly to shocks.

The existence of a floating system does not preclude the influence of monetary policies on real exchange rates. Monetary policies, however, do not affect equilibrium real exchange rates. These depend, under any nominal exchange rate regime, on real variables only. The wide swings in real exchange rates in the industrial countries in the past few years have become an important topic of analysis.[9]

The clearer case where monetary policies induce changes of the actual RER has been analyzed by Dornbusch (1976). Assuming that asset (including foreign exchange) markets adjust instantaneously, while nontradable goods markets adjust only slowly, a monetary expansion will result in an immediate jump of the nominal exchange rate that will exceed the long-run equilibrium nominal depreciation.[10]

---

[9]See Williamson (1983) for a meticulous analysis of the possibilities of RER misalignment under floating rates.

[10]The overshooting in the nominal rate is required in order for interest arbitrage to hold permanently. See Dornbusch (1976).

Prices of nontradables, in contrast, will remain constant in the short run. As time passes, however, domestic prices will rise toward a new equilibrium level compatible with the increased stock of money, and the nominal exchange rate will fall toward its new equilibrium.[11]

Parallel nominal exchange rates

Multiple exchange rates have traditionally had some appeal for developing countries, where they have recently become fairly common. With this system, different international transactions are subject to different nominal exchange rates, giving rise to the possibility of having more than one real exchange rate.[12]

With multiple exchange rates, the relation between macroeconomic policies and the rest of the economy will depend on the nature of the system. If, for example, the system consists of two (or more) *predetermined* (that is, fixed) nominal rates, it will work in almost the same way as under a single fixed rate, since multiple fixed rates are equivalent to a unified rate with taxes on certain external transactions.[13] In this case, as with unified predetermined rates, inconsistent macroeconomic policies will reduce international reserves, raise domestic inflation above world inflation, and result in RER overvaluation. Since this combination is unsustainable in the long run, the authorities will have to take corrective action.

A different kind of multiple rate system consists of a fixed official rate for current account transactions and an (official) freely fluctuating rate for capital account transactions. Although this arrangement has been more common in industrial countries, some developing countries (such as Mexico and Venezuela) have recently experimented with it. The main purpose is to uncouple the real economy from the effects of supposedly unstable capital movements.[14] Portfolio decisions in this case are strongly influenced by the expected rate of devaluation of the free rate.[15]

Under this type of system, even if no current account transactions slip into the free rate, a change in the free nominal rate will influence

---

[11]Notice that the direction of the departure of the RER from its equilibrium level is the opposite of that under fixed rates.

[12]There is a growing theoretical literature on the effects of macroeconomic policies under nonunified nominal rates. See Aizenman (1985) and Dornbusch (1986a and 1986b).

[13]See, for example, the discussion in Dornbusch (1986b).

[14]In fact, this type of dual rate system is an alternative to foreign exchange controls.

[15]The free rate, in turn, will be highly responsive to expectations about future events. Dornbusch (1986a) has recently discussed this type of regime.

the RER.[16] Suppose, for example, that domestic credit increases faster than the demand for domestic money, producing excess demand for goods and financial assets. As a result, international reserves will fall, the price of nontradable goods will rise, and the RER will appreciate. In addition, the demand for foreign assets will increase, resulting in a nominal devaluation of the free rate and changes in the domestic interest rate.[17] The devaluation of the free rate will have secondary effects on the official *real* exchange rate, through a wealth effect. But the essential point is that inconsistent macropolicies will eventually also become unsustainable as international reserves decline. By isolating the current from the capital account, all the dual rates system can do is delay the eventual crisis.

The analysis is more complex if some current account transactions are subject to the free exchange rate. In such a case, there will then be an additional RER—defined as the price of tradables subject to the free rate relative to nontradables—and changes in macropolicies will affect both real rates.[18] For example, an increase in domestic credit that exceeds growth of domestic money will now result in lower reserves, higher prices of nontradables, a higher "free" market nominal exchange rate, and increased foreign debt. The higher price of nontradables will generate an appreciation of the RER applicable to those goods subject to the official rate. For those goods subject to the free rate, what happens to the RER will depend on whether the nominal exchange rate determined in the free market increases by more or less than the price of nontradable goods. If its behavior is the same as under a freely floating rate, exchange rate overshooting is likely in this market: that is, the free rate will initially rise more than the price of domestic goods. The RER applicable to this type of good will, at least in the short run, depreciate. Under this dual exchange rate system, it is thus perfectly possible for an expansionary monetary policy to produce a real appreciation for goods subject to the official market and a real depreciation for goods subject to the free market.

Perhaps the most complex type of regime consists of an official pegged (or predetermined) exchange rate plus an illegal black market for foreign exchange. Some kind of black market for foreign

---

[16] Notice that if no current account transactions are subject to the free rate, the relevant rate—that is, the appropriate measure of competitiveness—is the fixed rate RER, because it is the one at which all goods transactions can take place.

[17] In this case, if there are no capital controls and we assume risk neutrality, the following relation will hold between domestic (i) and foreign (i^*) interest rates: $i = (e/f)i^* + (\hat{f})$, where e is the fixed nominal exchange rate, f is the free rate, and $(\hat{f})$ is the expected change in f.

[18] Dornbusch (1986b) analyzes this case in some detail.

exchange exists whenever there are exchange controls; sometimes it becomes very significant, even dominant.[19] Although the results of a fixed official rate coexistent with a black market are similar to those of the dual rates regime discussed above, there are important differences.

- To the extent that the black market is illegal, the expectations and costs of detection affect the premium—the difference between the official and freely determined nominal exchange rates.
- Expectations of political events are crucial, since they reflect possible future changes in exchange controls and other policies.
- Exporters have to decide how much of their foreign exchange earnings to surrender legally and how much to handle through the black market.[20] This decision, of course, will partially depend on the size of the premium itself.

With a generalized black market for foreign exchange, the marginal rate for import and import-competing sectors will be the black market rate. As for exports, the marginal rate will depend on the institutional arrangement and on whether exporters "have" to surrender a specified proportion of their export proceeds through the official market. If so, the marginal rate for exporters is a weighted average of the official and the black market rate. (If exporters have to surrender a given number of dollars, however, the black market rate is the marginal one.)

With a generalized illegal parallel market, an increase in the rate of domestic credit creation will boost domestic prices and the black market premium. Since in this situation it is likely that the central bank has no more international reserves to lose, this expansive monetary policy will push up the official RER, as well as lower the price of exports surrendered through the official market relative to those that use the parallel market.[21] As a result, a smaller proportion of export proceeds will be surrendered at the official rate, making the crisis even worse. Eventually, the inconsistent macropolicies will become unsustainable, and corrective measures will have to be taken. Then

[19] The extent and importance of the black market are basically determined by whether authorities allow some changes in international reserves. Under complete rationing, the authorities have no reserves, and legal export proceeds are the only source of foreign exchange.

[20] In a way, exporters also face this decision under an official dual system. It will still pay to convert export proceedings at the higher free rate.

[21] Depending on expectations, the nominal exchange rate determined in the parallel market can increase by more or by less than domestic prices.

the issue of exchange rate *unification* becomes important, since the-authorities will usually try to devalue the official rate, eliminating the multiple rates system.

III. Two Types of Real Exchange Rate Misalignment

For policy and analytical purposes, it is useful to distinguish between two types of RER misalignment. The first, *macroeconomic-induced misalignment*, occurs when inconsistencies between macroeconomic (and especially monetary) policies and the official exchange rate system cause the actual RER to depart from its equilibrium value.[22] As the previous section pointed out, if a monetary policy is so expansive that it becomes incompatible with maintaining the predetermined nominal exchange rate, the price of domestic goods will rise faster than world prices. As a result, the real exchange rate (EP_{T*}/P_N) will appreciate. Not only will there then be pressures on the price of nontradables; international reserves will also decline, (net) foreign borrowing will rise above its long-run sustainable level, and black markets will grow.[23]

The second type, *structural misalignment*, takes place when changes in the real determinants (or fundamentals) of the equilibrium RER are not translated in the short run into actual changes in the RER. One example is a worsening in a country's international terms of trade; the equilibrium RER will change, since a higher relative price of tradables will now be required to maintain equilibrium in the economy.[24] If the actual RER does not change in line with the equilibrium RER, misalignment will take place. Temporary changes in fundamental variables can sometimes result in significant divergences between the actual and equilibrium RER (Edwards (1986c)). Such disequilibriums can often be handled by, for example, running down (or building up) international reserves, using the compensatory facilities of the IMF, and so on. However, it is essential to distinguish between changes that are genuinely temporary and those that are inclined to persist.

---

[22]In a predetermined nominal system, this influence of monetary policies is reflected in changes in the price of nontradables; under fluctuating rates, it is reflected in changes in both the nominal rate and the price of domestic goods.

[23]Naturally, as the gap between the official and parallel market widens, so do the distortions associated with these dual rates.

[24]Strictly speaking, as a result of a worsening in the international terms of trade, the equilibrium RER could either appreciate or depreciate. As discussed above, however, under the most plausible circumstances, it will depreciate.

IV. Correcting Misalignments

RER misalignments result in severe welfare and efficiency costs, the
worst of which come from the exchange and trade controls that
usually accompany overvaluation. Such controls also encourage the
creation of strong lobbies, which compete for the rents the controls
generate (see Krueger (1974) and Edwards (1987)). And RER overvaluation greatly hurts exports; maintained for long periods, it can
even wipe out the agricultural infrastructure (see World Bank 1984,
Pfeffermann 1985). RER misalignment also generates massive capital
flight, which may be optimal from a purely private perspective, but
which imposes a substantial cost in terms of social welfare (Cuddington (1986)).

How should policymakers deal with RER misalignments? With
macroeconomic-induced misalignment, a necessary step is eliminating the inconsistency between macroeconomic policy and the nominal exchange rate. The authorities could then choose to wait for the
economy to adjust on its own, until the actual RER converges with the
equilibrium RER. However, this approach has various limitations that
can be particularly severe in the case of predetermined nominal exchange rates.

Once the inconsistent policies generating the macroeconomic-
induced misalignment are controlled, the RER will still differ from the
equilibrium RER. The question then is how to return the RER to its
equilibrium value. In the most common case, the RER misalignment
takes the form of real overvaluation and loss of international competitiveness. If nominal rates are fixed, a rapid return to RER equilibrium
will then require a drop in the domestic prices of nontradables.[25]
This is unlikely to happen quickly, so the RER misalignment will
persist for a long period—as will all its related costs.

These costs will be supplemented when (as is usually the case)
prices and wages are inflexible, for then unemployment will rise and
output will be squeezed. The cut in aggregate expenditure resulting
from the macroeconomic correction will generate an excess supply of
(or smaller excess demand for) all types of goods and assets. For
tradables, this excess will be reflected in a smaller trade deficit and
reduced foreign indebtedness. In the nontradables market, however,
the excess supply generated by the disinflation will require a drop in
the relative price of nontradables to reestablish equilibrium. If prices
are rigid, this realignment will not take place, and unemployment
will result.

---

[25]Since RER $= EP_{T^*}/P_N$ under fixed E, RER can only jump back to equilibrium
if P_N declines.

Devaluation

The restoration of RER equilibrium can be greatly aided by policies that help the domestic price of tradables to adjust. The most common of these policies is a devaluation of the nominal exchange rate.

In principle, the objectives of such devaluations are to improve both the international competitiveness of a country and its external position. Obviously, since RER = EP_{T^*}/P_N, a nominal devaluation that increases E will be effective in moving the RER toward its higher equilibrium value only if P_N does not go up in the same proportion as E.

In theory, and under the most common conditions, nominal devaluations will affect an economy through three main channels.[26] First, a devaluation has an *expenditure-reducing* effect. To the extent that domestic prices rise as a result of the devaluation, there will be a negative wealth effect that will reduce the real value of all assets (including domestic money) denominated in domestic currency. (Notice, however, that to the extent that there are assets denominated in foreign currency, there may also be a positive wealth effect.) If the negative wealth effect dominates, expenditure on all goods (including tradables) will be reduced, as will the trade deficit. Second, a nominal devaluation will tend to have an *expenditure-switching* effect.[27] To the extent that it succeeds in altering the relative price of tradables to nontradables, expenditure will switch away from tradables and production toward them. While the expenditure-switching effect boosts demand for nontradables, the expenditure-reducing effect cuts demand for all goods. Depending on which of these effects dominates, the demand for domestic home goods will either rise or fall. Third, a devaluation will boost the domestic currency price of imported intermediate inputs, pushing up the supply schedules for the final goods (including nontradables).[28]

With unified nominal exchange rates and no quantitative restrictions, a nominal devaluation is not discriminatory: it increases the domestic price of *all* tradable goods, services, and assets. But if there is a parallel (or dual) market, and only the official rate is devalued, then only those transactions affected by the official rate will be directly affected by the devaluation. However, transactions in the parallel market will be affected indirectly—though it is not possible to

---

[26]In some cases, however, if there are extensive quantitative import controls and parallel markets, some of these effects will be different. See the discussion below.

[27]We say it will "tend to have" because this assumes that the nominal devaluation is translated into a real devaluation.

[28]The combination of these effects may very well result in a *decline* of aggregate output as a consequence of the devaluation. See Edwards (1986a).

know in advance whether devaluing the official rate will increase or reduce the parallel market premium.[29]

When there are quantitative restrictions (QRs) on imports, devaluations will also fail to generate a uniform increase in the price of tradables (and other effects are also quite different; see Krueger (1983)). The domestic price of importables is endogenous in the sense that it reaches whatever level is required for that market to clear. In this case a nominal devaluation will tend to have no direct (first-round) effect on the domestic price of such importables. However, since the prices of exportables continue to be tied, through the exchange rate, to world prices, the devaluation will increase their price relative to rationed importables. Nonrationed importables will also be affected by the devaluation: their price relative to both rationed importables and nontradables will tend to change.

If a country implements a devaluation at a time when the RER is greatly overvalued, the devaluation will generally help to restore equilibrium. And if devaluation is accompanied by the appropriate macropolicies, it will generally have a mediumto long-run positive effect on the RER. But if the initial condition is one of equilibrium—that is, the actual RER does not diverge from its long-run equilibrium level—a nominal devaluation will have no medium- or long-run effect. The price of nontradables, P_N, will quickly increase, and the RER will not be affected.

Since a nominal devaluation—which increases E in the RER formula (RER $= P^*E/P_N$)—tries to eliminate misalignment by causing a real depreciation, it is imperative that it not be accompanied by an *equiproportional* increase in P_N. Such an increase could come about in several ways: expansive credit (or monetary) policies, expansive fiscal policies, and wage indexation. But if the nominal devaluation is implemented along with monetary and fiscal restraint and without wage indexation, it is likely to achieve a real devaluation and help the RER return to equilibrium.

Even if the accompanying macropolicies are restrictive, however, nominal devaluations will never result in equiproportional real devaluations in the medium to long run. Several forces will ensure some offsetting increase in the price level P_N. For example, nominal devaluation will boost the prices of imported inputs and consequently the cost of producing domestic goods. Over time, such

[29]Of course, the devaluation itself will affect the parallel rate. Theoretically, an official devaluation can generate either an increase or decline in the black market premium. The empirical evidence indicates that following the nominal devaluation, there is usually a drop in the parallel market premium. An important question when there are parallel markets refers to exchange rate unification. Lizondo (1986) has shown that the equilibrium nominal rate can be either above or below the black market rate.

effects will grow. Thus the nominal devaluation will, on impact, result in a large (and almost equiproportional) increase in the RER. Then, as the prices of imported goods (and in some cases wages) react to the nominal devaluation, the effect on the RER will be partially eroded. (See the final section for empirical results regarding the degree of erosion.)

Alternatives to devaluation

In principle, other policies can have effects similar to those a devaluation generates, though it is not easy to replicate every possible result.

Import tariffs and export subsidies

This combination will replicate only some of the effects of a devaluation. Import tariffs will boost the domestic price of importables; export subsidies will likewise boost the domestic price of exportables. As long as both tariffs and subsidies are at the same rate, the relative price between importables and exportables (the tradables) will not be affected, but their relative price with respect to nontradables will increase. This is the same consequence that results from a successful devaluation.

In other respects, however, the two policies differ quite sharply. First, a devaluation affects both visible and invisible trade; the policy of tariffs with subsidies affects only visible trade. Second, a devaluation affects the domestic currency price both of tradable goods and services and of tradable assets; tariffs with subsidies affect only the domestic price of tradable goods and services. Third, a devaluation will affect domestic interest rates if it breeds expectations of further devaluations. In this case, some fraction of the expected devaluation will be passed on to the domestic interest rate, even if the capital account is partially closed. By contrast, the tariffs with subsidies will not have such an effect on interest rates. Fourth, devaluations will generally have no direct effects on the fiscal budget; the tariffs with subsidies will generally result in fiscal imbalances. Fifth, the imposition of tariffs and export subsidies will prompt various interest groups to claim exemption for their particular industry—and history shows that they often succeed. This political reaction is avoided with a devaluation.

Multiple nominal exchange rates

The adoption of multiple rates constitutes a semidevaluation, inasmuch as the exchange rate applied to some transactions is altered. Thus, multiple rates are essentially discriminatory, whereas one of the most important properties of a devaluation (without rationing) is its neutrality. Furthermore, every variety of multiple rates system begs the important question of how (and at what level) to unify the different rates eventually.

Incomes policies

This approach will succeed in realigning the real rate only if the price of domestic goods falls relative to that of foreign goods. On this rule, the historical evidence is emphatic: incomes policies that are not supplemented by demand restraint have invariably failed to bring down inflation for more than a short period. Trying to realign the real exchange rate by controlling incomes policies alone is not only an inefficient approach; it is also very risky.

V. The Effectiveness of Devaluations: The Evidence

Empirical evidence strongly suggests that, accompanied by appropriate macroeconomic policies, nominal devaluations can produce a real depreciation and improve a country's external position. In his classic study, Cooper (1971) analyzed 24 episodes and found that most nominal devaluations were indeed associated with real devaluations. He also pointed out that most major discrete devaluations were accompanied by the kind of trade reforms that lifted quantitative restrictions or lowered tariffs. This finding has also been reported by Krueger (1978) and Edwards (1989).

Connolly and Taylor (1976 and 1979) found that nominal devaluations were translated into real devaluations in the short to medium run. Their 1979 paper suggests that, on impact, nominal devaluations have an important positive effect on relative prices, but this effect erodes slowly—until, nine quarters after the devaluation, the RER is back to the value it had two years before devaluation. Although the details differ, the same point is established in studies by Donovan (1981), Bautista (1981), and Morgan and Davis (1981).

More recently, Edwards (1986b) analyzed 29 devaluations between 1962 and 1979. He found that in some countries, nominal devaluation had succeeded in producing a sizable real devaluation. Table 1 shows an index of effectiveness of real devaluations for 28 of these episodes. This index is constructed as the ratio of the percentage change in the RER to the percentage change in the nominal exchange rate. As the table shows, the initial effects of devaluations are large. After 12 quarters, however, many or all of the benefits have been eroded. Indeed, the RER became even more overvalued in Bolivia (1979), Cyprus and Egypt (1962), Israel (1971), Jamaica (1967), and Nicaragua (1979). Edwards (1986b) showed that countries that had a

Table 1. Index of Effectiveness of Nominal Devaluation

Country	Year	Quarter of Devaluation	1 Quarter after	4 Quarters after	8 Quarters after	12 Quarters after
Bolivia	1972	0.68	0.66	0.36	0.09	0.03
	1979	0.51	<0	<0	<0	*
Colombia	1962	0.94	0.48	<0	<0	<0
	1965	1.00	0.88	0.50	0.57*	0.66*
Costa Rica	1974	0.82	1.04	0.75	0.75	0.83
Cyprus	1967	1.00	0.19	0.27	0.31	0.32
Ecuador	1961	1.05	1.06	0.93	0.51	0.03
	1970	0.88	0.74	0.73	0.59	0.66
Egypt	1962	1.03	1.03	0.98	0.85	0.32
	1979	0.99	1.05	0.98	0.93	0.76
Guyana	1967	1.03	0.96	1.10	1.31	1.42
India	1966	0.92	0.81	0.56	0.56	0.62
Indonesia	1978	1.00	0.98	0.73	0.64	0.61
Israel	1962	0.94	0.87	0.74	0.63	0.53
	1967	0.95	0.93	0.99	1.05	0.57
	1971	0.98	0.64	0.53	0.23	<0
Jamaica	1967	0.96	0.99	0.83	0.57	0.37
	1978	0.46	0.43	0.31	0.26	0.20
Malta	1967	0.93	0.88	0.99	1.12	0.99
Nicaragua	1979	0.17	<0	<0	<0	<0
Pakistan	1972	1.00	0.99	0.78	0.61	0.45
Peru	1967	0.89	0.65	0.40	0.41	0.36
Philippines	1962	0.97	0.89	0.87	0.73	0.69
	1970	0.72	0.65	0.49	0.47	0.55
Sri Lanka	1967	0.82	0.71	0.54	0.70	0.69
Trinidad	1967	0.82	0.71	0.54	0.70	0.69
Venezuela	1964	0.98	0.95	0.96	1.00	1.02
Yugoslavia	1965	0.67	0.46	0.42	0.29	0.26

Source: IMF, *International Financial Statistics*, various years.
Note: This index shows the percentage change in the real exchange rate between one quarter before the devaluation and the quarter given, divided by the percentage change in the nominal exchange rate during the same period. An asterisk indicates that a new devaluation took place.

large (or complete) erosion of the effect of the nominal devaluation were those that accompanied the exchange rate adjustment with expansive credit policies, large fiscal deficits, or wage indexation. Those countries that experienced only minor erosion usually implemented consistent macroeconomic restraint. Regression results in Edwards (1986b) indicate that, on average and all other things given, a nominal devaluation of 10 percent will result, in the first year, in a real devaluation of approximately 7 percent. However, the real effect of the nominal devaluation erodes (rather slowly) through time. After three years, the average effect on the real exchange rate of a 10 percent nominal devaluation will be only around 5 percent.

The most interesting finding in these regressions concerns the effect of changes in domestic credit creation. The results show that if a devaluation is accompanied by expansive credit policies, its corrective effect on the RER will be greatly diminished. If a nominal devaluation of 10 percent is accompanied by an acceleration of the rate of growth of domestic credit equal to 10 percentage points, the resulting depreciation in the RER will be reduced to only 2 percent in that year. After two years, the RER will again have become overvalued.

VI. Summary and Conclusions

Exchange rate misalignment has been a serious problem for developing countries in recent years. The distinction between nominal and real exchange rates is crucial to an understanding of these problems. Misaligned real rates have usually resulted from macroeconomic policies that have not been consistent with the exchange rate system, or from external shocks. These misalignments misrepresented the relative costs of production and consumption of tradables and nontradables. Stability of nominal exchange rates has not always implied stability of real exchange rates, and nominal (and real) exchange rates have not always moved smoothly to new equilibriums after disturbances. Trade barriers and multiple exchange rates, which have often been introduced in response to economic shocks, are not efficient instruments to adjust real exchange rates. Inappropriate monetary policies have often prevented nominal exchange rate adjustments from turning into real exchange rate changes.

Experience suggests, however, that exchange rate misalignment is susceptible to solution. A nominal devaluation undertaken with appropriate fiscal and monetary policies can generate a real depreciation and increase a country's ability to sell those goods that make it internationally competitive and to attract the investment needed for growth.

References

Aizenman, Joshua. 1985. "Tariff Liberalization Policy and Financial Restrictions. *Journal of International Economics* 19 (November): 241–55.
Bautista, Romeo. 1981. "Exchange Rate Changes and LDC Export Performance under Generalized Currency Floating." *Weltwirtschaftliches Archiv* 117(3): 443–68.
Calvo, Guillermo. 1986. "Fractured Liberalism: Argentina under Martínez de Hoz." *Economic Development and Cultural Change* 34 (April): 511–34.

Connolly, Michael, and Dean Taylor. 1976. "Adjustment to Devaluation with Money and Nontraded Goods." *Journal of International Economics* 6 (August): 289–98.

——.1979. "Exchange Rate Changes and Neutralization: A Test of the Monetary Approach Applied to Developed and Developing Countries." *Economica* 46 (August): 281–94.

Cooper, Richard. 1971. *Currency Devaluation in Developing Countries.* Essays on International Finance 86. Princeton, N.J.: Princeton University, International Finance Section, Department of Economics.

Cuddington, John. 1986. *Capital Flight: Estimates, Issues, and Explanations.* Princeton Studies in International Finance 58. Princeton, N.J.: Princeton University, International Finance Section, Department of Economics.

Donovan, Donal. 1981. "Real Responses Associated with Exchange Rate Action in Selected Upper-Credit-Tranche Stabilization Programs." *IMF Staff Papers* 28 (December): 698–727.

Dornbusch, Rüdiger. 1976. "Expectations and Exchange Rate Dynamics." *Journal of Political Economy* 84 (December): 1161–76.

——.1986a. "Special Exchange Rates for Capital Account Transactions." *World Bank Economic Review* 1 (September): 3–33.

——.1986b. "Special Exchange Rates for Commercial Transactions." In Sebastian Edwards and Liaquat Ahamed, eds., *Economic Adjustment and Exchange Rates in Developing Countries.* Chicago: University of Chicago Press.

Edwards, Sebastian. 1986a. "Are Devaluations Contractionary?" *Review of Economics and Statistics* 68 (August). 501–8.

——.1986b. "Exchange Rate Misalignment in Developing Countries: Analytical Issues and Empirical Evidence." CPD Working Paper. Washington, D.C.: World Bank, Country Policy Department.

——.1986c. "Tariffs, Terms of Trade and Real Exchange Rates in Intertemporal Models of the Current Account." University of California, Los Angeles, Department of Economics.

——.1987. "Sequencing of Economic Liberalization in Developing Countries," *Finance and Development* 24 (March): 26–29.

——.1988. *Exchange Rate Misalignment in Developing Countries.* Baltimore, Md.: Johns Hopkins University Press.

——.1989. *Real Exchange Rates, Devaluation and Adjustment: Exchange Rate Policies in Developing Countries.* Cambridge, Mass.: MIT Press.

Krueger, Anne O. 1974. "The Political Economy of the Rent-Seeking Society." *American Economic Review* 64 (June): 291–303.

——.1978. *Foreign Trade Regimes and Economic Development: Liberalization Attempts and Consequences.* Cambridge, Mass.: Ballinger.

——.1983. *Exchange Rate Determination.* Cambridge, Mass.: Cambridge University Press.

Lizondo, J.S. 1986. "Exchange Rate Reunification." Paper presented at Econometric Society Meetings, Cordoba, Argentina.

Morgan, Theodore, and Albert Davis. 1981. "The Concomitants of Exchange Rate Depreciation: Less Developed Countries, 1971–1973." *Economic Development and Cultural Change* 31 (October): 101–30.

Pfeffermann, Guy. 1985. "Overvalued Exchange Rates and Development." *Finance and Development* 22 (March): 17–19.

Willet, Thomas. 1986. "Exchange Rate Volatility, International Trade, and Resource Allocation." *Journal of International Money and Finance* 5 (March): Supplement 101–12.

Williamson, John. 1983. *The Exchange Rate System*. Institute of International Economics, Policy Analysis and International Economics Series 5. Cambridge, Mass.: MIT Press.

World Bank. 1984. *Toward Sustained Development in Sub-Saharan Africa*. Washington, D.C.

Exchange Rate Policy in Developing Countries 3

W. Max Corden

This paper distinguishes between two approaches to exchange rate policy in developing countries: the "real targets" and the "nominal anchor" approaches. It also looks at whether the exchange rate follows other policies and private sector price and wage setting or leads them. The real targets approach, which is now the orthodox policy, assumes that nominal exchange rate changes have prolonged real effects and that the exchange rate should adapt to other policies. The nominal anchor approach uses the exchange rate as an instrument of anti-inflation policy, as a way of constraining domestic policies and influencing private sector reactions. In examining the implications of the nominal anchor approach, the paper considers to what extent such an approach might explain the low-inflation experiences of the many countries in which exchange rates have been (more or less) fixed for long periods. The implications of increasing capital mobility for exchange rate policy are also examined, and some conclusions for policy are presented. The analysis draws on examples of exchange rate policies and the experiences of a group of 17 developing countries that have been studied as part of a World Bank project on macroeconomic policies and growth over a longer period.[1]

Note: The analysis in this paper draws on some of the findings of a World Bank research project (Little and others (1993)). The views expressed here are those of the author and should not be attributed to the World Bank. The author is indebted to Premachandra Athukorala for valuable comments on an earlier version of this paper.

[1] All references to developing countries are to this group or to individual members of the group. The countries include 2 that are members of the franc zone—Cameroon and Côte d'Ivoire—and so their exchange rates have been completely fixed; 4—Argentina, Brazil, Chile, and Colombia—that were "chronic inflation" countries before 1973, when they had quite high inflation rates and crawling peg or variable exchange rates even when most other countries had fixed rates and low inflation; and finally, 11 others—Costa Rica, Mexico, Morocco, Turkey, Kenya, Nigeria, India, Indonesia, Pakistan, Sri Lanka, and Thailand.

I. Two Approaches to Exchange Rate Policy

The real targets approach uses the nominal exchange rate, together with other policy instruments, to attain real objectives such as an appropriate (noninflationary) level of demand for home-produced goods and services (internal balance) and a desired current account target. In its assumption that a nominal policy instrument can achieve a real objective, this approach is essentially Keynesian. Furthermore, it assumes that the government can be trusted to make sensible use of the exchange rate and other instruments—that is, it does not need to be constrained. In addition, this approach assumes that the nominal exchange rate is a policy instrument distinct from domestic monetary and fiscal policies, although it must be applied together with these policies.

The assumption that the exchange rate is a policy instrument separate from domestic monetary policy is particularly important to the discussion. It means that a nominal exchange rate objective can be attained by sterilized intervention. It is thus assumed that effective exchange controls or other measures are used to ensure that international capital mobility is not high for the country.

The approach implies that a nominal devaluation has real effects that are sufficiently long lasting to be worth pursuing, at least provided expenditure policy avoids excess demand at the same time. Domestic prices and wages are assumed to be imperfectly flexible downward (in the simplest models, they are actually held constant). There is now strong evidence that, except in the chronic-inflation countries of Latin America, devaluations do have real effects that last for several years, provided appropriate credit policies are also followed. Thus the evidence seems to justify one of the key assumptions, at least for a period of, say, two to four years. Even in the case of high-inflation countries, continuous nominal depreciations may have real effects in the sense of preventing the real appreciations that would otherwise take place.[2]

The alternative, nominal anchor approach is a version of monetarism and used to be known as "international monetarism." The exchange rate is used to anchor the domestic inflation rate (broadly) to the inflation rate of trading partner countries. Possibly the exchange rate is adjusted on the basis of some predetermined scale to affect the

[2]On the basis of the real exchange rate indexes calculated by the IMF, it seems clear that, for many of the countries in our group, real and nominal (trade-weighted) exchange rates have moved together closely since 1981. For earlier years, there is strong evidence in Edwards (1989). But the effects do tend to get eroded, as evidenced both in Edwards (1989) and, for example, for Indonesia, in Warr (1984).

inflation differential with trading partner countries. It constrains domestic monetary policy (and hence possibly fiscal policy), making it endogenous. The exchange rate leads rather than follows other nominal variables, such as domestic price and wage inflation, in order to attain real objectives, such as maintenance of competitiveness. Apart from restraining governments, this approach is meant to send out clear and credible signals to private agents about prospects for inflation. The implication is that if the signals are clear and credible, the real economy will adjust appropriately to various shocks, including anti-inflationary exchange rate policy.

The approach—which focuses both on the need to restrain government inflationary tendencies through some kind of commitment and on the influence of the credibility of government monetary policies on private agents' expectations— is very much in tune with recent macroeconomic theorizing. For that reason, it is surprising that the current policy orthodoxy with regard to developing countries takes little account of it. Hence I discuss it at some length here.

II. Exchange Rate Policy Targeted on Real Variables

This section presents a systematic analysis of certain issues related to the real targets approach. How should the nominal exchange rate move in response to various "real" shocks or objectives, such as fiscal expansion or trade liberalization? What is the meaning of exchange rate "overvaluation" or "misalignment"?

The basic model: switching and expenditure adjustment

Chart 1 is the familiar "Swan diagram" (Swan (1963)), but it calls for careful interpretation here. It is assumed that the country is small in world markets, so that any changes in the terms of trade are exogenous.

The vertical axis shows the relative price of traded to nontraded goods in domestic currency terms, allowing also for the effects of tariffs, quantitative restrictions, and so on, that affect this relative price ratio. This is the S ratio, the S standing for either "Salter" or "switching."[3] It is sometimes called the "real exchange rate," a

---

[3] The reference is to Salter (1959), who presented the first systematic, diagrammatic model with traded and nontraded goods.

movement upward being a real depreciation.[4] The horizontal axis shows real expenditure or absorption (E), which can increase as a result of monetary or fiscal expansion or various other factors, such as higher incomes yielded by a terms of trade improvement. The curve Y_0 shows varying combinations of S and E that yield constant real income Y_0 resulting from constant demand for home-produced goods. Curve Y_1 represents a higher level of demand and income. Similarly, curve C_0 represents a constant current account balance, and curve C_1 a current account that is more in deficit.

Let us now look at the three crucial prices, namely, the prices of nontraded goods, imports, and exports.

First, there is a large category of nontraded goods N, with price p_n. This category contains two subclasses: (1) pure nontradables, which would be priced on the basis of domestic demand and supply even if there were free trade, and (2) goods that might have been imported under free trade but, because of prohibitive quantitative import restrictions, are priced on the basis of domestic demand and supply rather than in terms of the prices of competitive imports. The latter goods are the quantitative restriction-propelled nontraded goods—importables that have been converted into nontraded goods.

Second, there are imports M, whose domestic price is $e(1+t)p_m$, where p_m is the border price of imports in foreign currency terms, e is the nominal exchange rate defined as units of domestic currency per unit of foreign currency (an increase being a depreciation), and t is the tariff rate, whether explicit or implicit (quantitative restrictions), whichever effectively determines price. If import restrictions are tightened or their range is expanded within the broad category of M, t will rise.

Finally, there are exports X, where p_x is the foreign price of X, and ep_x is the domestic price.

Since there are two kinds of traded goods, weights must be attached to the two prices to get an average price of traded goods. The weights are a and $1 - a$. We thus get an expression for S, the relative price of

---

[4]The assumption is made here that imports and domestically produced importables are perfect substitutes—an assumption that is clearly unrealistic in a world of product differentiation. Hence it should be regarded as no more than a simplifying assumption. It should be noted that the real exchange rate, as well as being defined as the relative price of domestically produced tradables to nontradables, as here, could be defined as an index of "competitiveness"—that is, as the price of traded goods in foreign countries, adjusted for the nominal exchange rate, relative to their prices in the domestic economy. This definition, which is favored in Balassa (1987), hinges on the realistic assumption that foreign and domestic tradables are imperfect substitutes, so their prices, adjusted for the exchange rate, can indeed differ. The main arguments in this paper—especially in the comparison between the real targets and the nominal anchor approaches—apply fully when imports and domestically produced import-competing goods are imperfect substitutes; the latter, in terms of the (Salter) model of this paper, are, in effect, nontradables.

Chart 1. The Real Targets Approach

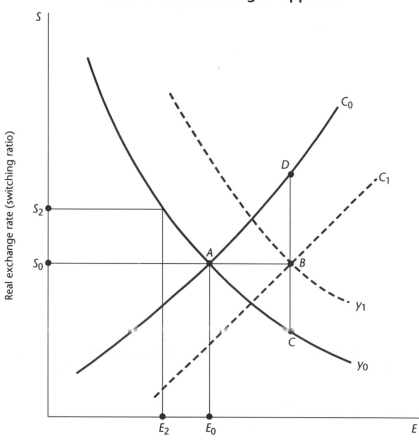

Real expenditure

traded to nontraded goods, taking into account trade restrictions and allowing for the possibility that the terms of trade (p_x / p_m) may change:

$$S = e \, [a(1+t)p_m + (1-a)p_x] / p_n. \qquad (1)$$

When the weights are held constant, S can change because of changes in the exchange rate, in protection, in one or two foreign prices, or in domestic (nontraded) prices, the last possibly because of a change in the nominal wage level. If a there is a nominal depreciation, that is, if e rises, and with p_n, t, p_m, and p_x given, S will increase. In that case, we can equate a change in S with a change in e, a movement upward in Chart 1 (positive switching) being a real depreciation or devaluation. An increase in p_n would lower S (negative switching). If p_n rises more than e (and with p_m, p_x, and t still constant), one might say that there has been real appreciation. When p_m, p_x, and t are constant, and only e and p_n vary, it seems appropriate in terms of conventional usage to use the real exchange rate concept, with positive switching resulting from real depreciation (e rising more than p_n). But a problem with this concept arises when p_x, p_m, or t changes.

A fiscal expansion: how should the exchange rate move?

Let us now consider a common situation in developing countries. A fiscal expansion is financed by borrowing, domestic or foreign. We take this as given. We also hold protection (t), and world prices (p_x, p_m) constant. Which way does S have to move? Should the exchange rate appreciate or depreciate?

It is not difficult to show that if the deficit is domestically financed and there are initial excess capacity and unemployment, the exchange rate needs to depreciate. In Chart 1, at a constant e and p_n, the movement would initially be from A to B, the net result of the fiscal expansion itself and possibly of some crowding out of private spending (as a result of a higher interest rate or of credit rationing brought about by the domestic financing). The current account worsens to C_1 and demand for nontraded goods rises, bringing demand for home-produced goods to Y_1. Clearly, a depreciation could restore the initial current account situation, provided it were possible to sustain higher domestic output. The system would go to D.

The more interesting case is that in which the deficit is foreign financed and the initial situation is one of full capacity or full employment (internal balance). In this case, the system cannot stay above Y_0, although it may move there initially, so S must fall to bring the country to C. This could be brought about by a rise in p_n, yielding a real appreciation. If a domestic price rise (temporary inflation) is to be avoided, nominal appreciation is required. The current account, of course, worsens. This negative switching reduces the profitability of export industries (and of any import-competing industries) and so yields the familiar Dutch Disease effect. It is caused by a fiscal expansion that is foreign financed or financed, at least temporarily, out of reserves when the starting point is one of internal balance.

(Given such a starting point, any transfer into the country, whether in the form of loans or aid, would have the same effect.)

It follows that the fiscal expansion may have to be associated with either a depreciation or an appreciation, depending on the extent to which the output of home-produced goods can be increased and the extent to which the deficit can be financed by foreign borrowing or the use of reserves.

Now suppose the country is at the last situation, at point C, with a current account deficit and internal balance. Reserves are running out or foreign borrowing is becoming difficult. Can we say that the exchange rate is "misaligned" or "overvalued"? We still hold p_x, p_m, and t constant. Should the country be advised to devalue?

If fiscal policy remained unchanged, a devaluation might temporarily bring the country back to B (or even to D), creating excess demand at home. But p_n would rise until S was back at C. *Given the fiscal policy*, the appreciated e is the correct one and is not overvalued. The fiscal expansion has to be reversed if the current account is to be improved. If it is impossible to reverse the fiscal expansion, there is no point in depreciating, since this would only cause temporary inflation. This point is often forgotten. It is wrong in this situation to advocate devaluation without the assurance that adequate fiscal contraction will also take place. But it would also be wrong to advocate fiscal contraction alone, leaving the exchange rate unaltered and p_n inflexible downward, since a recession would result. Given that the current account has to be improved, it is really the *package* of fiscal policy and exchange rate that is misaligned. A reversal of the fiscal expansion should be accompanied by a devaluation so as to undo the earlier appreciation of the currency.

Import restrictions and exchange rate misalignment

Protection—realistically, quantitative import restrictions—can now be introduced as a variable. To simplify, we hold p_n, p_m, and p_x constant. The two policy instruments are e and t, a rise in t representing a tightening or extension of restrictions. According to equation 1, a given S can be obtained with varying combinations of e and t. Suppose we start at the desired level of S, namely S_0 (in Chart 1), obtained by combining a particular level of e, namely e_0, with a positive level of t, namely t_0. Is the exchange rate then "misaligned"? The answer depends on whether the exchange rate *leads* or *follows*.

It is certainly possible that it follows. The level of protection may have been set at t_0 because this was desired as a long-term protectionist strategy or because tariffs are used to raise revenue. In that case, protection leads, and e_0 is then the equilibrium rate to ratify t_0, given the target S_0.

The currently more familiar story is that of trade liberalization. Again, the exchange rate is meant to follow. The much-repeated message is that trade liberalization requires devaluation to maintain both internal balance and the initial current account balance (see Corden (1971) and Krueger (1978)). This is an important example of the real targets approach. If the devaluation does not take place, trade liberalization cannot be sustained. In due course, import restrictions, although not necessarily the same ones as before, will be reimposed to deal with a current account problem that may have been caused by the earlier liberalization. In fact, this is the explanation for many failed liberalization attempts. The exchange rate is meant to follow but fails to do so (Krueger (1978)).[5]

A common experience in developing countries has been creeping overvaluation followed by increasing trade restrictions. A country starts at its desired internal and external position (point A in Chart 1) and with a low level of trade restrictions, say zero. But then because of domestic monetary expansion, domestic prices (p_n) rise faster than world prices. Therefore S would fall unless e were increased pari passu. Continuous nominal depreciation is needed to compensate for the excess of domestic inflation over world inflation. But the country fails to depreciate sufficiently for a variety of reasons, perhaps primarily to discourage further inflation. Therefore restrictions have to be continually intensified to maintain S_0 and hence equilibrium at A in Chart 1. This is a case in which the exchange rate leads when, from the point of view of the real targets approach, it should have followed. Restriction of imports turns out to be the residual policy, and it is not optimal.

Because of the increasing import restrictions imposed as a result of the continuous overvaluation of the real exchange rate, export industries are continuously squeezed.[6] Eventually, however, the limit of import restrictions will be attained: the country will be down to its bedrock level of imports. Then either S must fall below S_0, producing a current account deficit or an internal balance problem (depending on whether real expenditure, E, is raised or reduced), or the exchange rate must start depreciating.

Numerous examples of this pattern could be given. Indeed, there is hardly a country in our group of 17 that has not at some time gone through an episode like this, where rigidity of the nominal exchange rate leads to increasing import restrictions.[7] That this is an undesirable

[5] The point is also made in many papers by Bela Balassa.
[6] The term "real exchange rate" is used here in a particular way, namely to refer to the movement of ep_m/p_n or ep_x/p_n—that is, excluding the effect of the change in t. Alternatively, we could follow Edwards and van Wijnbergen (1987) and define the real exchange rate as S (equation 1 in this paper), in which case there would not necessarily be any real appreciation when a fall in ep_m/p_n led to a sufficient rise in t.
[7] It might be argued that the chronic-inflation countries of Latin America in our group have never been reluctant to depreciate. In particular, Brazil has been most ready to depreciate, and the nominal exchange rate has tracked domestic inflation with the aim of roughly maintaining the real rate over considerable periods. Nevertheless, Brazil has made much use of quantitative import restrictions. Wage indexation has often limited the ability of nominal exchange rate depreciation to bring about sufficient real depreciation. In the case of the other chronic-inflation countries in our group—Argentina, Colombia, and (at an earlier stage) Chile—there has also often been a reluctance to depreciate enough or quickly enough. Colombia has usually had a crawling peg, although, from the point of view of optimal switching and avoidance of restrictions, it has not always crawled fast enough.

outcome is, of course, a constant theme in the literature. The exchange rate should be adjusted appropriately. That is the essence of the real targets approach.

Nigeria presents a rather dramatic example of this kind of story. Inflation (consumer price index) was about 23 percent in 1983 and 40 percent in 1984, and yet the exchange rate stayed fixed. From the end of 1982 to the end of 1984, the real exchange rate (calculated by the IMF) increased by 64 percent (appreciated). Import restrictions were increasingly tightened. In 1985, the exchange rate was allowed to depreciate substantially, so that by mid-1986 the earlier real appreciation was more than fully reversed. But it was still far too high in real terms, mainly because of the precipitous fall in the price of oil in 1986. By that time, imports were certainly down to bedrock. A structural adjustment program was adopted in 1986 and implemented through 1987. Import licensing was abolished, and the exchange rate was floated. There was a massive nominal and real devaluation: the IMF index (in which a real depreciation is a decline) went from 114 in mid-1986 to 25 at the beginning of 1989 (which may also give some indication of the tariff equivalent of the import restrictions just before they were abolished).

Wage indexation: what difference does it make?

The implications of wage indexation for the real targets approach need to be considered. Wage indexation, explicit or implicit, has been a factor at certain times in all the Latin American countries, above all in Brazil, but much less so in the other countries of our group. At the same time, however, one cannot help noting the big drops in real wages that have taken place since 1981 in Argentina and Mexico (both countries with influential and centralized trade union movements), as well as in Chile (which had wage indexation from 1976 to 1981). Turkey has also seen a big decline in real wages since 1980, but in many of the other countries, wage indexation has not been a factor at all. Of course we cannot conclude that just because real wages have fallen substantially over some period, they can fall indefinitely. For example, in Mexico since 1988 there has been some degree of indexation as part of a social pact.

If there is formal or informal wage indexation, p_n will tend to rise, usually with a lag, when e rises. In the extreme case, a devaluation cannot bring about a change in S. How does this possibility affect the orthodox real targets model?

With the economy starting at internal balance (Y_0 in Chart 1), a devaluation in the absence of indexation would lead to an endogenous rise in p_n until internal balance was restored. This rise in p_n could be avoided by a simultaneous reduction in E. So, if a current account improvement is desired, E must fall; if internal balance is also to be maintained, then e must rise. There is a role for devaluation, but only as part of a policy package. By contrast, when there is indexation, p_n rises when e rises and would do so even if E were reduced. There is no role for devaluation at all, not even as part of a policy package. A reduction in E would be needed to improve the current account, but supplementing it with a devaluation would not affect S and thus could not maintain internal balance.

Suppose we observe that devaluations have been followed by increases in p_n, possibly causing the whole effect on S to be eroded after a while. There can be two explanations, and, from a policy point of view, it is important to know which is correct. One possible explanation is that E was not reduced sufficiently, so p_n rose because of excess demand. The conclusion then follows that a policy package that included contractionary aggregate demand policy should have been implemented or implemented more strongly. The second explanation could be that there was some tendency to indexation, formal or informal. In that case, a reduction in E would not have allowed S to rise—that is, would not have brought about positive switching, even though it was still required for a current account improvement. The policy implication in that case may be to try to end indexation.

There is some useful evidence about which explanation is likely to be more important. Edwards (1989, 264–69) analyzed the erosion of the real effects of nominal devaluations for a large group of developing countries (29 "stepwise" devaluations) and found that the rate of growth of domestic credit played a crucial role. In terms of our model, that would mean that a failure to reduce E would tend to lead to the failure of devaluation to have a sustained real effect. This suggests that indexation is relatively less important than adoption of the full policy package.

III. The Exchange Rate as Nominal Anchor

We now consider the alternative approach to exchange rate policy, in which the exchange rate is used as a nominal anchor, restraining government inflationary policies and sending out clear, credible signals to private agents about prospects for inflation. In this approach, the exchange rate leads. In terms of the model presented so far, p_n is no longer given: it becomes endogenous and depends on what happens—and what is expected to happen—to e. In this view, a readiness to devalue to achieve short-term real objectives means that this anchor is abandoned, and in the long run more inflation results. And when expectations are also allowed for, the long run may not be very long. Furthermore, the argument is that in the long run, real output will not be affected by the exchange rate or the level of nominal expenditure.

Domestic policies and private agents' reactions

There are three steps to the nominal anchor approach. (We continue to assume low capital mobility owing to effective exchange controls or other reasons.) First, the government makes a nominal exchange rate commitment. Second, the government is presumed to adjust its domestic monetary policies to this commitment as well. Since, to a great extent, monetary policy in developing countries is determined by fiscal policy (deficits tend to be monetized to varying extents), fiscal policy must adjust to exchange rate policy. To reduce the rate of money supply growth, a fiscal deficit will have to be reduced. Phrased in somewhat oversimplified form, in the nominal anchor approach the exchange rate leads and fiscal policy (insofar as deficits are monetized) must follow.[8] (This is in contrast to the real targets approach, in which fiscal policy leads and the exchange rate follows.)

Governments have two temporary ways of evading the constraint on monetary policies that a nominal exchange rate commitment is meant to provide. One way is to impose increasingly tight import restrictions to deal with the consequences of the incompatibility of monetary and exchange rate policies. The other way is to run down reserves and finance the growing current account deficit with foreign borrowing. The constraint imposed by the exchange rate can be—and often has been—evaded in these ways, with severely adverse effects. An example from Nigeria was given earlier, and many other examples could be given as well.

If the constraint is effective, however, then the third step is that in due course private agents adjust their price and wage setting to the fiscal, monetary, and exchange rate policies. If government commitment to the exchange rate itself and to any needed adjustment in domestic monetary policy has sufficient credibility and is clearly perceived by private agents, their price and wage setting may adjust quickly and without much loss of output when policy is designed to reduce the rate of inflation.

---

[8] This simplification does not apply when a fiscal deficit is financed by issuing domestic bonds or by foreign borrowing. The reference then is specifically to monetary, not fiscal, policy. As the experience of Côte d'Ivoire shows, a fixed exchange rate is compatible with a big budget deficit, provided foreign financing is available.

This nominal anchor approach thus hinges on both government and private behavior. It can fail, or work badly, either because domestic monetary policy (implying, usually, fiscal policy) is slow to adjust or evades the constraint completely, or because private price- and wage-setting agents are slow to adjust and devaluation has real effects for some time.

We might take the view that government does not need to be constrained, that it might have a genuine commitment to reducing inflation or maintaining price stability. It could achieve these goals either through an exchange rate policy to which domestic monetary policy is adjusted—as in the approach just discussed—or through a noninflationary or anti-inflationary domestic monetary policy to which the exchange rate is adjusted. Thus, again, the exchange rate could lead or follow, but this time the choice is between two ways of achieving the same nominal objective—that is, between two forms of monetarism—exchange rate and money supply (or nominal income) targeting.

The case in favor of using the exchange rate as the nominal anchor is that it is a very visible, very well-defined anchor, which increases the likelihood that private agents will adjust quickly. It is much more visible, and so more credible, than a money supply or normal expenditure target or a more general anti-inflation commitment. Its visibility is strengthened when the exchange rate is fixed to a particular currency, such as the dollar, rather than to a basket of currencies. The case against using the exchange rate as a nominal anchor is that exchange rate targeting is more likely to produce a balance of payments problem.

The last point is illustrated in Chart 2. We assume that the country starts at point A with a steady rate of inflation, nominal expenditure growth, and depreciation yielding a constant S and constant E at point A. To reduce the rate of inflation, one approach is to reduce the rate of depreciation. If the nominal expenditure reduction comes with a lag, the movement is thus first from A to B, with S falling and E constant (or even rising). The current account deteriorates from C_0 to C_1. In addition, output falls. Then real expenditure is reduced (the rate of growth of nominal expenditure is reduced) to restore the current account, and the system moves to D. Output falls further. Eventually the domestic rate of inflation declines and the system returns gradually to A, with output recovering. The movement from B to D represents the government's monetary policy reaction, and the movement from D to A the private agents' reaction. Of course, in the final equilibrium the inflation tax will have to be replaced by some other tax, or government expenditure will have to fall.

Chart 2. The Nominal Anchor Approach

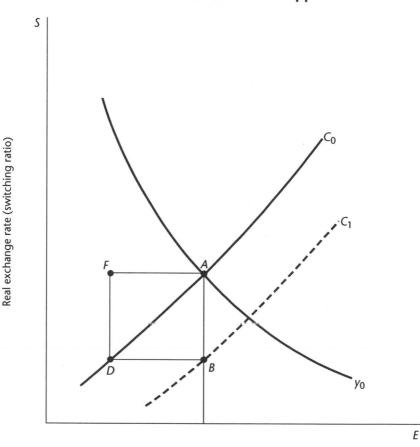

Real expenditure

Now we contrast this with the case in which domestic expenditure reduction leads rather than follows. First, the rate of growth of expenditure falls, while the exchange rate is not yet adjusted. The system moves to F, with the current account improving. Then, with the improvement in the current account, the real exchange rate appreciates (the rate of depreciation declines), bringing the country to D and restoring the original current account situation. The third stage—the move from D to A—is the same as in the case in which the exchange rate leads. The main point we notice here is that when the exchange rate leads (as it does in the nominal anchor approach), domestic policy adjustment might lag behind, resulting in a temporary balance of payments problem.[9] This possibility is avoided when domestic expenditure policy leads in the disinflationary process.

Experiences in five Asian countries and Turkey: have exchange rate policies actually constrained domestic policies?

The exchange rate experiences of the five Asian countries in our group may shed light on the relevance of the nominal anchor approach. At some stage between 1975 and 1984, these countries switched from a fixed exchange rate (tied to sterling or the dollar) to pegging to a basket, with some exchange rates more flexible than others. In general, these countries have had low inflation (with exceptions in some periods). To what extent have their exchange rate policies constrained domestic policies and provided nominal anchors? (Of course, a fully documented answer can hardly be given here, nor can their exchange rate policies be described in detail.)

Let us begin with the extreme case. Thailand's rate was fixed to the dollar from 1955 until 1984, with just one small devaluation (9 percent in 1981) during that period and a 15 percent devaluation at the end. Thailand did not even adjust its nominal exchange rate to its two severe adverse terms of trade shocks (the two oil shocks). The baht has tended to move with the dollar, even after formal pegging to the dollar ended.

India's rupee was fixed to sterling until 1975, with just one major devaluation (36 percent in 1966) during the postwar period before 1975. In 1975, India switched to a flexible peg tied to a trade-weighted basket. Since then, overt devaluations have been avoided, and there have been various movements in nominal and real rates. At times there seems to have been some tendency toward rigidity (but not actual fixing) in terms of the dollar; the real rate depreciated between late 1985 and 1988, reflecting dollar depreciation.

Pakistan's rate was unified in 1972, then devalued sharply (130 percent) because of the secession of Bangladesh. The rate was then pegged to the dollar until 1982. Since 1982 it has depreciated in terms of the dollar and in real terms.

In Indonesia, the nominal exchange rate was fixed to the dollar from 1970 to 1978, but there was substantial real appreciation owing to higher domestic inflation. This was made possible by the oil boom, which generated the Dutch Disease effect. In 1978 there was a 33 percent devaluation. Since then, the rupiah–dollar rate has been

---

[9] When expectations and capital mobility are introduced, a foreign exchange crisis can occur at this point.

kept fairly constant, apart from devaluations in 1983 (33 percent) and 1986 (31 percent).

Sri Lanka's exchange rate was fixed to sterling from 1952 to 1976 (with some devaluations after 1972). In 1977 the rate was unified, many exchange controls were removed, and there was a large (81 percent) depreciation. The rupee depreciated against the dollar until 1985 but stayed almost constant in trade-weighted nominal terms. During the period 1977–85, Sri Lanka's experience was somewhat similar to Indonesia's in 1970–78, with real appreciation resulting from some degree of rigidity of the (trade-weighted) nominal exchange rate.

So what can be said about the experience of these countries, in which the exchange rate was fixed in nominal terms for fairly long periods of time (either formally or effectively), sometimes to the dollar or sterling and at other times to a currency basket? Since 1973, the floating of the major currencies has clearly presented a problem—especially since 1981, when the dollar started appreciating and later depreciating. With the currency relationships among major trading partners changing so much, the concept of a clear nominal anchor became difficult to maintain and abandonment of the various pegs became inevitable—late though this was, in many cases, relative to the 1973 watershed year when the Bretton Woods system finally collapsed. We can sense that some of the Asian governments have wanted to maintain the credibility of a peg by moving with the dollar rather than firmly pegging to a basket, even after the formal peg to the dollar was ended. But this created problems by leading to unintended real appreciations or depreciations as the dollar moved up and down.[10]

Thailand, India, Pakistan, and Sri Lanka have been low-inflation countries, and even Indonesia (from 1969) could be categorized that way (certainly compared with the Latin American experience).[11] Did their exchange rate policies compel these countries to follow low-inflation fiscal and monetary policies in order to avoid balance

[10]This problem has been central to the literature on exchange rate policies for developing countries. How should developing countries fix their rates in a world where the major currencies are themselves floating? See Black (1976), Williamson (1982), and Joshi (1990).

[11]The average annual inflation rates (consumer price index) for the period 1965–88 have been 8.7 percent for Pakistan, 8.4 percent for Sri Lanka, 8.2 percent for India, and 6 percent for Thailand. For Indonesia, the inflation rates in each year during the period 1962–68 were well over 100 percent, but the average for 1969–88 was 14 percent. Figures for 1982–88 were 10.3 percent (Sri Lanka), 8.6 percent (India), 8.5 percent (Indonesia), 5.9 percent (Pakistan), and 3 percent (Thailand)—rather remarkable when seen from the Latin American perspective or, in the case of Thailand, from any perspective.

of payments and competitiveness problems? Can their low-inflation records be explained in terms of the exchange rate's function as a nominal anchor? The real commitment, I suspect, was not to the exchange rate as such, but to low inflation and hence to conservative domestic monetary and fiscal policies.[12]

What kept these countries off the South American road? What was the nature of their exchange rate commitment, especially up to 1981? Clearly, the commitment has not been absolute. There were devaluations before 1981 (and there have been significant real and nominal depreciations since 1982). In focusing on the pre-1982 period, it seems to me that the explanation for a considerable degree of the rigidity of nominal exchange rates lies in certain well-established beliefs.

One was a concern with prestige: devaluation was thought to represent an admission of failure. More generally, views about the desirability of fixed exchange rates remained widely held in these Asian countries even after the 1973 collapse of the Bretton Woods system. A second important factor was the thoroughly justified belief that devaluation was inflationary. In Sri Lanka's first macroeconomic crisis of 1968–70, devaluation was ruled out as an appropriate policy instrument because of concern with the adverse effect of a devaluation on newly established industries that depended heavily on imported inputs. Other countries have also had this concern.

When exchange rate pegging to a single currency came to an end, all five of these countries continued to follow low-inflation policies. Hindsight tells us that the spell of the fixed exchange rate may have backed up the anti-inflation commitment, so that there was some element of a nominal exchange rate anchor. But with substantial devaluations by some countries since 1973, and with large changes in bilateral nominal rates compelled by the fluctuations in the dollar, the spell has no doubt been broken by now.

Similar issues arise for various other countries in our group that maintained more or less fixed rates (sometimes with occasional devaluations) for long periods, namely Costa Rica until 1980 (with a devaluation in 1974), Kenya, Mexico until 1976, Morocco, Nigeria (to 1984), and Turkey. In all these cases, there have been long periods with fixed or near-fixed rates lasting well after the 1973 breakdown of the Bretton Woods system. Some of these countries—Costa Rica (briefly), Mexico, Nigeria, and Turkey—have gone through high-inflation episodes, while Kenya and Morocco have not. All have

---

[12] It must also be noted that all these countries used quantitative import restrictions and exchange controls for short-term balance of payments purposes (strongly so in the case of India, Pakistan, and Sri Lanka). So all had available a switching instrument that could substitute for devaluation—although not, of course, for continuous devaluation.

used quantitative restrictions for balance of payments purposes at various times. Only the two countries in our group that are part of the franc zone—Côte d'Ivoire and Cameroon—have had a true fixed exchange rate commitment, leading inevitably to low inflation and to real depreciations and appreciations that reflect movements in the franc-dollar rate.

The case of Turkey is particularly interesting. Since about 1977 the economy has moved from relatively low inflation to high inflation, a transformation associated with a switch in exchange rate regime from a fixed rate to a crawling peg.[13] From the point of view of the real targets approach, a very simple story can be told. For reasons that need not be discussed here, Turkey had its debt crisis from 1977 to 1979. The need to drastically improve the current account and to reverse the appreciation of the real exchange rate that occurred between 1974 and 1979 called for substantial real depreciation. As part of a major stabilization program, the nominal exchange rate was depreciated by about 70 percent in 1980. From 1981 on, the rate was adjusted daily. The net result was a substantial real depreciation of about 30 percent by 1984, followed quickly by a remarkable export boom. This episode was regarded by Balassa (1983) and others as a striking and praiseworthy example of the success of exchange rate policy and, above all, as evidence that export supply and demand elasticities were high.

How does this episode look from the point of view of the nominal anchor approach? The exchange rate was fixed to the U.S. dollar up to 1973, and during the period 1960–70 inflation averaged less than 5 percent. From 1971 to 1977, it averaged 18 percent. In 1980, an exceptional year, inflation was over 100 percent, reflecting the effects of the stabilization program, principally the big devaluation and large price adjustments by state enterprises. Inflation averaged 37.5 percent from 1981 to 1986 and has increased since then, reaching 75 percent in 1988 and 1989.

It is possible to argue that such a high rate of inflation sustained now for nine years after a drastic stabilization program can be explained only by the removal of the nominal anchor in 1980. If that is the case, we would have to say that Turkey faced a trade-off between the benefits of maintaining a more appropriate real exchange rate for some time and the longer-term costs of higher inflation. This could be described as an "exchange rate-adjusted Phillips curve" trade-off. It is the trade-off that is implied in conceding the validity of both the

---

[13] This discussion draws on the study on Turkey conducted for the World Bank project (Onis and Riedel (1993)).

real targets and the nominal anchor approaches. But against the view that the change in the exchange rate regime explains (or helps to explain) the relatively high inflation rate since 1981, it can be pointed out that the inflation rate was already beginning to increase in 1971 and had reached 44 percent by 1978.

A reasonable conclusion is that by 1980, substantial devaluation was essential and indeed inevitable. But a government more committed to low inflation might have tried to fix the exchange rate firmly at a new, more depreciated level. Yet this would have worked only if there had been a genuine long-term commitment to a noninflationary monetary policy (and hence fiscal policy) in support of the nominal anchor at its new level. This commitment would have required strong public support, including a willingness to accept the transitional costs.

Inflation and exchange rates in Latin American chronic-inflation countries

Any discussion of the exchange rate as a nominal anchor must refer to the much-discussed experiences of the four South American chronic-inflation countries in our group, as well as Mexico. Brazil and Colombia have practiced crawling peg policies over long periods, but it is clear in these cases that the exchange rate followed rather than led.[14] The aim of continuous nominal exchange rate adjustment was to avoid real appreciations—a clear example of the real targets approach in an inflationary context—not to slow up inflation by constraining government or sending signals to private agents. This "passive crawling peg" policy, as Williamson (1981) has called it, has also been practiced in Argentina, Chile, and Mexico since 1982.[15] Finally, Argentina and Chile had each experienced an earlier brief, but much discussed, nominal anchor episode.[16]

The Argentine episode of 1976–80 (under Finance Minister Martinez de Hoz) is now viewed as a classic case. A crawling peg

---

[14]See Urrutia on Colombia and Fendt on Brazil, both in Williamson (1981).

[15]With respect to Mexico, it should be added that, after six years of depreciation necessitated by high inflation, the Mexican peso was fixed to the dollar in 1988 and adjusted on the basis of an active crawling peg policy in 1989. Both episodes were part of the Mexican stabilization plan which, among other things, required limiting wage increases. But it is really not certain in this case that the exchange rate was the nominal anchor: the anchor was (and is, at the time of writing) the commitment to the whole stabilization plan.

[16]On Argentina see Calvo (1986); on Chile, Balassa (1985), Corbo (1985), and Edwards and Edwards (1987); and on both countries, Corbo, de Melo, and Tybout (1986) and Corbo and de Melo (1987).

exchange rate, with advance announcement of the devaluation rate (a *tablita*) operated for two years from 1979. In Williamson's (1981) classification, this was an "active crawling peg." A real appreciation resulted, and there was massive capital outflow. Domestic inflation failed to decline much because of continued high fiscal deficits. The failure of domestic inflation to decline sufficiently brought about the real appreciation. The failure was thus in the accompanying domestic policy, which led directly to a balance of payments problem and indirectly, because of the policy's lack of credibility, to a slow reaction by private agents.

In the case of Chile, the exchange rate was fixed to the dollar for a brief period from the end of 1979 until 1981 in order to bring inflation down from 33 percent. The policy succeeded, since inflation was 7 percent by the end of 1981. But there was still high unemployment and a large real appreciation (the U.S. dollar was appreciating during that period relative to other currencies, and Chilean inflation was still higher than U.S. inflation). Domestic monetary and fiscal policies were not out of line. To some extent, domestic prices and wages were slow to adjust to reduced inflation because of lagged wage indexation. But such slow adjustments in prices and wages in response to disinflationary policies could have been expected even if there had been no formal wage indexation. In addition, some degree of real appreciation was also to be expected because of massive capital in-flow. In my view, this much-analyzed episode cannot really be con-sidered a failure. Chile's subsequent problems arose because of excessive private borrowing during that brief period, a decline in the terms of trade, and a rise in real interest rates.

The two-year Chilean exchange rate commitment was a nominal anchor only insofar as the government chose to adhere to it. The fundamental commitment in Chile was to the objective of reducing inflation, just as in the five Asian countries the commitment has been to the objective of keeping inflation low.[17] The true anchor is the policymakers' conviction—usually rooted in and backed by widespread community conviction—that inflation is undesirable. Perhaps a fixed exchange rate has a role in signaling the government's anti-inflationary commitment to private agents. But they will always be alert—as they were in Argentina—to the possibility that the signal is a false one. If they are rational, they will look for the underlying commitment.

---

[17] A critique of the nominal anchor approach as applied to Chile can be found in Balassa (1985, 203–8).

IV. Capital Mobility: What Difference Does It Make?

Finally, in considering exchange rate policy, we cannot ignore the increase in capital mobility. Without going into the issue in detail, the judgment may be made that in many of the countries in our group—including Indonesia, Pakistan, Thailand, Morocco, Turkey, and all the Latin American countries—international capital mobility increased steadily during the 1970s and 1980s and is now high.[18] What is the implication of this finding for exchange rate policy?

In general, the appropriate model is still one in which sterilized intervention is possible—that is, in which domestic interest rate policy is distinct from foreign exchange rate intervention policy. Hence the model is one of imperfect capital mobility, whether owing to partially effective exchange controls or imperfect substitutability of domestic currency-denominated and foreign (usually dollar) assets.

The implication is that it is no longer possible to maintain for any length of time a nominal exchange rate that the market considers seriously overvalued. Such expectations would lead to capital outflow and thus to a balance of payments problem, unless domestic interest rates rose sufficiently. And the tightening of domestic monetary policy to sustain an exchange rate may have to be so severe that there are limits to this instrument. While the exchange rate does not have to float, the rate must be quickly adjusted when market expectations turn significantly against it.

Some countries' policies of maintaining exchange rates have been so consistent and hence so credible that market pressures against it hardly take place. Perhaps Thailand is the best example. But for most developing countries, the days of the Bretton Woods "fixed but occasionally adjustable" system are over. This consideration explains why many countries in our group have moved in the direction of more flexibility since 1982—usually, so far, to flexible pegs rather than floating rates (with the exception of Nigeria, which has had a floating rate since 1986).

---

[18] Measuring capital mobility is difficult (see Cumby and Obstfeld (1983), Cuddington (1986), various papers in Lessard and Williamson (1987), and Haque and Montiel (1990)). It is not sufficient to look at actual capital movements. There have been dramatic episodes of capital flight from Argentina and Mexico, so clearly mobility is high in those cases. But capital mobility may also be high in the case of a country such as Brazil where, until recently, incentives for capital outflow were not as strong—because the flexibility of the nominal exchange rate was designed to maintain the real rate. In other countries, interest rates are raised quickly when there is a tendency toward capital outflow; in still other countries, notably Pakistan and Turkey, the flow of remittances from citizens working abroad is likely to vary to some extent in response to exchange rate expectations.

The Bretton Woods system broke down in 1973 largely because of increasing capital mobility and the failure of the United States, and perhaps others, to pursue credible domestic policies to sustain particular rates. Thus the developed world moved into the floating rate stage. By contrast, the developing countries (other than the four chronic-inflation countries of South America) generally tried until around 1982 to maintain either fixed rates or a fairly inflexible peg, with intermittent adjustments. But capital mobility increased for them as well, although with a lag, and many of these economies became destabilized as a result of the recession and debt crisis of 1980–82. With a few exceptions, their exchange rate regimes have now become much more flexible, and it seems unlikely that they could go back to the fixed but adjustable regimes of the earlier period.

This has implications for both the real targets and the nominal anchor approaches. Both call, at any point in time, for a policy-determined nominal rate. It might be an active crawling peg, but this still means that it is fixed at a point in time. Yet such a rate cannot be sustained unless the market is convinced it will be sustained. It is true that expectations of depreciation can be offset by sufficiently high domestic interest rates. But the need to target domestic monetary policy on sustaining the exchange rate when the market expects substantial depreciation is itself a constraint on the attempt to fix the exchange rate.[19]

It follows that the whole package of policies that goes with an exchange rate commitment—whether to achieve a real target or a nominal anchor—must be thoroughly credible if an exchange rate is to be maintained. This is conceivable when a country has been following consistent policies in the past (like Thailand or like Mexico up to 1973) and is perhaps keeping the rate constant or crawling on some steady basis. In the absence of such credibility, the actual rate

[19]The problem arises only when expected depreciation substantially exceeds expected domestic inflation, so that a high real interest rate is required to sustain the current nominal exchange rate. But a high real exchange rate has adverse effects both for private investment and for the budget. This problem is intensified when inflationary expectations are excessive (when actual inflation falls below expected inflation). In addition, in many developing countries the domestic free market rate exceeds the international (U.S.) rate by a substantial risk factor. The net effect of all these factors is exemplified by Mexico's experience. In 1989, when Mexico practiced an active crawling peg policy, its real rate of interest as usually calculated was around 30 percent, while the U.S. rate was closer to 4 percent. The usual calculation assumes that the expected rate of inflation is equal to the current rate, but there is little doubt that in this case the expected rate of inflation in Mexico exceeded the remarkably low current rate, so that the true real rate of interest must have been less than 30 percent.

would have to follow the direction in which the market expects it to move.

The policy implication is that, when there is high capital mobility, it is no longer possible to have extensive discussions about the appropriate real exchange rate and what this implies for the nominal rate, and then to make a major adjustment, perhaps as part of a stabilization program. Changes have to be made quickly, and normally they must be small and more frequent. This is the direction in which countries have been moving. When large changes are expected—and it is rare for a large change to be unexpected[20]—the market will force an early adjustment. If particular changes are desired in order to achieve real targets, the domestic policies that go with them must be in place or credibility about policy intentions must first be established. If there is a change in the fundamentals, such as a change in the terms of trade or a major trade liberalization, a nominal exchange rate change will be expected and cannot be delayed. If quick policy action does not bring it about, the market will force it.

While all the issues connected with the two approaches remain relevant when there is capital mobility, and the basic trade-offs remain the same, credibility now becomes crucial. If either approach calls for a particular nominal exchange rate and the market does not believe it will be sustained, two steps will need to be taken quickly. First, domestic monetary policy will need to be tightened sufficiently to maintain the rate immediately. Second, signals will need to be sent out—for example, through fiscal policy decisions—that will convince the market the rate will be sustained. Argentina's short episode in 1979–80 under Martinez de Hoz clearly shows what happens when this is not done.

V. Conclusion

Is it possible to conclude with some simple policy recommendations? I would suggest four propositions that have important repercussions. First, in general, the real targets approach to exchange rate policy is the right one. The exchange rate should follow rather than lead, taking into account the various shocks or changes in other variables—notably fiscal policy, trade policy, and terms of trade changes.

---

[20]The one example from our group of countries of a large unexpected devaluation is the 33 percent Indonesian devaluation of 1978, the motive for which was "exchange rate protection" of the tradables sectors, not a balance of payments problem (see Warr (1984)). It appears from the low forward premium that the 15 percent Thai devaluation of 1984 was also unanticipated.

Second, exchange rate policy should be associated with an appropriate noninflationary monetary policy. Normally, there has to be a direct commitment to the anti-inflation objective if inflation is to be avoided. In the absence of such a commitment—with monetary policies being inflationary—exchange rate policy must still be aimed at the real target (the real exchange rate) unless there is reason to believe that this would significantly affect the commitment itself.

Third, because of capital mobility, delayed exchange rate adjustments must be avoided; if the rate needs to be changed, it should be done quickly.

Fourth, there is some role for the nominal anchor approach for the two groups of countries at opposite extremes of the inflation scale. One group includes countries that have long-established fixed exchange rate systems (with occasional devaluations) and relatively noninflationary records. These countries may be well advised to stay with such a system, since their commitment will be credible. I think here especially of Thailand (and possibly Indonesia) and, of course, of the African countries in the franc zone. But only a few countries in our group could fall into this category now, although many more would have in 1973.[21]

At the other extreme are countries with a history of high inflation that are ready to stabilize by radically shifting their policies and making the necessary commitment. These countries may find a fixed exchange rate (or an active crawling peg) a valuable anchor in helping to constrain government monetary policies and in achieving credibility with the markets (including the labor market). Possibly Argentina, Brazil, and Mexico are in this category. But whenever a fixed rate regime or an active crawl is chosen, there is likely to be some cost because of the real exchange rate misalignment (the exchange rate-adjusted Phillips curve trade-off), at least for a limited period.

[21]We might even wonder about the franc zone countries. As a result of a public spending boom in Côte d'Ivoire in 1976–80, inflation increased, causing a real appreciation, which led to increased tariff and nontariff import restrictions. Latin American-style inflation has certainly been avoided in spite of a prolonged fiscal crisis, but import restrictions and a severely reduced growth rate have not.

References

Balassa, Bela. 1983. "Outward Orientation and Exchange Rate Policy in Developing Countries: The Turkish Experience." In *Change and Challenge in the World Economy*, edited by Bela Balassa. London: MacMillan.

———.1985. "Policy Experiments in Chile, 1973–83." *The National Economic Policies of Chile*, edited by Gary M. Walton. Greenwich, Conn.: JAI Press.

———.1987. "Effects of Exchange Rate Changes in Developing Countries." DRD Discussion Paper 291. Washington, D.C.: The World Bank, Development Research Department.

Black, Stanley W. 1976. *Exchange Policies for Less Developed Countries in a World of Floating Rates.* Essays in International Finance No. 119. Princeton, N.J.: Princeton University, International Finance Section, Department of Economics.

Calvo, Guillermo. 1986. "Fractured Liberalism: Argentina under Martinez de Hoz." *Economic Development and Cultural Change* 34 (April): 511–33.

Corbo, Vittorio. 1985. "Reforms and Adjustments in Chile during 1974–84." *World Development* 13: 893–916.

Corbo, Vittorio, and Jaime de Melo. 1987. "Lessons from the Southern Cone Policy Reforms." *The World Bank Research Observer* 2 (July): 111–42.

Corbo, Vittorio, Jaime de Melo, and James Tybout. 1986. "What Went Wrong with the Recent Policy Reforms in the Southern Cone?" *Economic Development and Cultural Change* 34 (April): 607–40.

Corden, W. Max. 1971. *The Theory of Protection.* Oxford: Oxford University Press.

Cuddington, John T. 1986. "Capital Flight: Estimates, Issues and Explanations." Princeton Studies in International Finance No. 58. Princeton, N.J.: Princeton University, International Finance Section, Department of Economics.

Cumby, R.E., and M. Obstfeld. 1983. "Capital Mobility and the Scope for Sterilization: Mexico in the 1970s." In *Financial Policies and the World Capital Market*, edited by Pedro Aspe Armella. Chicago: University of Chicago Press.

Edwards, Sebastian. 1989. *Real Exchange Rates, Devaluation, and Adjustment: Exchange Rate Policy in Developing Countries.* Cambridge, Mass.: MIT Press.

Edwards, Sebastian, and A. Cox Edwards. 1987. *Monetarism and Liberalization: The Chilean Experience.* Cambridge, Mass.: Ballinger.

Edwards, Sebastian, and Sweder van Wijnbergen. 1987. "Tariffs, Real Exchange Rate, and the Terms of Trade: On Two Popular Propositions in International Economics." *Oxford Economic Papers* 39 (September): 458–64.

Haque, Nadeem, and Peter Montiel. 1990. "Capital Mobility in Developing Countries: Some Empirical Tests." IMF Working Paper 90/117. Washington, D.C.: International Monetary Fund.

Joshi, V. 1990. "Exchange Rate Regimes in Developing Countries." In *Public Policy and Economic Development: Essays in Honor of Ian Little*, edited by Maurice F. Scott and Deepak Lal. Oxford: Oxford University Press.

Krueger, Anne. 1978. *Foreign Trade Regimes and Economic Development: Liberalization Attempts and Consequences.* Cambridge, Mass.: Ballinger.

Lessard, Donald R., and John Williamson. 1987. *Capital Flight and Third World Debt*. Washington, D.C.: Institute for International Economics.

Little, Ian, Richard Cooper, W. Max Corden, and Sarath Rajapatirana. 1993. *Boom, Crisis, and Adjustment: The Macroeconomic Experience of Developing Countries*. New York: Oxford University Press for the World Bank.

Onis, Ziya, and James Riedel. 1993. *Economic Crisis and Long-Term Growth in Turkey*. World Bank Comparative Macroeconomic Studies. Washington, D.C.: The World Bank.

Salter, W.E.G. 1959. "Internal and External Balance: The Role of Price and Expenditure Effects." *Economic Record* 35 (August): 226–38.

Swan, T.W. 1963. "Longer Run Problems of the Balance of Payments." In *The Australian Economy: A Volume of Readings*, edited by H.W. Arndt and W. Max Corden. Melbourne: Cheshire.

Warr. P.G. 1984. "Exchange Rate Protection in Indonesia." *Bulletin of Indonesian Economic Studies* 20 (August): 53–89.

Williamson, John, ed. 1981. *Exchange Rate Rules*. New York: St. Martin's Press.

Williamson, John. 1982. "A Survey of the Literature on the Optimal Peg." *Journal of Development Economics* 11 (August): 39–61.

Inflation Stabilization and Nominal Anchors 4

Guillermo A. Calvo and Carlos A. Végh

Since the late 1940s, many developing countries have suffered from chronic inflation. Chronic inflation is characterized by high—relative to industrial countries—and persistent inflation (Pazos (1972)). Unlike hyperinflation, which is measured in terms of months and exhibits an explosive nature, chronic inflation may last several decades and is relatively stable. By Harberger's (1981) definition—annual inflation of 20 percent or more for at least five consecutive years—countries such as Argentina, Brazil, Chile, Israel, Mexico, Peru, and Uruguay have experienced long periods of chronic inflation.

Repeated attempts to eliminate chronic inflation have often met with only temporary success, after which inflation has returned with a vengeance. More often than not, the failure of stabilization plans reflects the absence of a lasting fiscal adjustment. Although Chile, Israel, Mexico, and, more recently, Argentina have all succeeded in reducing inflation to under 15 percent per year, even some fiscally sound programs (for instance, the Chilean and Uruguayan programs of the late 1970s) faced insurmountable hurdles.

The Southern Cone programs of the late 1970s in Argentina, Chile, and Uruguay were characterized by an initial boom that made reducing the inflation rate of nontraded goods particularly difficult. The recessionary effects that, according to conventional wisdom, should follow from inflation stabilization came only later in the program. The Southern Cone programs thus gave rise to the intriguing idea—captured by the expression "recession now versus recession later"—that the choice between using the money supply or the

Note: This is a revised version of a paper presented at the Western Economic Association International 67th Annual Conference, San Francisco, July 9-13, 1992, in a session organized by John Welch of the Federal Reserve Bank of Dallas. The authors are grateful to José Fajgenbaum, Carlos Medeiros, Gerald O'Driscoll Jr., Ratna Sahay, Pierre Siklos, Peter Wickham, conference participants, and two anonymous referees for helpful comments and discussions. A previous version of this paper was issued as an IMF working paper (PPAA 92/4). The views expressed in this paper are those of the authors and do not necessarily represent those of the International Monetary Fund.

exchange rate as the nominal anchor may mean choosing the *timing* of the recession. With money-based stabilization, the output costs are paid up front (recession now), whereas with exchange rate-based stabilization, the costs are paid at a later stage (recession later).

The experience of the Southern Cone programs also led some observers to argue that a single nominal anchor might not be enough to ensure rapid disinflation, as lack of credibility, backward indexation, and nonsynchronized price setting tend to cause inflation to persist (see, for instance, Edwards and Edwards (1991)). These considerations prompted the introduction of additional nominal anchors—most notably incomes policies—in the programs of the mid-1980s in Argentina, Brazil, Israel, and Mexico.

This paper examines the role of nominal anchors in inflation stabilization programs in chronic-inflation countries. Section I reviews aspects of the experience of chronic-inflation countries undertaking inflation stabilization programs. Section II interprets the evidence in an analytical framework, and Section III analyzes the use of multiple anchors. Section IV presents policy conclusions.

I. Inflation Stabilization: Empirical Evidence

Reviewed here are the main empirical regularities associated with inflation stabilization in chronic-inflation countries.

Exchange rate-based stabilization

The following 11 major programs in Latin America and Israel are considered: (i) the heterodox programs of the 1960s in Argentina, Brazil, and Uruguay; (ii) the orthodox programs of the late 1970s (the *tablitas*) in Argentina, Chile, and Uruguay; (iii) the heterodox programs of the mid-1980s in Argentina, Brazil, Israel, and Mexico; and (iv) the 1991 Convertibility plan in Argentina (see, for instance, Kiguel and Liviatan (1992a) and Végh (1992)).

These programs share several characteristics.

Slow convergence of inflation to the rate of devaluation

The four-quarter inflation rate has remained above the four-quarter devaluation rate (Table 1).

Real appreciation of the domestic currency

Given the slow convergence of inflation, it should come as no surprise that the domestic currency has appreciated substantially in real terms (Table 1).

Table 1. Inflation, Devaluation, and Real Exchange Rate Appreciation in Selected Exchange Rate-Based Programs

| Programs | Period[1] | Quarter Before Program | | Last Quarter of Program | | Real Exchange Rate Appreciation (in percent)[3] |
		Devaluation Rate (4Q change)[2]	Inflation Rate (4Q change)	Devaluation Rate (4Q change)	Inflation Rate (4Q change)	
Argentina 1967	1967.2–1970.1	85.6	26.6	0.0	8.5	25.0
Brazil 1964	1964.2–1968.2	188.0	95.4	18.6	20.7	26.6
Uruguay 1968	1968.3–1971.3	183.1	167.2	0.0	23.6	28.6
Argentine *tablita*	1979.1–1980.4	67.9	167.3	23.1	88.7	46.3
Chilean *tablita*	1978.1–1982.1	60.5	66.3	0.0	7.6	28.8
Uruguayan *tablita*[4]	1978.4–1982.3	28.3	41.9	15.1	25.2	48.2
Argentine Austral	1985.3–1986.3	1,462.2	1,036.2	33.5	59.4	4.6
Brazilian Cruzado	1986.2–1986.4	211.0	263.5	42.0	76.7	9.3
Israel 1985[5]	1985.3–1990.2	434.0	386.1	3.3	16.4	16.7
Mexico 1987[5]	1988.1–1992.4	139.3	148.4	1.4	13.2	36.6
Arg. Convertibility[6]	1991.2–1992.4	106.8	453.0	−0.8	17.8	20.2

Sources: Bufman and Leiderman (1993), Di Tella (1983), Kiguel and Liviatan (1989), Machinea and Fanelli (1988), and IMF's *International Financial Statistics* (various years).
[1]Quarters during which the program was in effect. If a program started late in a quarter, the following quarter is taken as the first quarter.
[2]Four-quarter (4Q) change indicates percentage change over same quarter of previous year.
[3]Cumulative real appreciation (i.e., fall in the real exchange rate) during the program. Yearly data was used for Brazil 1964, Uruguay 1968, and Israel 1985.
[4]Last quarter for devaluation and inflation refers to 82.1, before the devaluation rate was increased.
[5]Duration of program has been arbitrarily set at five years.
[6]Program in progress; terminal date determined by data availability.

Deterioration of the trade balance and the current account

The current account normally worsened during the programs (Table 2). A similar pattern holds for the trade balance (Végh (1992)).[1] Large trade account imbalances, fueled by imports of durable goods, were usually responsible for the current account deficits.

Initial increase in real activity (i.e., real private consumption and real GDP) followed by a later contraction

Table 3 shows the growth of private consumption before and after stabilization; real GDP figures follow a similar pattern (Végh (1992)). In Israel, the late slowdown occurred in spite of the program's success. The Mexican program proved to be an exception, in that no late

[1]The improvement in the current account in Israel is related mainly to the fall in investment and the rise in unilateral transfers (see Bufman and Leiderman (1993)). There was, however, a trade deficit during the five years following the program that averaged 7.1 percent of GDP.

Table 2: Current Account and Real Interest Rates in Selected Stabilization Programs

| Programs | Period[1] | Current Account Balance (as percent of GDP) | | Real Interest Rates[2] (in percent per year) | | |
		Three Years Before Program	During Program	Four Quarters Before Program	First Four Quarters	Last Four Quarters
		(average)				
Exchange Rate-Based						
Argentina 1967	1967–70	1.4	−0.2	...	...	...
Brazil 1964	1964–68	−1.2	0.0	...	...	...
Uruguay 1968	1969–71	1.7	−1.7	...	...	...
Argentine *tablita*	1979–81	2.1	−2.5	0.7	−2.8	5.9
Chilean *tablita*	1978–82	−3.1	−8.6	70.9	43.0	46.4
Uruguayan *tablita*	1979–82	−2.8	−4.6	18.2	−7.2	24.9
Argentine Austral[3]	1986	−2.8	−3.6	20.0	48.0	−7.5
Brazilian Cruzado[3]	1986	−1.1	−1.7	−4.5	8.5	−9.5
Israel 1985[4,5]	1986–90	−2.5	1.1	−2.0	21.2	11.0
Mexico 1987[4]	1988–92	0.7	−3.9	−2.9	29.2	2.0
Arg. Convertibility[6]	1991–92	−0.6	−2.6	38.1	−2.0	4.0
Money-Based						
Chile 1975[7]	1975–77	−3.1	−3.1	...	127.2	58.0
Argentine Bonex	1990	−3.6	1.7	−7.4	112.7	—
Brazilian Collor[8]	1990	3.2	2.0	−8.1	−2.4	—
Dominican Rep. 1990[6,9]	1990–92	−4.5	−3.8	...	15.1	13.7
Peru 1990[6]	1990–92	−4.0	−4.6	−17.3	235.0	48.1

Sources: Baliño (1991), Barkai (1990), Bufman and Leiderman (1993). Castro and Ronci (1991), Cukierman (1988), Kiguel and Liviatan (1989), Peréz-Campanero and Leone (1991), IMF's *International Financial Statistics* (various years), and country authorities.
[1] Calendar years during which the program was taken to be in effect for the purposes of current account figures.
[2] Quarterly real lending rates unless otherwise indicated. Periods specified in Tables 1 and 4 apply. Ellipses indicate data are not available. Dashes indicate data do not apply.
[3] Real interest rates are reported for two-quarter periods and exclude the initial price shock.
[4] Duration of program has been arbitrarily set at five years.
[5] Real interest rate before program refers to two quarters before.
[6] Program in progress.
[7] Annual real interest rates.
[8] Monthly averages of overnight interest rates on government securities. Real interest rate after the program refers to first three quarters.
[9] Real interest rates for 1991.3 and 1991.4. Before January 1991, interest rates were subject to controls.

recession occurred. The boom-recession cycle was usually more pronounced for durable goods consumption, as shown in Table 3 for Israel.

Ambiguous response of domestic real interest rates

While ex post domestic real interest rates fell in the early stages of the *tablitas* and Argentina's Convertibility plan (although in Chile they remained extremely high), they appear to have increased substantially in the early stages of the heterodox programs of the mid-1980s (Table 2).

Table 3. Private Consumption in Selected Stabilization Programs
(Annual rate of growth, in percent)

Programs	Period[1]	Three Years Before Program (average)	First Year	Second Year	Third Year	Fourth Year	Fifth Year
Exchange Rate-Based							
Argentina 1967	1967–70	6.8	2.6	4.0	6.4	4.1	4.4
Brazil 1964[2]	1964–68	3.6	3.3	0.7	4.3	9.6	10.2
Uruguay 1968	1969–71	0.5	8.2	6.4	1.0	−0.2	—
Argentine *tablita*	1979–81	−4.2	14.4	5.6	−3.6	−13.3	—
Chilean *tablita*	1978–82	1.0	7.5	6.5	6.8	10.1	−12.1
Uruguayan *tablita*	1979–82	0.2	9.0	5.0	2.4	−9.7	−9.1
Argentine Austral	1986	1.2	7.9	0.7	—	—	—
Brazilian Cruzado	1986	2.8	6.4	−0.9	—	—	—
Israel 1985[3] Total[4]	1986–90	0.6	14.8	9.0	4.3	0.0	5.3
Durables		−6.2	49.7	13.2	5.8	−12.8	17.1
Mexico 1987[3]	1988–92	0.3	1.8	6.3	5.7	5.0	4.9
Arg. Convertibility[5,6]	1991–92	−2.1	6.7	10.8	—	—	—
Money-Based							
Chile 1975	1975–77	−6.3	−11.4	0.3	16.0	7.5	—
Argentine Bonex	1990	−1.2	−1.8	6.7	—	—	—
Brazilian Collor	1990	−0.5	−2.5	3.9	—	—	—
Dominican Rep. 1990[6,7]	1990–92	−0.3	−12.9	7.5	...	—	—
Peru 1990[6,7]	1990–92	1.5	−15.3	10.8	−1.1	—	—

Sources: Bufman and Leiderman (1993), Favaro and Bensión (1993), Kiguel and Liviatan (1989), Lustig (1992), Medeiros (1993), Viana (1990), IMF's *International Financial Statistics* (various years), World Bank tables, Fundacion Mediterranea, country authorities, and IMF staff estimates.

[1] Calendar years during which the program was taken to be in effect. Figures reported include data up to one year after the program ended. Ellipses indicate data are not available. Dashes indicate data do not apply.

[2] Average before the program corresponds to two years before.

[3] Duration of program has been arbitrarily set at five years.

[4] Total (durables and nondurables) private consumption.

[5] Figure for second year corresponds to total (private and public) consumption.

[6] Program in progress.

[7] Figures correspond to quarterly real GDP and refer to the four-quarter rate of growth in the quarter before the program, two quarters after the program, and then every four quarters.

Money-based stabilization

Five major programs will be considered: the 1975 Chilean plan; the 1989 Bonex plan in Argentina; and the 1990 programs in Brazil (the Collor plan), Peru, and the Dominican Republic (see Edwards and Edwards (1991), Kiguel and Liviatan (1992b), and Medeiros (1993)).[2]

---

[2] In the Dominican Republic plan, dual exchange rates were in place for a year before being unified into a single floating rate (see Medeiros (1993)). Under dual rates, however, money is still the nominal anchor.

Table 4. Inflation, Money Growth, and Real Exchange Rate Appreciation in Selected Money-Based Programs

Programs	Period[1]	Quarter Before		Last Quarter		Real Exchange Rate Appreciation (in percent)[3]
		Money Growth (4Q change)[2]	Inflation Rate (4Q change)	Money Growth (4Q change)	Inflation Rate (4Q change)	
Chile 1975	1975.2–1977.4	234.6	363.6	113.0	66.3	41.8
Argentine Bonex	1990.1–1990.4	4,096.2	4,144.8	1,070.5	1,629.1	51.2
Brazilian Collor[4]	1990.2–1990.4	6,791.5	6,232.4	2,382.7	1,476.6	9.7
Dominican Rep. 1990[5]	1990.3–1992.4	40.2	40.8	16.9	6.2	9.0
Peru 1990[5]	1990.3–1992.2	1,823.6	2,085.6	73.7	86.9	25.5

Sources: Corbo (1985), IMF's *International Financial Statistics* (various years), Instituto Brasileiro de Economia, country authorities, and IMF staff estimates.

[1] Quarters during which the program was in effect. If a program started late in a quarter, the following quarter is taken as the first quarter.

[2] Four-quarter (4Q) change indicates percentage change over same quarter of previous year.

[3] Cumulative real appreciation (i.e., fall in the real exchange rate) during the program.

[4] Monthly data; program period is 90.03–90.12. Real appreciation was computed using parallel exchange rate.

[5] Program in progress; terminal date determined by data availability.

Given the small number of money-based programs in chronic-inflation countries, the evolution of the macroeconomic variables presented here should be viewed only as suggestive.

Slow convergence of inflation to the rate of monetary growth

Inflation persisted in some money-based programs, although it seemed to converge more quickly than in exchange rate-based programs (Table 4).

Real appreciation of the domestic currency

The real exchange rate appreciated in all five programs, often substantially (Table 4).

No clear-cut response in the trade balance and current account

The trade balance and current account showed an ambiguous response (Table 2). If anything, the external accounts showed a short-run improvement.

Initial contraction in economic activity

As Table 3 suggests, money-based stabilization appears to have caused a sharp (though short-lived) contraction in economic activity at the beginning of the programs.

Initial increase in domestic real interest rates

The liquidity "crunch" associated with a money-based stabilization resulted in sharp increases in real interest rates (Table 2).

II. A Basic Analytical Framework

Since the model has been formally developed elsewhere (Calvo and Végh (1990 and 1993)), the assumptions will be reviewed only briefly and the results explained intuitively. The economy is small and open, with perfect capital mobility. On the demand side, the public consumes traded and nontraded (or home) goods. Consumers must use money to purchase goods and so face a cash-in-advance constraint. As a result, the opportunity cost of holding money (i.e., the nominal interest rate) affects the cost of consumption (i.e., the *effective* price of consumption). A fall in the nominal interest rate reduces the effective price of consumption by lowering the opportunity cost of holding money.

On the supply side, the supply of traded goods is fixed and the supply of nontraded goods determined by demand. Firms that produce nontraded goods stagger prices, taking into account the expected path of aggregate demand and the aggregate price level. This nonsynchronization in price setting implies that while the *aggregate* price level is fixed at each point in time, the inflation rate is free to adjust instantaneously.

Exchange rate-based stabilization

Policymakers may announce a reduction in the rate of devaluation. If the announcement is fully credible—in the sense that the public believes the reduction in the devaluation rate will be permanent—inflation falls immediately to the new equilibrium value determined by the lower rate of devaluation. Furthermore, there are no real costs associated with eliminating inflation at one fell swoop. This exercise may be useful in interpreting the end of hyperinflations (Végh (1992)).

Given the history of failed stabilizations, however, policies in chronic-inflation countries are not likely to be fully credible. So the announcement may not be credible, in the sense that the public expects the higher rate of devaluation to resume at some point. The fall in the nominal interest rate (due to perfect capital mobility) is then viewed as temporary, reducing the cost of present relative to future consumption. The ensuing increase in aggregate demand leads to expanded output and a trade deficit. The overheated economy keeps inflation above the rate of devaluation, resulting in a sustained real appreciation. Over time, the real appreciation reduces excess aggregate demand for home goods, causing output to decline. Eventually, the economy falls into a recession.

The model is thus able to rationalize most of the empirical regularities described in Section I. (See Reinhart and Végh (1992) for a quantitative analysis.) Furthermore, the boom-recession cycle occurs whether or not the program is eventually abandoned. Hence, the model may also explain recessions occurring in successful programs, such as Israel's. Domestic real interest rates fall in the model; the decline is consistent with the evidence on orthodox programs. The high real interest rates observed in the heterodox programs may be explained by the use of additional nominal anchors (see below).

Money-based stabilization

Alternately, policymakers may announce a reduction in the rate of growth of the money supply. (The results that follow require that real money demand be interest-rate elastic, something that is not essential to exchange rate-based stabilization.) If the announcement is credible (i.e., the lower rate of money growth is expected to be permanent), the long-run demand for real money balances increases. Inflation must then fall below the rate of monetary growth to generate higher real money balances over time. The initial drop in inflation reduces the nominal interest rate, increasing real money demand. Since the real money supply is given on impact (given that the price level is sticky), there is excess demand for real money balances. Money market equilibrium can be restored only by a recession that reduces the demand for real money balances.[3] This recession is brought about by higher real interest rates (which reduce today's demand for home goods relative to tomorrow's) and a real exchange rate appreciation (which decreases the demand for nontraded relative to traded goods).

If the announcement is not credible, the picture remains qualitatively unchanged, because, with an exogenous money supply and sticky prices, the results are driven primarily by the fact that the real money supply cannot change at the time the plan is implemented. The only difference is that the current account, which remains in balance if the announcement is fully credible, goes into

---

[3]In theory, this initial recession could be avoided simply by engineering an initial once-and-for-all increase in the *level* of the nominal money supply at the same time that the *rate of change* of the money supply is being reduced. In practice, however, this is likely to be interpreted as a lack of commitment to a tight monetary policy that would severely undermine the credibility of the program.

deficit as people anticipating the policy's reversal consume more. *Quantitatively*, however, credibility plays a crucial role: the less credible the program, the smaller the initial fall in inflation. Lack of credibility also mitigates the initial recession, because the nominal interest rate does not fall by much—it is not "anchored" exogenously at a lower level as it is with exchange rate-based stabilization—so real money demand increases very little. A lack of credibility is not costly, in the sense that lower benefits go hand in hand with lower costs.

The model's predictions for money-based stabilization are consistent with the facts discussed above: the initial drop in inflation is accompanied by a recession, real appreciation, and high real interest rates. When a policy is not credible, the model predicts a current account deficit, although the evidence on this is not clear-cut.

III. Multiple Anchors

This section discusses the use of monetary and credit constraints and incomes policies as additional nominal anchors.

Tight monetary and credit policy

Too much liquidity in the initial stages of an exchange rate-based program may prove dangerous, because it finances the initial consumption binge and contributes to an initial real exchange rate appreciation. Therefore, policymakers have frequently attempted to use additional anchors to put a lid on the forces unleashed by too much liquidity. The 1985 Israeli plan, for example, included an explicit target for bank credit, which was to be implemented by increased reserve requirements, a higher discount rate, and a tightening of existing controls on short-term capital flows (Barkai (1990)). The ensuing liquidity "crunch" provoked a sharp initial rise in real interest rates (Table 2), perhaps explaining the initial (albeit brief) downturn in economic activity that preceded the consumption boom. Analytically, Calvo and Végh (1993) show that using money as an additional nominal anchor results in high real interest rates, real exchange rate appreciation, and an initial recession.

Sterilized intervention is a popular method of insulating the domestic money stock from the expansionary effects of capital inflows at the beginning of a program. But even if it proves effective in temporarily controlling the money supply, sterilized intervention may impose a severe fiscal burden, as the government is forced to pay higher interest rates on the public debt than it receives on the world market for its reserves (see Calvo, Leiderman, and Reinhart (1993)).

Price and wage controls

Inflation inertia (defined as inflation of nontraded goods that remains above the growth rate of the nominal anchor) has characterized many programs. It may result from, among other factors, lack of credibility (as in the model discussed above) or widespread backward indexation (Pazos (1972)). Price and wage controls have usually been advocated in the belief that they help fight inflation inertia and that they may make a program more credible. However, removing the controls too soon may unleash the same problems with credibility and inflation inertia the controls were supposed to address in the first place. Removing them too late may result in highly distorted relative prices with ensuing real costs.

More importantly, however, the use of incomes policies does not seem to alter the outcome of exchange rate-based stabilization: both orthodox and heterodox plans share similar characteristics, as discussed in Section I. This finding suggests that price and wage controls cannot solve the underlying problems related to lack of credibility. Rather than resorting to price controls, the best hope is probably to switch from backward- to forward-looking indexation—that is, to adjust wages at the beginning of the program according to expected inflation.

IV. Policy Conclusions

The preceding analysis suggests several policy conclusions.

- Although a recession seems unavoidable when a stabilization policy lacks credibility, the *timing* of the downturn appears to depend heavily on the choice of the nominal anchor.
- A lack of credibility may be more disruptive when exchange rates are predetermined than when they are floating. With money-based stabilization, lower credibility reduces the benefits (i.e., inflation falls by less) but the real effects tend to vanish as well. With exchange rate-based stabilization, lower credibility also reduces the benefits (inflation may even increase) but the real disruptions are magnified. If the public is perceived as highly skeptical, a money-based strategy can be less risky. On the other hand, if credibility is high (because there is a new administration taking over, for example), the exchange rate should probably be favored as a nominal anchor, as it allows for a speedier adjustment of real money balances.
- Attempting to pursue a disinflationary policy while maintaining a competitive real exchange rate is likely to be self-defeating. Both theory (see Section II) and evidence (see Section I) suggest that real appreciation is an unavoidable byproduct of lowering

inflation. Moreover, the public's perception that the authorities may be pursuing both objectives at the same time is bound to undermine credibility further. The experience of Israel and Mexico suggests that in exchange rate-based programs, adjustments in the nominal exchange rate (i.e., devaluations or changes in the rate of devaluation) aimed at correcting the real appreciation should be postponed, if possible, until the fundamentals are perceived to be well under control. Initial large devaluations aimed at making room for the inevitable real appreciation also proved helpful in the cases of Israel and Mexico.

- It should be stressed that the dynamics of disinflationary policy discussed in this paper are unrelated to fiscal problems. This fact is particularly worrisome because it illustrates the stabilization programs' vulnerability to the private sector's beliefs about the economic or political sustainability of such programs. A serious fiscal adjustment may not be enough to ensure the success of a program if, for some reason, the public believes that the plan will eventually be abandoned. Policymakers must be able to convince the public that a policy will be sustained over time.
- Currency substitution, a widespread phenomenon in chronic-inflation countries, appears to tilt the balance in favor of the exchange rate as the nominal anchor (Calvo and Végh (1992)). If the elasticity of substitution between foreign and domestic currency is very high—which is bound to be the case after many years of high inflation—then the system may be left without a nominal anchor under flexible exchange rates. Otherwise, floating rates do provide a nominal anchor to the system. Currency substitution may make the initial liquidity "crunch" and the ensuing recession more severe as the public attempts to switch from foreign to domestic currency. But other things being equal, currency substitution appears to render the exchange rate more attractive as the nominal anchor.

References

Baliño, Tomás J.T. 1991. "The Argentine Banking Crisis of 1980." In *Banking Crisis: Cases and Issues*, edited by V. Sundararajan and Tomás J.T. Baliño. Washington, D.C.: International Monetary Fund.

Barkai, Haim. 1990. "The Role of Monetary Policy in Israel's 1985 Stabilization Effort." IMF Working Paper 90/29. Washington, D.C.: International Monetary Fund.

Bufman, Gil, and Leonardo Leiderman. 1993. "Israel's Stabilization: Some Important Policy Lessons." Tel Aviv University, Department of Economics. Mimeo.

Calvo, Guillermo A., Leonardo Leiderman, and Carmen M. Reinhart. 1993. "Capital Inflows and Real Exchange Rate Appreciation in Latin America: The Role of External Factors." *IMF Staff Papers* 40 (March): 108–151.

Calvo, Guillermo A., and Carlos A. Végh. 1990. "Credibility and the Dynamics of Stabilization Policy: A Basic Framework." IMF Working Paper 90/110 (Washington, D.C.: International Monetary Fund). Forthcoming in *Advances in Econometrics*, edited by Chistopher Sims. Cambridge and New York: Cambridge University Press.

———.1992. "Currency Substitution in Developing Countries: An Introduction." IMF Working Paper 92/40. Washington, D.C.: International Monetary Fund.

———.1993. "Exchange Rate-Based Stabilisation under Imperfect Credibility." In *Open-Economy Macroeconomics*, edited by Andreas Worgotter and Helmut Frisch. London: MacMillan Press.

Castro, Paulo Rabello de, and Marcio Ronci. 1991. "Sixty Years of Populism in Brazil." In *The Macroeconomics of Populism in Latin America*, edited by Rüdiger Dornbusch and Sebastian Edwards. Chicago and London: The University of Chicago Press.

Corbo, Vittorio. 1985. "Reforms and Macroeconomic Adjustments in Chile during 1974–84." *World Development* 13 (August): 893–916

Cukierman, Alex. 1988. "The End of High Israeli Inflation: An Experiment in Heterodox Stabilization." In *Inflation Stabilization: The Experience of Israel, Argentina, Brazil, Bolivia, and Mexico*, edited by Michael Bruno, Guido Di Tella, Rüdiger Dornbusch, and Stanley Fischer. Cambridge, Mass.: MIT Press.

Di Tella, Guido. 1983. *Argentina under Perón, 1973–76: The Nation's Experience with a Labor-Based Government*. New York: St. Martin's Press.

Edwards, Sebastian and Alejandra C. Edwards. 1991. *Monetarism and Liberalization: The Chilean Experiment*. Chicago and London: The University of Chicago Press.

Favaro, Edgardo and Alberto Bensión. 1993. "Uruguay." In *Costa Rica and Uruguay*, edited by Simon Rottenberg. Washington, D.C.: The World Bank.

Harberger, Arnold C. 1981. "In Step Out of Step with the World Inflation: A Summary History of Countries, 1952–1976." In *Development in an Inflationary World*, edited by M. June Flanders and Assaf Razin. New York: Academic Press.

Kiguel, Miguel, and Nissan Liviatan. 1989. "The Old and the New in Heterodox Stabilization Programs: Lessons from the 1960s and the 1980s." PPR Working Paper 323. Washington, D.C.: The World Bank, Country Economics Department.

———.1992a. "The Business Cycle Associated with Exchange Rate Based Stabilization." *The World Bank Economic Review* 6 (May): 279–305.

———.1992b. "Stopping Three Big Inflations." Washington, D.C.: The World Bank. Mimeo.

Lustig, Nora. 1992. *Mexico: The Remaking of an Economy*. Washington, D.C.: The Brookings Institution.

Machinea, Jose Luis, and Jose Maria Fanelli. 1988. "Stopping Hyperinflation: The Case of the Austral Plan in Argentina, 1985–87." In *Inflation*

Stabilization: The Experience of Israel, Argentina, Brazil, Bolivia, and Mexico, edited by Michael Bruno, Guido Di Tella, Rüdiger Dornbusch, and Stanley Fischer. Cambridge, Mass.: MIT Press.

Medeiros, Carlos. 1993. "The Dominican Republic's Stabilization Program 1990–92: Was It a Monetary Stabilization Program?" Washington, D.C.: International Monetary Fund, Western Hemisphere Department. Mimeo.

Pazos, Felipe. 1972. *Chronic Inflation in Latin America.* New York: Prager Publishers.

Peréz-Campanero, Juan, and Alfredo M. Leone. 1991. "Liberalization and Financial Crisis in Uruguay (1974–1987)." In *Banking Crisis: Cases and Issues*, edited by V. Sundararajan and Tomás J.T. Baliño. Washington, D.C.: International Monetary Fund.

Reinhart, Carmen M., and Carlos A. Végh. 1992. "Nominal Interest Rates, Consumption Booms, and Lack of Credibility: A Quantitative Examination. Washington, D.C.: International Monetary Fund, Research Department. Mimeo.

Végh, Carlos A. 1992. "Stopping High Inflation: An Analytical Overview." *IMF Staff Papers* 39 (September): 626–695.

Viana, Luis. 1990. "Uruguay's Stabilization Plan of 1968." Centro de Estudios de la Realidad Económica y Social (Uruguay). Mimeo.

Comment

Hans M. Flickenschild

My talk will be organized around two points. First, I will respond to the positions taken by W. Max Corden and Guillermo Calvo. Then I will discuss two countries I have been involved with in recent years—Bolivia and Poland—from the point of view of the exchange rate regimes chosen under their stabilization and adjustment programs. My discussion of these country cases is less an attempt to give the a priori reasons for the choices the authorities made than it is an effort to justify these choices ex post facto in the light of Mr. Corden's and Mr. Calvo's remarks.

I. Exchange Rate Choices and Fiscal and Monetary Policy

After listening to the two speakers, I find that some of my concerns about their taking what at first may appear to be polar positions have been allayed. Although IMF staff work in country-specific situations—which are always gray zones, mixing elements of the two extremes—we nonetheless need the orientation that the theories in their simplification and extreme position give us.

Mr. Corden's discussion of the real targets approach seems to reach the conclusion that this approach is the "right" one. Such a statement risks bringing up an old, contentious issue between the IMF and World Bank staffs. In the Bank, the time horizon is the medium or long term, while in the IMF, we realize that the medium or long term is made up of many short terms. The IMF usually deals with countries where a medium-term real exchange rate objective, although important for the general orientation of policies, is not the most immediate policy concern. We usually come into a situation of great instability and need to advise countries on how to reduce inflation rapidly. Mr. Corden acknowledges these situations when he mentions two types of countries that are potential candidates for nominal exchange rate targeting: countries that have had low inflation in the past, and high-inflation countries, which may need to resort to pegging the nominal rate in order to break entrenched expectations. I would add a third exception to this list to cover countries that suffer sustained exogenous shocks, such as a severe terms of trade shock. In this situation, the real rate needs to be changed and adjustments made based on the new rate. With a nominal anchor policy, it will be essential in such cases to explain clearly to the population why the nominal rate has been changed, so that no adverse expectations are created.

I could not agree more with the second point in Mr. Corden's conclusions. Appropriate noninflationary monetary policy must accompany any exchange rate policy that is chosen. According to the orthodox view, an appropriately tight fiscal policy is also necessary—the two things are often equated. They become different instruments only when capital mobility is sufficiently high.

Mr. Corden also observes that because of the current high degree of capital mobility, exchange rate changes should be made quickly and, if possible, in small installments. I agree with this position and less with Mr. Calvo's, which would postpone exchange rate adjustments until the economic fundamentals are right. With the size and speed of capital movements in today's world, waiting is likely to be a luxury governments cannot afford, especially in chronic-inflation countries, such as those in the Southern Cone.

Mr. Calvo maintains that the choice of the nominal anchor is crucial to the timing of recessions, the occurrence of which he views as almost inevitable, and suggests that recessions come early with money-based programs. At first glance, Bolivia's experience seems to confirm this idea, because the country's GDP experienced its sixth consecutive annual decline after the stabilization program was initiated. But I think there are good explanations in this case (which we will examine more closely in a moment), including the fact that the shocks were largely external and not necessarily the result of the type of anchoring. On the other hand, Mr. Calvo maintains that recessions occur late in a program if the exchange rate is pegged. In Poland, the exchange rate was pegged, yet the economy entered a recession at the very start. Again, there may be special factors at play, which we will examine more closely later on.

I certainly agree with Mr. Calvo's second point: that lack of credibility is more disruptive under a pegged exchange rate regime than under a monetary anchor. Lack of credibility was one of the reasons Bolivia adopted a more flexible exchange rate arrangement. I also agree with Mr. Calvo's statement that implementing disinflationary policy while trying to maintain the real exchange rate is self-defeating. This point embodies my major objection to the real exchange rate rule. My opposition to real rate rules was hardened by my involvement with Peru in the first half of the 1980s, when the IMF staff and Peruvian authorities tried to preserve international competitiveness by adjusting the nominal exchange rate in an attempt to offset the inflation differential. As a result, absent any serious constraint on bank-financed fiscal deficits, inflation climbed every year until there was a change of government. There is little

Chart 1. Bolivia: Effective Exchange Rate Indices, 1979–92
(1980=100)

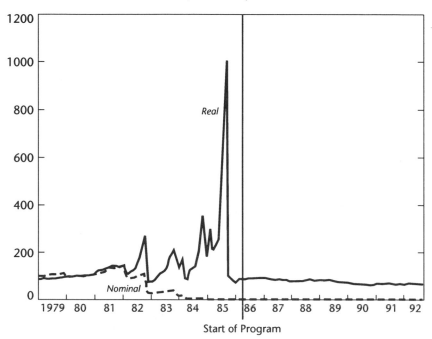

Start of Program

Source: IMF staff estimates.

solace in the fact that, without IMF assistance, the new government made matters worse. Because of such experiences, I think IMF staff in general are very much inclined to prefer a nominal anchor in a program. On the other hand, not every program leads to real exchange rate appreciation. It is not the necessary byproduct of an anti-inflationary program, as I hope Bolivia's experience will show (see Chart 1).

On Mr. Calvo's fourth point, I agree that currency substitution is a very important factor in deciding which exchange rate regime to adopt. In Bolivia, currency substitution was not an issue, but it was in Poland, where it had reached large proportions. Measured at market-determined exchange rates, almost two thirds of the money supply was in foreign exchange. High volatility of the exchange rate, which Poland experienced before stabilization, results in large fluctuations in the perceived value of financial assets of economic agents. In the end, the authorities may lose control over monetary policy.

With regard to Mr. Calvo's final point—that the dynamics of disinflationary policy are "unrelated to fiscal problems"—I would say this: fiscal adjustment alone may not be enough, but it is the crux of a successful stabilization program, and no recent program has succeeded without it. However, credibility—acceptance of a government's policies and the belief that they will hold—is also very important to a program's success, and I do not see how a government can achieve credibility in the presence of a large fiscal imbalance and rapidly rising public debt.

I would not claim that IMF staff went systematically through all these points with the authorities of Bolivia and Poland in choosing exchange rate systems. Nonetheless, as will become apparent, the choices actually made—a floating rate for Bolivia and a pegged one for Poland—were the correct ones. For each country, the exchange rate regime adopted was consistent with the basic criteria relevant to such a decision.

II. Bolivia and Poland

The Bolivian program was initiated in late August 1985 and received IMF support in the form of a stand-by arrangement in June 1986. The arrangement had been negotiated earlier, but there was some fiscal slippage. In addition, the country's terms of trade deteriorated sharply in late 1985. For these reasons, the program had to be renegotiated. Some people believe that Bolivia had actually fixed its exchange rate, but this notion is far from true: the IMF staff was strongly encouraging the authorities to keep the rate flexible. In a formal sense, Bolivia had adopted a "Dutch auction" system, under which the Central Bank was auctioning foreign exchange (which it received from state enterprises) on a daily basis (Table 1). I say "formal" because in fact the Central Bank had an undisclosed minimum reservation price and was very much inclined, to the extent that it had foreign exchange, to increase the supply elastically when demand increased. Hence, the rate tended to be relatively stable over protracted periods of time. But when demand increased sharply on a sustained basis, then indeed there was upward flexibility under the adopted system. With the Dutch auction system, every successful bidder had to pay the price submitted in the bid. Over time, however, the bids converged almost completely, because the participants in the market learned by trial and error what the Central Bank's reservation price was in a given period. That price was not changed frequently, so bidders clustered their bids closely, often keeping the maximum and minimum within a spread of 2 percentage points.

In Poland, the situation was quite different. The stabilization and adjustment program initiated at the beginning of 1990 was soon followed by IMF support in the form of a stand-by arrangement that had been negotiated with the Polish authorities in November-

Table 1. The Choice of a Nominal Anchor:
How Two Countries Managed

	Bolivia	Poland
Exchange rate regime	Managed float (Dutch auction)	Nominal anchor (US$ peg)
Situation		
International reserves	None; arrears	Substantial but negative foreign exchange position
Stabilization fund	No	Yes
Currency substitution	No	Yes
Capital mobility	Yes	No
Credibility	Low	High
Other	Heavy terms of trade losses, exchange rate determination depoliticized as a result of float	Terms of trade losses
Supporting policies		
Fiscal policy	Energy price increases, wage freeze, tax reform	Subsidy and real wage cuts, end of income tax relief
Monetary policy	Liberalized interest rates, credit ceiling	Increased refinance rate, credit ceilings
Structural policies	Price liberalization, decentralization, privatization	Tax-based incomes policy, liberalized prices, privatization

After one year	1986		1990	
	Result	Objective	Result	Objective
Growth (percent)	–3	0	–12	–5
Inflation (12-month rate, percent)	66	84	249	94
Change in net international reserves (US$, millions)	–110	–51	4,442	245

December 1989. Accordingly, there was ample opportunity to discuss the exchange rate system. Once a decision had been reached to peg to the U.S. dollar, fairly complex calculations were necessary to justify the level of the peg. Using different assumptions, the IMF staff and Polish authorities came up with a scatter of rates between 8,300 and 11,700 zlotys; the rate picked was 9,500 per dollar.

What were the initial situations in the two countries that justified adopting a floating rate with a monetary anchor in one and a fixed rate with endogenous money in the other?

Reserves

One criterion was the reserve situation at the beginning of the program. Bolivia had no usable liquid reserves when it launched its stabilization effort in the second half of 1985. Under a democratic government, the country had been in political and social turmoil for several years and had finally entered hyperinflation. The measured inflation rate during the 12–month period ending in August 1985 was 23,000 percent. Actually, inflation had been running at an annual rate of about 60,000 percent in the final months before stabilization. Reserves were depleted, and arrears were accumulating rapidly. The government had not paid banks or other creditors, and there were no lines of credit to draw on for intervention. In this type of situation, it is risky to peg the exchange rate, since it is possible to set the wrong rate.

The reserve situation in Poland was quite different. There were substantial foreign exchange reserves in the banking system—especially in the National Bank of Poland (NBP). However, one factor was of great concern to the Polish authorities: the large foreign exchange liabilities to residents. The Polish system permitted both households and enterprises to hold foreign currency deposits, and the net foreign exchange position—in contrast with the international reserve position—was substantially negative. The Polish authorities were concerned about this "overhang" of foreign exchange liabilities. They could intervene by drawing on their substantial reserve assets but in doing so would risk favoring residents who wanted to take capital out of the country.

Stabilization fund

The Bolivian Government had no access to foreign credit at the time it began its program. Its predecessor had spoiled its reputation with international creditors, and the situation had been unstable for so long that initially nobody was willing to believe the authorities would stay the course. Bolivia had made six stabilization attempts between 1982 and 1985, all of which ended in failure. Nobody was willing to put up a stabilization fund to support a pegged exchange rate. On the other hand, Poland received an outpouring of international support that reflected the historical importance of the country's attempt to break away from communism. Western countries—notably the United States and Germany—rapidly put together a fund amounting to $1 billion in the few days between Christmas 1989 and the New Year.

Currency substitution

Bolivia, unlike many other Latin American countries, had no foreign currency deposits in its banking system at the start of the stabilization program. The economy had been "de-dollarized" by decree in 1982. There was, of course, de facto dollarization in the form of widespread holdings of currency notes (mattress money) among the population, but the measured dollarization was zero. In Poland, however, it was quite high: foreign currency deposits amounted to 63 percent of the total money supply, as valued at the exchange rates prevailing when the exchange markets were unified at the start of 1990.

Capital mobility

In a bold but realistic move, the Bolivians threw open their exchange system completely at the outset. There was no way to police the borders for current transactions—essentially, foreign trade—so trade and payments restrictions attendant on these transactions could not very well be enforced. And capital controls would have been very difficult—if not impossible—to enforce, considering the general incompetence and run-down condition of the public administration. Poland's approach was more nuanced. It adopted what amounted to convertibility for most current account transactions for the enterprise sector and full convertibility for the household sector. As a result, some capital flows, especially those the large state enterprises could initiate, remained under control.

Credibility

In Bolivia, both internal and external credibility were at rock bottom. The new President, the leader of the 1952 revolution, had handed over the Government in 1956 with a high inflation rate that the IMF had been called in to stabilize. In his fourth presidency (as the head of a party called the Movement of the Revolutionary Left), he was not expected to follow a conservative path to domestic stabilization, and Bolivia had no external credit standing. Polish credibility, by contrast, was high. The Solidarity Movement had just scored a resounding victory by winning all the contested parliamentary seats in the elections. The Communists were out of power, but a perceived external threat still existed in the guise of the Soviet Union. The Polish electorate appeared both united and determined to "tough it out," and the authorities had both internal and external credibility.

Other factors

Two other criteria militated for a flexible exchange rate in Bolivia. First, the country had experienced heavy terms of trade losses. In a stroke of bad luck, the international tin agreement collapsed in November 1985, less than three months after the stabilization effort was launched. The price of tin—one of Bolivia's two main exports—fell by 50 percent. The price of natural gas—the other important export—began to slide in the wake of declining oil prices in late 1985 and early 1986. And there was a third exogenous shock in mid-1986—a drug interdiction operation by the United States. U.S. troops, which had been invited into the country, disrupted activities in the coca-growing areas. As a result, the price of coca leaf fell to one tenth of what it had been. It has been estimated that the combined effect of these shocks accounted for the entire drop in GDP observed in 1986. Poland was also facing terms of trade losses, especially in transactions with member countries of the Council for Mutual Economic Assistance (CMEA). The CMEA was still functioning at the time, but it was clear that Poland's imports of oil and gas from the Soviet Union would become much more expensive and that its exports of manufactured goods to other CMEA members would have to be sold at much lower prices. However, the relative importance of the terms of trade loss was not as great in Poland as in Bolivia.

In Bolivia, domestic politics provided an additional reason for a flexible exchange rate system. Because past governments had been known to fall as a result of devaluations, ministers and presidents did not want to take responsibility for new devaluations. The auction system provided an excellent way to depoliticize the process of setting the exchange rate.

Supporting policies and results

The supporting macroeconomic and structural policies of both countries are described briefly in Table I. On the whole, these policies were not out of the ordinary, except that Poland had a well-publicized second nominal anchor constraining wages. In Poland, wage bill increases were indexed to a fraction—initially, a very small fraction—of cost of living increases. Bolivia imposed a wage freeze of nine months in the public sector, but this second anchor was never a center of attention.

Table I also shows the objectives and the results of the first year of the programs. Bolivia suffered a loss of reserves. Under the program, a portion of the resources provided by the IMF was supposed to be used for intervention, but Argentina fell behind on gas payments, and thus the reserve loss was higher than envisaged. In Poland, the

Chart 2. Poland: Effective Exchange Rate Indices, 1980–92
(1980=100)

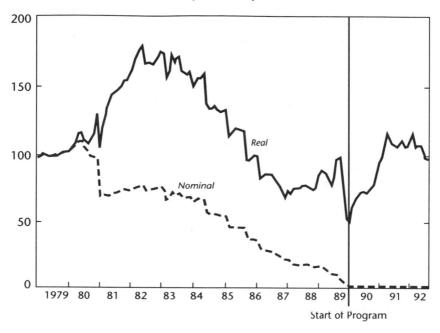

Start of Program

Source: IMF staff estimates.

increase in reserves exceeded all expectations, reflecting both an unexpected export boom and much lower imports (despite a sharp real appreciation of the exchange rate (see Chart 2)), as well as favorable, private capital movements.

Summary of Discussion

The discussion centered on the different functions of the exchange rate and the advantages and drawbacks of using the exchange rate as a nominal anchor. The distinction was made between real fundamental variables, which determine the equilibrium real exchange rate, and nominal macroeconomic variables, such as the exchange rate and nominal wages (among others), which affect the actual real rate. Measuring the real effective exchange rate is to a large extent an art that is partly a function of the weighting scheme adopted for different components of the current account. In particular, it was agreed that the guiding principle in devising a weighting scheme should be to measure movements in competitiveness as accurately as possible. While the equilibrium real effective exchange rate of a country undergoing rapid structural change is likely to shift as a result of the changes, it is nevertheless important to try to assess the impact of the changes. In measuring the real exchange rate, it is important to distinguish between a tariff imposed to influence long-term resource allocation (e.g., for the protection of domestic industry), and a tariff imposed as a measure to slow the loss of reserves, which should not affect the equilibrium real rate.

The economic impact of a devaluation on a country was discussed in terms of propensities to consume, the effect of expectations on investment, and the structure of the government budget. Devaluation was judged to have a significant effect even if export elasticities were low, as imports would be rationed by higher prices rather than by quantitative restrictions. The effect on prices would be determined by the supporting monetary policy, as a devaluation would generate only a one-time rise in prices. Further discussion on devaluation highlighted the government credibility factor and the impact of a devaluation on domestic absorption.

Regarding government credibility, the point was made that it was essential for the government to maintain its credibility after a devaluation; this could be done more easily if there was a history of government credibility or if a new government devalued soon after coming into power. If the public realized that there would be a devaluation whenever a real exchange rate misalignment occurred, the government would completely lose its credibility and ability to control inflation.

While a devaluation would normally cut real wages and consumption and absorption, the opposite effect on absorption could occur if profits were raised as a result of the devaluation, leading to expectations of increased future profits and, consequently, higher investment expenditures. In Mexico, for example, a devaluation combined with other policies contributed to an investment boom that benefited primarily export industries. In terms of the fiscal effects of a devaluation, evidence suggested that absorption depended on the particular country's revenue structure and debt service profile.

It was made clear that a nominal exchange rate anchor was just one of several possible nominal anchors. While some participants favored an exchange rate anchor, others were afraid that it would erode competitiveness. It was agreed that if exchange rates were used to maintain competitiveness, the problem of inflation would remain unsolved unless another nominal variable was used to anchor prices. It was important that the nominal exchange rate anchor be viewed as credible, and in this context there was some support for a large one-step devaluation prior to the introduction of the fixed rate anchor, so that another devaluation would not be needed soon. There was considerable opinion, however, that most countries with an independent central bank should not commit themselves permanently to a fixed exchange rate. Exceptions would be desirable only for very small countries and countries with a long tradition with a fixed rate. Several cases were also mentioned in which a nominal exchange rate anchor was unlikely to be successful if the underlying fiscal imbalances were not first addressed.

External Liberalization, Currency Convertibility, and Implications for Exchange Rate Policy 5

Anupam Basu

I. Introduction and Broad Policy Framework

In general, countries have tended to reform and liberalize their external sector policies within the context of comprehensive macroeconomic and structural adjustment programs aimed at increasing real economic growth, lowering inflation, and achieving external viability. The primary rationales for countries to liberalize and open up their external sectors are improved access to world markets, better allocation of resources as a result of external competition, and closer linkage between the domestic and world prices of tradables.

In order to reap these benefits, reforming countries have been implementing IMF-supported adjustment programs since the mid-1980s. These programs represent broad-based efforts to adjust initial financial imbalances (particularly weak fiscal positions), correct relative price distortions, reform repressed financial systems, and liberalize restrictive and distorted foreign trade and exchange regimes. By addressing these issues within a comprehensive policy framework, policymakers have been faced with at least three unavoidable constraints. First, success in resolving the problems in any one area depends on progress in the other two areas. Second, because the immediate as well as the future consequences of policy decisions must be considered together, intertemporal trade-offs between short-term costs and long-term gains have to be weighed carefully. This consideration is particularly important for investors and producers, who need a long-term perspective on the policy environment in order to restructure their operations. Third, even when problems of macroeconomic stabilization (including domestic resource mobilization and use) are addressed, relative price distortions corrected, and domestic prices liberalized, policymakers must deal with a wide range of institutional rigidities that have prevented economies from responding to the new "market-oriented" environment. These rigidities include a lack of clearly defined property rights and bankruptcy procedures; limited entry and exit for firms; nontransparent public accountability and regulatory provisions; and a weak prudential and supervisory role for the central bank in the financial sector.

In the eyes of the public, the credibility of a program of reforms depends on how consistently the reforms are applied in different policy areas, how efficiently they are sequenced over time, and whether institutional and systemic reforms aimed at helping the economy respond to the new incentives are implemented in a timely manner. Sustained external liberalization that increases the scope of external transactions backed by currency convertibility also strengthens policy credibility.[1]

II. The Unsustainable Costs of Foreign Trade and Exchange Restrictions

In many reforming countries, the initially restrictive and distortionary foreign trade and exchange regimes in part reflected a desire to have the government direct resource allocation (e.g., Algeria, Ethiopia, and Tanzania in the late 1970s and early 1980s). More importantly, however, they represented a vicious circle of trade and exchange restrictiveness that led to further restrictiveness as the countries' domestic financial positions, external positions, and growth performances became increasingly weak. The dynamics of the vicious circle referred to here can be illustrated with examples of countries that relied heavily on trade-based taxes and tried to address external imbalances by restricting imports and external payments (for example, Tanzania in the late 1970s and early 1980s, and Uganda in the 1970s). This approach reduced domestic tax bases and increased fiscal deficits, allowing adverse pressures on weak external positions to continue.

In cases such as those cited above, excessive restrictions on and taxation of external transactions contributed to the emergence of parallel exchange markets, the growth of unrecorded trade, and the steady shrinking of the official exchange market. These developments made the task of macroeconomic stabilization more difficult and contributed to obvious relative price distortions in the marketplace. There is also evidence that countries relying heavily on restrictive foreign trade and exchange controls for long periods experienced serious shortages of imported inputs and capital, unproductive inventory buildup, severe deterioration of essential infrastructure and productive capital, and fundamentally weaker growth. These problems were clearly evident in the countries of the former Soviet Union and Eastern Europe prior to the advent of market-

---

[1]For the purposes of this paper, currency convertibility is broadly defined as the absence of official restrictions on the exchange of domestic for foreign reserve currencies, for both external current and capital account transactions.

based reforms. Under such circumstances, foreign trade and exchange reforms were certainly desirable, not only because of the potential gains from foreign trade-led expansion and greater domestic efficiency, but also because the old trade and exchange regimes were headed toward collapse.

In devising measures to correct the relative price distortions of restrictive foreign trade and exchange regimes, attention had to be given at the outset to two key issues: (1) the appropriate measures for liberalizing exchange rate policy and unifying the exchange system; and (2) the appropriate reforms for both liberalizing the trade regime and correcting its anti-export bias (resulting, for example, from the stronger incentives that protective trade policies provide for the production of importables and other domestic goods). Both sets of issues had to be addressed, because the wedge or link between world prices (in foreign currency) and domestic prices (in local currency) is determined by both the exchange rate and trade measures, and because no trade reform can be initiated without addressing currency overvaluation and distortions in the foreign exchange system. Moreover, given the time needed to complete the trade reforms, early, decisive actions—plus a preannouncement of the timing of future reforms—would prove helpful, allowing economic agents to adjust their production, investment, and savings decisions.

III. Liberalization and Reform of the Exchange System

The exchange system reforms that have been undertaken vary widely, depending in large part on the nature of the initial distortions.

In many cases, the de facto segmentation of exchange markets into a shrinking official market and a widespread parallel market characterized the prereform situation (e.g., The Gambia, Nigeria, Tanzania, and Uganda in the first half of the 1980s). In these cases, the prevailing exchange restrictions in the official market for current external transactions were progressively liberalized. In particular, exchange restrictions were removed for all trade and other current transactions, licensed and unlicensed. (In the prereform period, it was the presence of such restrictions that led to the emergence of parallel markets and excessive premiums in the free market price of foreign exchange.) In terms of nontrade transactions, care was taken to allow foreign investors to repatriate profits and dividends in order to maintain incentives for inflows of direct investment.[2]

---

[2]The issue of sequencing the liberalization of external current and capital accounts is discussed in Section VI.

Second, in a number of cases, the parallel market was initially believed to be dominant, foreign reserves were relatively low, and recovery of foreign exchange receipts through the official exchange market was uncertain and expected to increase only gradually. Moreover, the authorities typically found it difficult to determine the equilibrium (fixed) exchange rate. In these situations, the official exchange rate policy was to ensure that the rate was market determined and thus realistic. A variety of systems were used, including (1) an official and unified auction administered by the central bank (as in Zambia in 1985–87); (2) a unified floating interbank arrangement, with the float either bounded within a band or free (e.g., the free float introduced in The Gambia in 1986 and the float within a band in Sri Lanka in 1990); (3) a managed or administered (unified) rate constrained within a declining percentage differential from the parallel market rate (as in Zambia in 1989–92 and Uganda in 1983–84); and (4) an official dual exchange market, with a temporary segmentation between transactions using the official market-determined rate and those using a more appreciated rate administered by the central bank (as in Uganda in 1982 and Guyana in 1990). In countries where the initial foreign reserves were adequate or the projected exchange receipts during the reform period were considered sufficient to build some reserves and defend an exchange rate after the initial correction, consideration was given to a fixed or adjustable fixed peg policy.

The main risk in both the floating and the adjustable fixed rate approaches has generally been the exchange rate variability that results from inadequate supporting fiscal and monetary policies. Both approaches required repeated tightening of fiscal and monetary policies at the same time that the exchange rate was adjusting in response to permanent external shocks (e.g., trend declines in the terms of trade or external financing inflows). When it seemed that financial policies were creating inflationary pressures, policies were, in general, tightened (as in Kenya, Malawi, and Nigeria in the early 1990s). (Nominal depreciation would have been an inefficient substitute in these cases.) The recommended approach in such cases—which would help avert the serious risk of inflation—was to weaken wage indexation, alleviate labor market rigidities, strengthen fiscal adjustment, and achieve productivity gains. In some chronic-inflation countries (e.g., Argentina and Brazil in the second half of the 1980s), policymakers found it difficult to successfully implement such fixed exchange rate-based programs, on account of weak incomes policies and inadequate adjustment of the fiscal deficit. Mexico (1988) and Israel (1985–86) are well known for their successful experiences in combating inflation inertia through tight incomes policies during stabilization efforts.

IV. The Role of the Central Bank and Government in the Exchange System

In operating the reformed exchange systems, the central banks have had a key role to play in three important areas. First, a clear separation had to be made between the banks' intermediary functions for the government and any market interventions. The intermediary role has included conducting transactions on behalf of the government (for example, paying for government purchases of goods and services abroad and externalizing public debt service payments) and building up official foreign reserves to targeted levels. But it was clearly understood that while central banks may usefully smooth out temporary shocks in the exchange market, they should not embark on unsustainable intervention against market trends.

Another aspect of central bank policy has had to do with building or strengthening the institutional framework of the exchange system by increasing the number of participants in the official exchange market. Thus, countries have taken steps to broaden the participation of banks, foreign exchange bureaus, hotels, and other institutions by licensing them to operate within the official exchange market, subject to appropriate prudential regulations and supervision regarding capital adequacy, as well as to limits on foreign exchange working balances and exposure to uncovered foreign exchange positions. Following appropriate institutional reforms, some countries have moved from auctions administered by the central bank to floating interbank-cum-dealer arrangements that signal a reduction in administrative interference in the official exchange system. To give a similar signal, some countries have transferred the daily administration of the reformed exchange control regime to commercial banks. The basic objective is to ensure that exchange control regulations are transparent and administered in a nonarbitrary and predictable manner.

Central banks and governments have had to cooperate closely to ensure not only that fiscal and monetary policies are adequately restrictive (as noted in Section III) but also that government transactions remain predictable and do not crowd the nongovernment sectors out of the foreign exchange market. To this end, governments (including those in the reforming countries noted in Section III) have gradually shifted their transactions to the more liberalized segment of the official exchange market and restrained their own net demands for foreign exchange. In general, these shifts have provided the market with more information on official transactions and allowed other market participants to discount appropriately for government demands.

The governments of reforming countries have often mobilized foreign financing, in the form of import support, to move to external current account convertibility. In many cases, inflows of foreign financing in various forms (such as grants, loans, and debt relief) have significantly facilitated government efforts to eliminate the overhang of outstanding external payments arrears, create a reformed and well-functioning exchange system, and help relieve the initial import scarcity and foreign reserve shortages. These flows have been particularly helpful in the case of the import support programs that multilateral and bilateral donors have financed in recent years in several countries, including Mozambique, Tanzania, and Uganda. At the same time, tying foreign aid to lists of imports that vary across donors and to specific donor-based policy conditionalities has not improved the delivery of aid and at times has made operating exchange systems unnecessarily complicated.

V. Reforming Foreign Trade

The foreign trade reforms many developing countries embarked upon in the 1980s have involved two primary sets of actions.[3] First, countries have taken steps to liberalize quantitative restrictions (QRs) and other nontariff barriers by raising quotas stepwise, eliminating them altogether, and introducing positive import lists (these are expanded and eventually replaced by negative lists that generally prohibit imports considered hazardous to security and health). At this stage, there has often also been a shift from QRs to tariffs, which roughly reflect the prereform black market premiums in the prices of quota-based imports. These premiums at times reflected not only import quotas but also the monopolistic or oligopolistic market position of domestic traders; the new tariffs, however, have been introduced simultaneously with the freeing of the domestic trading environment and other measures aimed at improving the performance of public sector monopolies. In some cases, data from import license auctions have been used to set tariff levels that reflect the premium in the auction price. It has also been necessary to bear in mind the tariff levels in neighboring countries. In fact, a common second phase of trade reform measures has included steps to rationalize the tariff structure and progressively reduce its dispersion and average level, with a view to gradually narrowing the band of tariffs. Such far-reaching reforms of the import trade regime were particularly evident in the 1980s in Chile, Korea, Mexico, and Turkey.

[3] In the 1980s, trade liberalization was undertaken with varying degrees of intensity in Bangladesh, Chile, Colombia, Ghana, Jamaica, Korea, Madagascar, Malawi, Mauritius, Mexico, Morocco, the Philippines, Senegal, Thailand, and Turkey.

In sequencing the trade reform measures, two key issues have had to be addressed. First, from the viewpoint of efficient resource allocation, policymakers needed to progress from a nontransparent, nonneutral incentive regime to a transparent and neutral incentive structure. Unlike QRs, tariffs were levied on both outputs and inputs. In narrowing the tariff band structure, then, reductions at both the high and low ends were important (as in Kenya in 1983–85, Tanzania in 1981–83, and Thailand in 1980–83). Also, the tariff rates for various products were adjusted according to the degree of processing required, ensuring some neutrality across industries on a value-added basis. Assessing the prereform, anti-export bias of incentives, required that a broad assessment of incentives be undertaken for both import substitutes and exports, because trade taxes and subsidies existed alongside other types of incentives (including domestic tax exemptions, subsidized domestic credit, and subsidized input sales).

Second, a three-pronged approach has been used to address the need to promote exports. Initially, any obvious impediments to exports were removed or alleviated through a variety of steps, including an exchange rate depreciation sufficient to restore the export sector's profitability;[4] efficiency-enhancing and cost-reducing measures for public sector exporters (often combined with increased private sector participation); removal of disparate rates of export subsidies; liberalization of imports to allow the export sector to benefit from both improved access to imported inputs and a reduction of the bias toward import substitution; and investment in supportive public infrastructure.[5] A key point here is that export promotion has often been accompanied by import liberalization, particularly in Jamaica, Mexico, Senegal, and Turkey. This dual approach has helped in two ways: by alleviating input supply bottlenecks for the export and complementary sectors, and by reducing the risk of inflation and exchange rate appreciation from the monetization of export surpluses not offset by imports.

VI. The Role of Supporting Policies in External Liberalization

In general, the process of external liberalization must be accompanied by adequately restrictive fiscal and monetary policies in order

[4]Notably, Chile, Colombia, Ghana, Mauritius, and Morocco relied on exchange rate depreciation.
[5]Bangladesh and Mauritius introduced export promotion schemes, such as duty drawbacks, exchange retention privileges, and other measures. Public investment in infrastructure was given high priority in Chile, Colombia, Korea, Malawi, Mexico, and Turkey.

to avoid serious pressures on the balance of payments and prevent inflationary pressures from undermining the relative price incentives and competitiveness of the tradables sector. Moreover, the fiscal impact of the envisaged trade reforms—potential revenue losses from lower trade taxes—has to be considered.

To ensure a supportive fiscal policy, the various reforming countries introduced tax initiatives that (to different degrees) cover a wide range of measures. These measures have included shifting from foreign trade-based taxes to domestic tax bases (as in Jamaica, Malawi, Mauritius, Mexico, Morocco, the Philippines, and Turkey) and strengthening tax administration and collection (as in Ghana and Thailand). Efforts have also been made to rationalize consumption taxes to cover both domestic and imported goods and to eliminate tax exemptions on imports as well as on other tax bases. Measures to reduce expenditures have been aimed at avoiding public outlays on projects that are unlikely to strengthen growth performance and debt-servicing capacity, reducing quasi-fiscal deficits to ease the burden of budget subsidies, and rehabilitating infrastructure and sectors (parastatals and financial institutions) considered essential to recovery and export growth. A special effort has been made to improve the financial performance of public enterprises and subject their operations to hard budget constraints. With these measures, the overall pace of fiscal adjustment is geared to reducing excess demand, especially in inflationary circumstances, and adjusted in response to major exogenous shocks (such as those affecting the terms of trade). In addition to minimizing the risks of payments imbalances and inflationary pressures, fiscal adjustment also helps to reduce the burden of adjustment on monetary policy and to facilitate financial sector reform.

Monetary policy has played a key role in supporting external liberalization and ensuring a stable, noninflationary environment in reforming countries. Since the real exchange rate is a relative price, monetary policy has had to be tight enough to prevent competitiveness from being eroded by domestic inflation. In this way, the external position has been protected during the process of trade reform without too much reliance on frequent and recurrent exchange rate depreciations. Unstable inflation and exchange rates could weaken the signaling effects of the relative price changes introduced by structural reforms.

The key financial sector reforms in reforming countries have included a movement away from administered interest rates, selective credit controls, stringent reserve requirements, and other portfolio constraints on banks' assets. The result has been a less repressed financial sector and a shift by the authorities to indirect methods of monetary management. Moreover, the authorities have strengthened prudential standards and the supervision of the banking sector.

These essential steps have helped make the domestic financial sectors of the reforming countries more competitive prior to external capital account liberalization.

In most countries, foreign trade reform and the liberalization of external current account transactions have preceded the opening up of the external capital account, for two reasons. First, structural reforms of fiscal and monetary policies, domestic pricing and marketing systems, foreign trade and current account exchange controls, and institutional and regulatory rigidities—especially in the financial sector—must be well advanced before the external capital account is opened up. The inflow of foreign resources can be used efficiently only after domestic distortions have been largely corrected. Secondly, the premature opening up of the external capital account during the process of current account liberalization and macroeconomic stabilization could, in some situations, cause the exchange rate to appreciate, hindering the progress of the trade liberalization process and weakening the competitiveness of the tradables sector. These problems have generally arisen in countries where interest rates rose above world levels (as in Argentina, Chile, and Uruguay in the late 1970s) because of relatively high domestic inflation rates and weak fiscal positions. Indeed, such problems have been a matter of concern recently in some middle-income countries (including in Latin America) that are well along in the process of structural reform.

Comments

Claudio M. Loser

Convertibility is what we understand it to be. I see convertibility as a liberalization of external transactions compatible with the open system provided for under the IMF's Articles of Agreement. During the process of economic reform in Latin America, we have assumed that moving toward a system that seeks to liberalize transactions is the correct path, because a system offering greater freedom of movement for goods, services, and capital will help enhance the prospects for economic growth.

For reform to succeed, however, more is required than just convertibility (which has been generally accepted in Latin America in the sense just given). No matter what exchange regime a country uses, the macroeconomic fundamentals must be right, including the fiscal situation and monetary management. In addition, over the longer term the process of reform must permit the economy to compete effectively with the rest of the world. Otherwise, the fiscal and monetary reforms the authorities pursue may not last. In terms of external liberalization—which is part of structural reform— experience shows that trade, or current account, reform must be accompanied by capital account liberalization. If the capital account is liberalized too soon without underlying trade reform, then it is very likely—as was shown in the southern cone of Latin America in the late 1970s—that the reforms may fail. And, as said before, the exchange system may or may not function, depending on whether these conditions are met.

In addition, the characteristics of the exchange system will again be a function of the government's ability to control the monetary and fiscal situation, and therefore countries will choose a fixed, flexible, or managed exchange rate on the basis of these macroeconomic considerations. And I certainly agree with Mr. Basu that a government should not be rigidly linked to any particular system, because the country's underlying strengths will determine its future course. The fact is that no exchange rate system offers the perfect solution to every country's problems. Policymakers know this.

A good point of reference for discussing recent developments in structural reform, exchange rates, and exchange rate management in Latin America is 1982, the year of the debt crisis. At that time we were confronted with the sudden interruption of the flows of foreign financing on which the region depended. Before 1982, Latin

123

American economies were characterized by weak macroeconomic policies, high public sector deficits, significant state control of the means of production, and controls on foreign trade. During the 1970s, however, this method of governance did not create clearly adverse effects because of the availability of ample foreign financing linked to existing oil surpluses. Countries were able to maintain some distortions in their domestic policies and still spend well in excess of their revenues.

Certain countries—for example, oil producers like Venezuela and Mexico—and the rest of the world believed that oil prices would continue to increase. Based on those expectations and low real interest rates, Latin American governments borrowed heavily. But an inflationary environment in the late 1970s resulted in a tightening of financial policy in the United States and Europe, higher real interest rates, and a decline in the prices of commodities, including oil. The results were a sharp decline in exports and reduced access to financial resources. In these circumstances, in a world that had moved slowly toward greater integration, where export orientation was the key, the countries of the Western Hemisphere had to confront this crisis by revising their policies. Latin America thus faced a very difficult political, economic, and institutional process. In response, some countries developed a three-pronged strategy for reform, though not all at the same time. Chile, for instance, had already begun the process in the 1970s. Other countries, such as Mexico, started in the early 1980s. Still others, including Argentina, started but failed in the early 1980s and have returned to reform only in recent years.

The three-pronged strategy consisted of macroeconomic adjustment, structural reform, and the settlement of external debt. The key elements were the improvement of macroeconomic and in particular fiscal performance, combined with monetary discipline. A related issue was management of the exchange rate; in the early 1980s, there was a tremendous shift from overvalued rates to rates that would make an economy more competitive. Structural reform touched on many areas. Financial sector reforms were very important in Chile and Mexico, where the systems were modernized. Domestic trade and direct investment were liberalized and public enterprises privatized.

These reforms were a question not of dogma but of economic efficiency. The private sector, it was believed, with appropriate conditions of competitiveness, could provide better services and make better use of resources. In certain cases, the public sector itself modernized, resulting in significantly improved efficiency. At the same time, the trade and exchange systems were modified to eliminate dual or multiple rates (a source of inefficiency and corruption). The result was simple, transparent exchange rate systems with either fixed exchange rates (Argentina), floating exchange rates (Bolivia), some type of crawling peg, or auctions. In Mexico, there has been a preannounced rate of depreciation, and in Chile and Brazil, a rule of depreciation linked to inflation.

Foreign financing, the third element in the equation, fell into two categories, private and public sector. During the last ten years, there has been a tremendous effort on the part of the debtor and creditor countries, multilateral agencies, and commercial banks to bring the public sector external debt to more manageable levels through either debt reduction or restructuring. Normalizing the relations between public sector and external creditors has been crucial to improving Latin America's attractiveness to foreign investors and has helped create the conditions that allow the private sector to make use of foreign financing, either through credits, direct investment, or the reversal of the capital flight of previous years. The reversal of these capital flows was in fact an aftereffect of the new domestic policies.

The overall result of the policies was that the fiscal performance in Latin America in the 1980s strengthened tremendously. Central government deficits improved an average of four percentage points of GDP from the period 1981–1983 to 1990–1992, providing a major contribution to adjustment by helping reduce aggregate demand and inflationary pressures. As a consequence, national savings have increased by two to three percentage points of GDP for countries in the region. Investment has increased, although by a smaller amount— some 1 percent of GDP—and therefore the current account deficits have tended to shrink.

The experience, however, varies tremendously from country to country. In Brazil, for instance, the current account has been in surplus or has shown only a very small deficit. Other countries, like Mexico, have experienced a sharp increase in the current account deficit in recent years. Notwithstanding the fact that many countries' balance of payments have shown current account deficits, foreign reserves have increased significantly. International reserves were very low—maybe $6 billion gross—at the beginning of the 1980s; in 1992, they were estimated to be on the order of $60 billion for the region as a whole. While only a few countries hold most of these reserves, the increase has been a general trend for all countries in the region. The external debt ratios increased initially, but the structure of the debt improved significantly. Exports over the last ten years have grown rapidly, notwithstanding the fact that growth in industrial countries has been slow and that oil prices, in real terms, are probably as low as they were in 1986.

Output growth in the region has been in the order of 3–4 percent in recent years, although some countries have been growing at a much faster rate. Chile is currently growing at the rate of about 7 or 8 percent annually, Argentina at about 6 percent, and other countries at some 3-4 percent. In general, there has been an upward trend, and it seems that growth has been sustained. Of equal interest is the fact that the rate of inflation in the region has tended to decline. Of course, some countries, Brazil among them, still have high rates of inflation. But in broader terms, 10 years ago 12 countries had inflation rates that were under 10 percent per year; today, that number has risen to 20. In the early 1980s, six countries had inflation rates of more than 50 percent, but today only Brazil and Peru have rates that high. Furthermore, Peru's inflation rate fell from over 50 percent for the 12 months ending in November 1992, to about 35 percent.

While there has been a tremendous improvement in the region, new policy dilemmas have emerged. The economic systems have become more open and the exchange systems more liberal, resulting in a significant increase in capital inflows as the private sector responds to the changed policies. Some of these inflows have come in as direct investment or other types of long-term capital, but others have been purely speculative. In principle, as capital flows come in, the exchange market comes under pressure, and the exchange rate tends to appreciate in order to accommodate the inflows. In these circumstances, policymakers need to decide whether the inflows are a short- or long-term phenomenon and to develop an appropriate response. Some Latin American countries have simply let the capital flow in, allowing the economy to adjust without intervention. Some have had occasional current account deficits that reflect the increased investment. Others, concerned about controlling monetary aggregates, have tried to sterilize these movements by placing bonds in the market, resulting in relatively high interest rates. Capital has continued to flow into these countries, putting upward pressure on either the nominal exchange rate or the domestic inflation rate and weakening external performance.

As noted earlier, these events reflect the private sector's changed view of economic conditions in the region. As economic performance improves, increased capital flows have resulted in growing aggregate demand, putting pressure on overall resources and inflation. In response, the authorities have sought to tighten fiscal policy, a tactic that has helped reduce the level of aggregate demand, curtail inflationary pressures, lower interest rates, and ease upward pressure on the local currency. While this type of solution seems the most effective one, individual countries must assess their own situations. Short-term flows might better be offset with some type of monetary policy. Experience shows, however, that capital inflows have continued despite such policies.

Some Latin American academicians and policymakers fear that because many countries once more have high current account deficits and are again tremendously dependent on foreign financing, the region will face the same crisis it experienced ten years ago.

However, I believe that today's situation is very different from that of the early 1980s, owing to significant structural reform, a public, sector that has improved its finances (and so does not depend entirely on foreign financing), and a generally better understanding of the need for governments to establish clear rules. Because of these changes, the potential dangers to the region are much lower today, and the Latin American economies are better able to compete effectively in an increasingly integrated world.

John R. Dodsworth

My focus will be on the policy issues of currency convertibility and stabilization, but from an Asian perspective.

The accepted wisdom on currency convertibility is that it should come late in the reform process, because it can be destabilizing. Following conventional tenets, several Asian countries that opted for currency convertibility—including Japan and the Republic of Korea—introduced it after they had liberalized their current accounts and the accounts had strengthened. In fact, these countries moved to currency convertibility because they had very large current account surpluses that were themselves posing a threat to price stability. In Japan, the delay between current account liberalization and currency convertibility was some 20 years or more. It was not until the late 1980s that the Republic of Korea accepted the obligations even of Article VIII—a fairly narrow definition of convertibility—of the IMF's Articles of Agreement. In Korea, capital account convertibility is still under way.

The motivation for establishing convertibility in Singapore and Thailand was somewhat different. Despite current account deficits, they undertook currency convertibility as part of an overall development strategy. But even Singapore and Thailand waited until their overall payments balances had grown very strong before undertaking the move to Article VIII status.

Unlike many Asian countries, most of the countries of Eastern Europe and the former Soviet Union have set aside balance of payments considerations and are pressing for the convertibility of their currencies. Currency convertibility has become part of a comprehensive policy package to get relative prices right and as such amplifies the need to move on a number of fronts at once. Asia's experience, however, suggests that unless there are strong policies and adequate external support, steps toward currency convertibility in the former centrally planned economies may be premature.

With respect to a country like Sri Lanka, which has now decided to move at a fairly early stage toward current account convertibility while simultaneously undertaking structural adjustment, the issue of currency convertibility is extremely important. There are risks involved in this decision, because convertibility requires additional policy discipline. It is important in this case that (1) the necessary instruments to stabilize the economy are developed, or (2) the political will to take necessary measures is present. In the absence of either of these conditions, the country takes certain risks in moving to an entirely open exchange system.

A second question concerns capital inflows, which arise from successful economic reform but can cause complications for policies. About three years ago, Sri Lanka had practically no international reserves and was experiencing a severe balance of payments crisis. After stronger adjustment policies and structural reforms were adopted, the economy turned around, reigniting capital inflows. At that time, Sri Lanka did not have the policy instruments to deal with the inflows. The IMF advised Sri Lanka to develop a treasury bill market to help mop up this liquidity. Although treasury bill auctions helped to reduce monetary growth, the capital inflows continued and the authorities were forced to allow the exchange rate to appreciate at a time when the competitiveness of the country's exports was in question. The situation called for fiscal adjustment, but fiscal adjustment on the necessary scale may not be realizable in the very short run.

In such a situation, a policy dilemma develops: while seeking fiscal adjustment, what does a country do with respect to exchange rate and monetary policy? It may be argued that the exchange rate should not be revalued, on the grounds that capital inflows will eventually change the structure of the economy and restore competitiveness. But to support this view, we would need to know the nature of the capital inflows. Are they really going to change the structure of the economy and increase efficiency, or are they short term, subject to reversal and flight? On a practical basis, it is very difficult to differentiate between these types of flows.

Summary of Discussion

The discussion focused on the implications of capital account convertibility. The point was made that the degree of international capital market integration is such that country authorities could do little to move effectively against the general tendencies of capital flows. Central banks might have to intervene, however, in order to slow capital flows that are clearly short-term fluctuations rather than part of a trend.

A related issue was whether or not governments should stand ready to bail out the private sector when the private sector was not able to service its debt. Most participants felt that the public sector needed to give clear signals that it would not bail out private sector enterprises experiencing foreign debt servicing problems. In this way, it would be possible to avert the Latin American experience of the early 1980s, when the exchange risk of private sector debt was transferred to governments. However, simply announcing this intention might not be seen as a credible response by either the international financial system or the domestic private sector. In the event of excessive inflows of nondirect investment capital, governments might be better off imposing exchange controls. Fortunately, circumstances in the 1990s differed from those in the early 1980s. Most countries' fiscal positions were substantially improved, and foreign borrowing was now directed mainly at investment rather than at supporting consumption.

Most participants felt that the capital account should not be liberalized before real sector reforms were implemented. Real sector reforms, however, were judged to be relatively difficult to implement, perhaps more so than macroeconomic reforms. The former—which include modification of the trade system, privatization of public enterprises, and reform of the domestic distribution system, among others—required a strong and persistent commitment from the authorities, in part because of potential conflict of interest. It was important for governments to try to eliminate other distortions in the economy, in particular those resulting from a restrictive trade system, before moving to currency convertibility.

Finally, the consensus was that there was no single solution or unique sequencing of steps that could be used as a model in the timing of reforms; rather, advice regarding currency convertibility would need to be tailored to individual country circumstances.

PART **III**

Experiences with Alternative
Exchange Rate System

Recent Experience with Floating Exchange Rates in Developing Countries   6

Peter J. Quirk

A major change in the exchange regimes of developing countries in the 1980s and early 1990s has been the adoption of floating exchange rates. Prior to the 1980s, it was widely believed that operating a competitive floating exchange rate regime required a level of institutional development these countries did not possess, although there had been a few isolated instances of floating among developing countries in the postwar period. Thirty have since adopted independently floating arrangements.

In 1987, the IMF examined its experience with these regimes through the mid-1980s and concluded that the early experience, although not definitive, indicated that floating exchange rate systems can be operated satisfactorily by developing countries with diverse economic structures, including those with a small number of commercial banks.[1] Floating was not found to lead to free fall or greater exchange rate instability, which instead depend on the quality of domestic economic policies.

The IMF has continued to play a major role in the adaptation and application of market-determined exchange rate systems in developing countries. The purpose of the present paper is to provide a brief update of this experience since 1985, a period in which a number of developing countries have adopted floating exchange rates.[2] Experience with floating exchange rates in Eastern Europe and the former Soviet Union (FSU) is covered in this paper only to a limited extent because these exchange rate regimes have been operating for a very short time.

In large part, the main issues with floating exchange rate regimes continue to be those relating to the long-standing debate between the merits of a floating exchange rate regime and the alternative, fixed or "anchor" regimes. To some extent this debate has been conducted

[1] Peter J. Quirk, Benedicte Vibe Christensen, Kyung-Mo Huh, and Toshihiko Sasaki, *Floating Exchange Rates in Developing Countries; Experience with Auction and Interbank Markets*, IMF Occasional Paper No. 53 (Washington: International Monetary Fund, 1991).

[2] Afghanistan, Bolivia, Brazil, Bulgaria, Costa Rica, Dominican Republic, El Salvador, The Gambia, Ghana, Guatemala, Guyana, Haiti, Honduras, Mozambique, Nigeria, Paraguay, Peru, Romania, Russia, and Venezuela.

along parallel tracks: supporters of floating regimes argue that such arrangements are inevitably implemented when, for example, international reserves are low or nonexistent, and supporters of fixed rates underline the optimality of fixed exchange rates because of their stability. Another issue that has emerged in some of the more successful "floaters," with perhaps surprising force, has been how to handle intervention and sterilization policies so as to counter the expansionary effects of large capital inflows.

The paper is organized as follows: Section I examines the experience with adopting and operating market-determined exchange rates, including the reasons for floating, institutional arrangements in the exchange market, the role of the IMF, and accompanying measures. Section II reviews economic developments under floating exchange rate regimes, both in the exchange markets themselves and in terms of macroeconomic performance. The Annex sets out some technical considerations in setting up market arrangements for floating.

I. Introducing and Operating Floating Regimes

All developing countries that adopted floating exchange rates in the period 1985–92 did so in response to severe balance of payments difficulties. Most made the change as a prior action or performance criterion in the context of discussions for an IMF-supported economic program. The exceptions were Brazil, Haiti, and Peru (Table 1).

Reasons for floating

These governments' reasons for adopting independent floating exchange rates rather than other exchange arrangements—such as pegs to single currencies or currency baskets, or managed floating, whereby the exchange rate is moved administratively according to various economic indicators—have become clearer in recent years as debate on the issue has grown. As noted above, the arguments for floating regimes have tended to concentrate on the inevitability of such arrangements in a range of circumstances, particularly those that marked the debt crisis of the 1980s and its aftermath.

Insufficient reserves

Lack of reserves has been the most conspicuous reason for allowing the exchange rate to float. Without sufficient reserves, a commitment to defend a fixed or crawling peg exchange rate is not credible and is quickly tested by the exchange markets. Because foreign exchange transactions now top US$1 trillion a day worldwide and

Table 1. Independently Floating Exchange Rate Arrangements in Developing Countries (Including Elements in Fund-Supported Economic Programs), 1985–92

Country	Date of Program	Date of Adoption of Independent Floating	Floating Arrangements Linked to Program		Prior Use of Official Multiple Exchange Rate (Introduced as part of the program[1])
			Performance Criteria	Other	
Afghanistan	—	December 1991	—	—	Yes (—)
Albania	August 1992	June 1992	Yes	No	Yes (No)
Bolivia	June 1986	August 1985	Yes[2]	Yes	Yes (No)
Brazil	August 1988	March 1990	No	No	Yes (No)
Bulgaria	April 1992	February 1991	No	Yes	Yes (No)
Costa Rica	—	February 1992	—	—	No (—)
Dominican Republic	August 1991	January 1991	Yes	No	Yes (No)
El Salvador	August 1990	June 1990	No	Yes	No
Gambia	September 1986	January 1986	Yes[2]	Yes	No
Ghana	August 1984	September 1986	Yes	No	Yes (Yes)
Guatemala	October 1988	November 1989	Yes	Yes	Yes (No)
Guyana	July 1990	February 1991	Yes	No	Yes (No)
Haiti	September 1989	June 1991	No	Yes	Yes (No)
Honduras	June 1992	February 1992	Yes	No	No
Lithuania	—	November 1992	—	—	Yes (—)
Mozambique	June 1990	April 1992	No	No	Yes (No)
Nigeria	December 1986	September 1986	Yes[2]	Yes	Yes (No)
Paraguay	January 1991	February 1989	No	No	Yes (No)
Peru	March 1984	August 1990	No	No	Yes (No)
Romania	May 1992	June 1992	No	Yes	Yes (No)
Russia	August 1992	June 1992	Yes	Yes	Yes (Yes)
Venezuela	June 1989	March 1989	No	No	Yes (No)

Sources: IMF staff and country authorities.
Note: Dashes indicate that data is not applicable.
[1]The reference here is to a dual exchange market other than the illegal parallel market that was present in most cases at the time floating rates were instituted.
[2]Program was tentative at time of introduction.

information on even the remotest speculative or arbitrage possibilities flows almost instantaneously by satellite or wire, governments need large resources to hold a rate against market sentiment. Before they floated their exchange rates, Bolivia, El Salvador, The Gambia, Guatemala, Guyana, Haiti, and Venezuela had the equivalent of three months' or less imports in gross official international reserves. Brazil, Ghana, Nigeria, and Paraguay had more, but they were limited in their ability to sell the reserves because of large external payments arrears and other liabilities.

Lack of information

Another major reason for adopting floating systems is a shortage of information that will aid in determining a sustainable equilibrium exchange rate under fixed or crawling regimes. Particularly in the context of extensive structural reforms and liberalization—such as those underway in Eastern Europe and the FSU—computation of a fixed or crawling rate is subject to considerable uncertainty. Errors that require resetting a fixed or crawling rate undermine the often tenuous credibility of government policies in the early stages of reform.

Macroeconomic instability

Continuing high rates of inflation in the early stages of reforms or in the absence of sufficiently strong programs necessitated independently floating arrangements in several countries in the 1985–92 period (Brazil, Peru, Romania, Russia, and Zaïre). In these circumstances, fixed or crawling exchange rates could not be adjusted quickly enough to keep up with prices and squeeze out significant arbitrage possibilities against the black market exchange rate. In order to avoid the flight of economic activity to the black market— with adverse consequences in the form of tax evasion, criminalization, and loss of economic control—the authorities have had little option but to allow the market to determine the exchange rate directly. Full currency board arrangements (such as those recently adopted in Estonia) can provide strong support for the credibility of macroeconomic policies, provided they do not prove overdeflationary—and therefore politically unsustainable—in their effects on output.

Political considerations

The choice of an exchange regime cannot be divorced from political considerations. In most instances, the authorities saw considerable merit in relinquishing political responsibility for adjusting the exchange rate and allowing it to be determined by market forces.

Institutional arrangements

The main issue facing the authorities in setting up a floating exchange market has been the extent to which the system will be centralized. In essence, deciding this issue has involved two parameters of institutional arrangements: (1) auction versus private sector ("interbank") markets, and (2) within the latter, whether or not to permit the functioning of nonbank foreign exchange dealers.

The 1987 IMF study concluded that the initial experience with auction foreign exchange markets had not been particularly satisfactory.[3] Auctions have been subject to destabilizing intervention, ad hoc controls, and discontinuities in the supply of foreign exchange to the market. Since the mid-1980s, auction markets have been introduced only as supplements to extensive commercial bank markets or as limited secondary dual markets. In Nigeria, an auction market was used to distribute the foreign exchange proceeds of oil to banks and from there to the foreign exchange market, and in Russia the auction market has played a similar role for export proceeds of enterprises (although nonbank residents also participate in the auctions). The Nigerian auctions were marked by large spreads between the auction and market exchange rates, leading to sustained excess profits for participating banks. The Russian auctions, which were introduced only in April 1991, have not been marked by such problems. So far, the main lesson appears to be that auctions require a significant commitment on the part of the authorities to ensure transparency and competitiveness. However, the very choice of this centralized arrangement has in some instances been a signal that the commitment is not sufficiently strong.

Most of the larger developing countries have enough banks to make cornering of the foreign exchange market by a bank or group of banks unlikely. Nevertheless, most also have licensed nonbank dealers that work alongside the banks. On the other hand, the continued use of capital controls has led some authorities to question whether or not nonbank dealers can be monitored as well as banks, given the extensive reporting requirements and prudential oversight of banks.[4] Providing that a comparable system is extended to the

---

[3]Quirk and others, pp. 32–33.

[4]However, the widespread capital flight of the 1980s—despite extensive capital controls in developing countries—raises questions regarding the effectiveness of any monitoring of banks or nonbanks.

licensed dealers, the gains of a better customer service network and insurance against market rigging greatly outweigh any costs in terms of monitoring requirements.[5]

The role of the IMF

Exchange rate flexibility has played an important role in many members' IMF-supported financial programs. Conversely, these programs have played an important role in the adoption of independently floating exchange arrangements. The 1987 review noted that one quarter of all programs in the period 1983–86 called for the adoption or maintenance of such arrangements. This close association has continued: 13 of the 44 stand-by, extended, or Structural Adjustment Facility/Extended Structural Adjustment Facility (SAF/ESAF) arrangements outstanding as of September 30, 1992 were with countries maintaining independently floating arrangements. Further, of the 22 independently floating arrangements adopted in 1985–92, 15 were implemented either as a performance criterion or an associated action in the context of an IMF program.

Multiple exchange rates run contrary to members' obligations under Article VIII of the IMF's Articles of Agreement, and in most instances the adoption of a floating exchange rate gave members an opportunity to unify a relatively appreciated official or commercial exchange rate and a freely (or almost freely) determined secondary exchange rate used primarily for nontrade transactions. In the previous review, it was noted that some countries took a gradualist approach to unification: six temporarily adopted dual exchange markets in the context of IMF programs. In contrast, in the period 1985–92, only two such programs (Ghana's and Romania's) included the introduction of temporary dual markets, reflecting increased recognition of the serious distorting effects, lack of transparency, and difficulties in enforcing the practices such an arrangement involves.

In those cases where the new rates were adopted in the context of an IMF-supported macroeconomic program, the IMF staff provided assistance in adapting the technical foreign exchange market arrangements to the particular circumstances of the member. Such assistance, previously provided by the IMF's Exchange and Trade Relations Department and, since 1992, by the newly constituted Monetary and Exchange Affairs Department, has included providing advice on the broad policy and technical aspects of market design, drafting foreign exchange laws and regulations in association with

---

[5] Technical considerations in setting up a competitive foreign exchange market are summarized in the annex to this paper.

the IMF's Legal Department; integrating the new practices with quantitative trade, capital restrictions, and monetary policies; establishing central bank foreign exchange operations; developing regional payments systems; introducing new national currencies; and developing forward foreign exchange markets.

II. Developments Under Floating Exchange Rates

It must be emphasized, for it is often neglected in discussions of exchange rate regimes, that it is the rate itself and not the regime that is important. Large differences between official and market-determined (black or parallel) exchange rates signal that the market does not view the official exchange rate as realistic. Before proceeding with a discussion of floating rate cases, it is useful to consider some evidence that parallel market-determined rates are more than mere indicators of sentiment.

Monetary determinants and black market rates

Limited cross-country investigation has been undertaken of the behavior and determinants of black market exchange rates, although regional and single-country studies tend to confirm the importance of monetary determinants.[6] Table 2 sets out the results of econometric tests of the relationship between black market exchange rates and broad money (lagged one period) for a broad sample of 13 major developing countries over the period 1977–89. These results show a remarkably consistent and strong bivariate relationship in all the countries except Korea and suggest that, while governments have maintained official exchange rates at differing and often inappropriate levels, at least one part of the private sector has consistently weighed and acted on the realities of monetary policy strengths or weaknesses.[7]

Such results point to the value of investigating the role of differences between the black and official market rates as a disequilibrium variable in prompting other macroeconomic developments. A number of studies have incorporated the variable into tests of covered interest parity. One finds the variable to be a significant

[6]See Sanjeev Gupta, "An Application of the Monetary Approach to Black Market Exchange Rates," *Weltwirtschaftliches Archiv* (Germany), Vol. 116 (No. 2, 1980), pp. 235–52; and Peter E. Koveos and Bruce Scifert, "Market Efficiency Purchasing Power Parity, and Black Markets: Evidence from Latin American Countries," *Weltwirtschaftliches Archiv*, Vol. 122 (No. 2, 1986), pp. 313–26.

[7]Exchange rate data are provided by correspondents to *Pick's Currency Yearbook* and, more recently, *International Currency Reports*.

Table 2. Black Market Exchange Rate Determination, 1977–89: Econometric Results

| | T-values | | | |
	Constant	Broad money[1] coefficient	$\overline{R^2}$	D.W.
Argentina	−1.4	219.6	1.00	1.6
Brazil	−1.1	153.4	1.00	1.9
Chile	3.4	7.8	0.85	0.9[2]
Colombia	1.4	23.6	0.98	1.9
Egypt	9.6	22.6	0.98	1.0[2]
Korea[3]	10.7	1.9	0.17	0.8[2]
Mexico	0.7	10.4	0.90	1.8
Nigeria	−3.7	10.2	0.90	1.0[2]
Peru	0.9	84.0	1.00	2.0
Philippines	3.5	6.7	0.79	1.1[2]
Turkey	2.3	18.4	0.97	1.6
Uruguay	2.4	27.8	0.98	0.8[2]
Venezuela	−3.3	14.6	0.95	2.0

[1] Broad money (annual average) in period preceding exchange rate.
[2] Serial correlation of errors is indicated.
[3] Results are generally insignificant.

determinant of long-run growth performance in a group of East Asian and Latin American economies.[8]

Exchange market developments

With the caveat that underlying developments in market-determined exchange rates—be they official or black market rates—are determined not by the system but by the stance of monetary policies, it is nevertheless interesting to look at the evolution of rates before and after the adoption of floating arrangements.

A striking feature of exchange rate movements after floating is that they are broadly similar to those that occurred before floating. The fixed or managed regimes did not eliminate or even greatly smooth official exchange rate movements, which broadly followed those of the black market rates, but with a considerable lag.[9] The exceptions

[8] Peter J. Quirk, "Exchange Rate Policies and Management: A Model for Successful Structural Adjustment: The Experience of Southeast Asia," in *Strategies for Structual Adjustment: The Experience of South Asia*, edited by Ungku A. Aziz (Washington: International Monetary Fund, 1990).

[9] Chart 1 shows official and parallel bilateral exchange rates against the U.S. dollar, as well as real and nominal exchange rates, in the period 1980–91 for the following group of countries: Bolivia, Brazil, El Salvador, Guatemala, Guyana, Lebanon, Nigeria, Paraguay, Peru, Philippines, South Africa, Uruguay, Venezuela, and Zaïre. Effective exchange rate series are from the IMF's information notice system.

are Brazil—and Zaïre some five years after it adopted the float—where the depreciation of official rates has accelerated sharply in recent years. In several countries, the official exchange rate remained less depreciated than the black market rate after floating, reflecting either market imperfections (Nigeria, as discussed above) or an illegality premium associated with continuing exchange controls (Guatemala, Guyana, Philippines, Peru, South Africa, and Uruguay). In some others, the black market rate was less depreciated than the official exchange rate after floating (Brazil, Venezuela, and Zaïre), indicating either the influence of strong capital inflows into the entire system (Venezuela) or growing avoidance of the official arrangements.

In many countries, the independently floating arrangements continued a process of real effective depreciation and improving competitiveness that was already underway (Guyana, Nigeria, Philippines, South Africa, Uruguay, Venezuela, and Zaïre). The exceptions were Brazil and Peru, where inflation was particularly rapid; El Salvador and Guatemala, where a small appreciation in the one or two years following floating reflected a strengthening of economic policies; and Paraguay, owing to large depreciations in neighboring countries. In Bolivia, the shift to floating reversed a deterioration in competitiveness beforehand.

Macroeconomic performance

The consequences of systemic reforms for specific macroeconomic variables are difficult to trace. First, economic developments depend on many factors, of which the exchange rate is but one. Second, there are well-known problems with "before and after" tests, but better methodology requires more data. Noting these caveats, the 1987 review found somewhat better balance of payments performances under floating arrangements and broadly similar inflation and output.

Updated data are shown in Charts 1 and 2. Of the 12 countries surveyed, inflation declined in 6 following floating (Bolivia, Brazil, The Gambia, Peru, Philippines, and Venezuela) and accelerated in one (Nigeria). Inflation was broadly unchanged in Paraguay following an initial upturn. The adoption of independently floating exchange rates (most often in the context of IMF-supported programs) between 1985 and 1992 has been associated with the surprisingly positive output performance of the 11 countries shown in Chart 2. Six experienced faster GDP growth after floating (Bolivia, with a one-year lag; Nigeria; Peru; Philippines; Uruguay; and Venezuela, after a one-year lag). In two countries (Brazil and Paraguay), growth performance deteriorated.

Chart 1. Consumer Price Developments
in Selected Countries, 1980–91

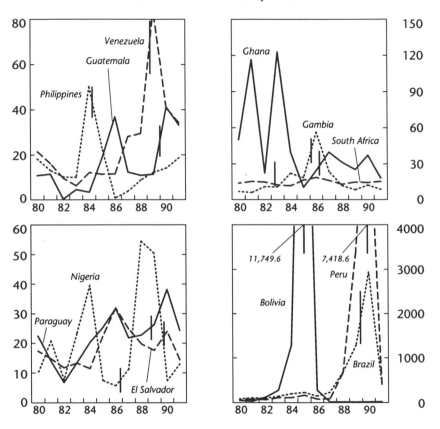

Sources: IMF, *International Financial Statistics* (various years).
    Note: Percentage change; 12-month change in consumer prices. Vertical slashes indicate the beginning of floating exchange regime.

Intervention policies and sterilization

Questions of appropriate intervention policies arise immediately following the adoption of floating. In industrial countries, intervention (in the context of floating exchange rates) usually means purchases and sales of foreign exchange by the central banks. In many developing countries, however, central banks will probably undertake official intermediary transactions in the exchange market that must be distinguished from direct intervention aimed at achieving a

Chart 2. Developments in GDP
of Selected Countries, 1980–91

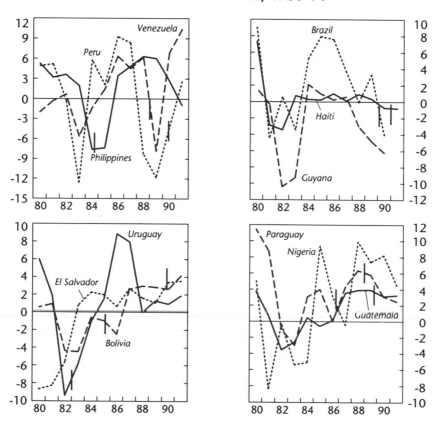

Sources: IMF, *International Financial Statistics* (various years).
Note: Percentage change in GDP (1985 prices). Vertical slashes indicate the beginning of a floating exchange regime. Guyana moved to a floating regime in February 1991.

specific exchange rate. Basically, it is convenient to define as intermediation rather than intervention (1) sales of foreign exchange by the central banks in accordance with the normal business of applying public sector foreign exchange receipts to public sector current payments,[10] and (2) purchases toward an established quantitative target

[10]Examples are sales of oil receipts by the Bank of Venezuela and the auctioning of enterprise receipts by the Moscow exchange.

for the recumulation of foreign exchange reserves over a period of time, within the context of the economic program.[11] In contrast, intervention involves the use of international reserves—either by adding foreign exchange to reserves, selling from reserves to the market, or taking a position in the forward market—with the principal objective of changing or supporting the exchange rate.

Under the market exchange system, a central bank trading desk should generally refrain from direct intervention in the early stages of exchange reform and limit foreign exchange transactions to those consistent with its intermediary function for the government and with the overall target for the stock of international reserves. Intervention to forcefully appreciate the currency cannot be sustained during the initial reform period, because reserves are generally low.

Later in a successful stabilization and reform process, there may be a need for direct intervention to prevent the exchange rate from appreciating and undermining competitiveness in case of reverses in terms of trade improvement or an unsustainable reflow of private capital. Such intervention should be coordinated with monetary policy actions to sterilize any undue expansion of liquidity. A central bank absorbs all or part of the reversible inflow of foreign exchange by (1) purchasing foreign exchange from the spot market into reserves and (2) offsetting money aggregates by reducing net domestic assets.

While reflows of capital in several of the countries that floated and liberalized were anticipated in principle, they were nevertheless surprising in terms of the speed of the turnaround and the size of the inflows. Reversals to capital inflows (indicated by short-term private capital and errors and omissions in the balance of payments) occurred in El Salvador, Nigeria (in the first year of the economic program), and Venezuela. Such a reversal has also taken place recently in Jamaica, which floated its currency in 1983 and eliminated the remaining exchange controls and interest rates in 1991. The main lesson of these episodes, as noted earlier, has been that it is necessary to adjust fiscal policies by reducing credit to government in order to sterilize the threat that foreign exchange purchases for international reserves pose for domestic liquidity. Sterilization by contracting credit to the private sector not only raises interest rates but accelerates and perpetuates the capital inflows; it therefore tends to be ineffective beyond the very short run.

---

[11] The aim of increasing reserves to a certain minimum level should not be considered intervention because the focus is on a quantity of reserves considered necessary (with the exchange rate as a "residual").

ANNEX

Technical Considerations in Establishing Floating Regimes

Under a market-determined exchange system, the central bank undertakes regulatory and prudential functions that include monitoring for "fair trading" (spreads, rates for small transactions, and the like), monopolistic practices, collusion, capital adequacy, and dealer licensing arrangements.

Fair marketing requires that dealers make open and honest quotations to all customers. The central bank requires that dealers post openly, in a public place, quotes for smaller transactors, including "live" (not indicative) buying and selling rates for major currencies, without excessive spreads and/or commissions. (Existing exchange rate spreads narrow considerably with the elimination of exchange taxes.) The market is monitored for abuses on a sample basis by the central bank, and continued abuses can lead to the suspension or withdrawal of dealers' licenses. Customers are free to choose their dealers and dealers to make transactions with one another. However, nonperformance is penalized—first, by the imposition of penalty fees and, with continuing nonperformance, by exclusion from the market. The nonperforming customer or dealer bears all exchange losses, if any. Dealers make suitable arrangements for monitoring and exchanging information on creditworthiness and performance, and the central bank similarly monitors the dealers.

For purposes of macroeconomic policymaking, the banking system and other dealers need to provide the central bank with up-to-date information on foreign exchange flows and main financial aggregates. Timely and accurate information is critical to prevent the destabilization of output, prices, and the balance of payments. For example, the central bank should receive, on a daily or weekly basis, aggregate data on each bank's or dealer's long and short positions in foreign exchange (spot and forward separately). These data provide early information on inward capital movements that are larger than expected, possibly requiring sterilization.

Controls on the spot and forward positions of market participants, which need to be handled delicately, pose several problems. Experience has shown that it is difficult to impose limits that prevent the undue accumulation of foreign exchange but permit dealers to amass working balances sufficient for conducting business efficiently. The central bank can monitor dealers' exposure relative to capital adequacy through normal prudential supervisory functions, consulting with the affected dealers and the association of dealers when exposure exceeds levels the central bank considers healthy for the bank in question. In any event, dealers will not accumulate excessive balances or attempt to corner the market, because they will be subject to two-way exchange rate risk under a floating system and, once they have been punished by losses, will keep their exposure to a minimum. The central bank can also act against any monopolistic or collusive tendencies by licensing further dealers, including nonbank dealers, to ensure competitiveness in the market.

The most important feature of the foreign exchange market in terms of ensuring competition is allowing creditworthy applicants free access to the market. To deepen the market, participation should be extended to all banks not experiencing financial difficulties that could call into question their ability to honor exchange contracts. In addition, in order to improve retail service, head off any collusion between the banks, and tap into the parallel market, *bureaux de change* could be licensed.

Consideration also needs to be given to delegating to the licensed dealers responsibility for ensuring compliance with foreign exchange monitoring requirements. The central bank supervises the bank's performance of this responsibility by spot checks, as well as by aggregative data.

Although most basic operations necessary for the new market will be extensions of the existing exchange market, there are several areas in which strengthening and new development of the market will generally be needed. Communications links in the interbank market may need to be strengthened, including telephone connections and a Reuters or similar screen for most recent representative transactions (banks' and dealers' bid-ask prices, amounts, and so forth).

Opening and closing hours for the exchange market need to be decided primarily with the interests of customers in mind. In general, this will mean longer rather than shorter market hours. Arrangements also need to be made for foreign exchange services at major points of entry and exit from the country.

All interdealer purchases and sales orders are drawn up on a final basis. However, if both parties agree, orders may be drawn up on a provisional basis specified clearly at the outset. Orders in the interbank market may be made by telex or by telephone; in the latter case, the selling dealer confirms the sale on the same day by telex (with a test number) or letter. The confirmation provides the type of currency, the amount bought or sold, the name of the correspondent bank abroad, the value date, the applicable exchange rate, and the local currency equivalent.

Foreign exchange for a valid customer purchase order must be delivered within two working days from the day of payment, in local currency in respect of spot transactions or within two working days of the fixed future date in respect of forward transactions.

Dealers should move in time to offer services in forward exchange (primarily three and six months). This activity is essential to achieving the maximum benefit from the increased confidence and availability of the credit lines expected to result from the new private sector-based arrangements. Following the introduction of the market, the central bank should generally consider coordinating seminars for market participants, particularly the smaller ones, in more sophisticated aspects of the market, including forward operations. (Correspondent banks often offer assistance from their home offices in this respect.)

Case Study of Ghana

Reinold H. van Til

Ghana's experience with the reform of its exchange and trade systems is an interesting one.[1] The country worked through a number of steps in its move from a fixed exchange rate to a floating regime. It was some seven years before the system reached the stage of maturity, and the road was at times bumpy. To understand why it took so long, we must take into account the dismal initial economic and financial conditions. In 1983, the economy had a severely weakened external sector, large external payments arrears, a minimal official market for foreign exchange, a flourishing parallel market, and virtually no official international reserves. Since then, as a result of the steadfast implementation of a coherent set of financial and structural policies, Ghana's economic and financial situation has improved steadily, as evidenced by its sustained economic growth and greatly strengthened external position.

The first wave of exchange rate reforms took place between 1983 and 1986. Ghana's currency, the cedi, had been at a fixed rate of ¢ 2.75 per dollar for more than five years. During this time, the differential between the official and parallel market exchange rates had grown very large, and the real effective exchange rate had appreciated by more than 400 percent. In April 1983, the authorities introduced a system of bonuses of 750 percent of the official exchange rate on specified export transactions and surcharges of 990 percent on foreign exchange payments, which resulted in exchange rates of ¢ 23.38 and ¢ 29.98 per dollar, respectively. In October 1983, this cumbersome scheme—introduced to postpone an unavoidable official devaluation—was abolished and a unified official rate of ¢ 30 per dollar adopted. During 1984, exchange rate policy was guided by a real exchange rate rule, on the basis of which the rate was adjusted quarterly for the inflation differential between Ghana and its trading partners. As a result, by the end of 1984 the official rate had depreciated from ¢ 30 to ¢ 50 per dollar. The real exchange rate rule was subsequently abandoned and, with an eye on

---

[1] A detailed account of developments is contained in Ishan Kapur, Michael T. Hadjimichael, Paul Hilbers, Jerald Schiff, and Philippe Szymczak, *Ghana: Adjustment and Growth, 1983–91*, IMF Occasional Paper 86 (Washington, D.C.: International Monetary Fund, 1991).

fiscal and balance of payments developments, the authorities implemented a series of discrete devaluations, bringing the rate to ¢ 60 per dollar by the end of 1985 and to ¢ 90 per dollar by the beginning of 1986. Despite these adjustments, the differential between the parallel and official exchange rates remained sizable, making it clear that a more market-oriented approach to exchange rate management was desirable.

On September 19, 1986, as a precursor to a full float, the Ghanaian authorities introduced a dual exchange rate system consisting of a fixed rate and a floating rate. As in 1983, when the move was made from a rigid fixed rate to a more flexibly managed rate, the authorities exercised caution, testing the market before relinquishing all controls. For the fixed rate, which applied mainly to government transactions and export receipts from sales of cocoa and gold, the cedi was traded at ¢ 90 per dollar. The more flexibly managed rate was determined in a weekly retail auction, where authorized banks could bid on behalf of their customers. When the auctions were first implemented, the currency was trading at ¢ 128 per dollar, but by the end of 1986 the auction rate had depreciated steadily to ¢ 152 per dollar.

In conjunction with this reform of the exchange system, the import licensing system was liberalized considerably, increasing access to the official foreign exchange market and reducing the spread between the auction and parallel market rates. Under the new licensing system, import licenses and access to the auctions could be obtained for virtually all nonconsumer goods. Traders in consumer goods were allowed to import with their own foreign exchange resources, which meant in practice through the parallel market.

Having tested the auction system, the authorities felt confident enough to unify the exchange system in mid-February 1987 by introducing an auction market for all official foreign exchange transactions. This market operated until the beginning of 1990, but the progressive liberalization of the trade regime—which ultimately led to the elimination of the import licensing system at the beginning of 1989—broadened the official market demand for foreign exchange over the years. At the same time, the strengthened external position allowed the central bank to increase the supply of foreign exchange to the auctions.

Despite the significant broadening of the official foreign exchange market, the parallel market for foreign exchange remained an important phenomenon during these years, and integrating and legalizing this market became an urgent objective. Accordingly, on February 1, 1988, the authorities allowed the establishment of foreign exchange bureaus. This decision was viewed with some skepticism in certain quarters, as it abandoned the "official" unified market and reintroduced a dual exchange system. This skepticism was reinforced by the strict separation of the foreign exchange bureaus and the auction market, which led to a persistent spread between the auction and bureau rates. The foreign exchange bureaus did not have access to the auction market, and the "no-questions-asked policy" and minimum reporting requirements governing the bureaus contrasted sharply with the rules in the official market.

Nonetheless, the bureaus brought what had been hidden in the parallel market into the open and were ultimately instrumental in establishing an integrated and market-determined foreign exchange system. Most importantly, however, they changed the public's perception that access to foreign exchange was reserved for the privileged. Once the bureaus were established, foreign currency, like any other commodity, became available to everyone. Moreover, the bureaus underscored the point that market forces, not a central authority, were responsible for exchange rate developments.

The process of integrating the foreign exchange bureaus and the auction market started at the end of 1989 and was completed by the end of April 1990, when licensed bureaus were granted access to the market. Authorized dealer banks and bureaus were then able to buy foreign currency for themselves and their customers, transforming the retail auction into a wholesale market. In addition, foreign exchange dealers could trade among themselves and with their customers, and thus an interbank market for foreign exchange developed. Not unexpectedly, the unification of the foreign exchange market caused the spread between the auction and foreign exchange bureau rates virtually to disappear. The last step in this process came with the development of the interbank market for foreign exchange: the auction market lost its importance in the pricing and distribution of foreign exchange and was replaced by a fully operational interbank market in March 1992.

Ghana's transition from a fixed exchange rate system to a floating regime was a carefully planned and controlled experiment, in which the policymakers closely monitored every step with a view to consolidating the gains achieved in previous stages of the reform process. I do not wish to suggest that this approach is the model for all developing countries, especially since I have often wondered whether a more rapid transformation would not have contributed to a speedier and more successful adjustment process in Ghana. In this respect, several factors need to be considered.

- First, the degree of gradualism a country can usefully follow depends on the external resources available to finance the adjustment process. The considerable external support that Ghana obtained as a result of its successful adjustment program gave the authorities more time than they would otherwise have had.

- Second, the speed of exchange rate adjustment is a function of the speed of trade liberalization, and coordination between the two is essential in controlling the process.
- Third, political and social consensus on the need for and speed of macroeconomic and structural adjustment dictates the phasing of reforms. In many cases, economic policymakers may be ahead of the rest of the political establishment, which must be fully in agreement for the program to be successfully implemented.

As Peter Quirk noted, the exchange rate itself, not the regime, is the primary factor in achieving stability. However, it is also clear that certain institutional settings may inhibit needed reforms, and in that sense a reform of the exchange system may be a necessary condition for achieving an equilibrium exchange rate.

A question was raised about the extent to which a floating regime contributes to exchange rate instability and whether it is preferable to maintain a fixed exchange rate regime to assure a stable exchange rate. It is important to emphasize that exchange rate stability also depends heavily on the stance of monetary and fiscal policies. Exchange rate stability can be meaningfully achieved only if the exchange rate is consistent with external and internal equilibria.

Case Study of Venezuela

Lorenzo L. Perez

Assessing Venezuela's experience with a floating exchange rate system requires discussing the exchange regime that existed prior to the floating of the currency in March 1989. In the face of a balance of payments crisis in 1983, Venezuela imposed a multiple currency practice system and introduced payment restrictions. By the end of 1988, the year before the floating of the bolivar, there were three exchange rates pegged to the U.S. dollar, plus a market-determined exchange rate. The bolivar was seriously overvalued in the three-pegged exchange rate markets, which were used primarily for servicing private and public debt and for authorized imports of goods and services. Tourism, nontraditional exports, and nonregistered private capital flows were channeled through a free exchange market.

This system of multiple exchange rates entailed complex administrative controls and, together with associated trade restrictions, led to severe distortions that curtailed growth and international trade. The cost of the system was borne by the public sector through the quasi-fiscal losses of the Central Bank, as well as through the decreased oil revenues of the government and the state oil company (the state petroleum company's oil export receipts were converted to bolivars at one of the appreciated exchange rates). The system, of course, created large economic rents for its beneficiaries, and by 1988 it had become increasingly clear to the private sector that the system was not sustainable. Along with capital flight, there was an anticipatory buildup of inventories of imported goods brought in at preferential exchange rates and financed by guaranteed letters of credit. These developments led to a sharp drop in international reserves and a balance of payments crisis.

I. The 1989 Reform

By the beginning of 1989, with official reserves at a very low level, transactions outside the free market were reduced to minimal amounts, and de facto devaluation and unification began. In these circumstances, and in support of reforms to liberalize the trade and financial systems, the new administration of President Carlos Andres Perez abolished the multiple exchange rate system on March 13,

1989, allowing the bolivar to float against the U.S. dollar in a free interbank market. The authorities' action was prompted by the difficulty of establishing an equilibrium exchange rate, as well as by the impending significant liberalization of the trade and financial systems, which would require an exchange rate settled at the outset of the float at a level close to that prevailing in the free market. With the adoption of the unified rate system, all exchange controls were eliminated, and all external transactions of the public and private sectors were channeled through the interbank market.

As was the practice prior to 1989, under the new exchange rate system the state oil company (PDVSA) continues to surrender its foreign exchange earnings—about 80 percent of total exports in recent years—to the Central Bank, which, in turn, intermediates by selling foreign exchange to the interbank market. As a result, the Central Bank has been and continues to be both a net seller of foreign exchange to the interbank market and a major participant. Foreign exchange proceeds of loan disbursements to the public sector are also surrendered to the Central Bank to service external debt. Although some 30 commercial banks and several exchange houses now participate in the interbank market, forward exchange market transactions have developed only on a limited basis.

In summary, the new exchange rate system has not been operating as a clean float, with the exchange rate clearing the market and no changes in net international reserves. As an operating principle, the Central Bank has set a target for its average daily sales of foreign exchange in the market, taking into consideration monetary objectives, including growth of base money consistent with growth in output and prices, and a net international reserve target for the year in question. Given the level of intermediation of foreign exchange established by the Central Bank, market forces play a role in determining the value of the bolivar in the foreign exchange market. However, in practice, the Central Bank occasionally intervenes in the interbank market, varying the amount of its daily foreign exchange sales with a view to achieving exchange rate objectives.

II. Experience with the Flexible System

When the bolivar was floated in March 1989, the authorities intended not just to implement a flexible exchange rate system; they also believed that the level of reserves needed to be raised significantly, given the experience of the late 1980s. With this idea in mind, the Central Bank limited its sales of foreign exchange receipts from the oil sector. Yet the reserves increased only marginally due to the large repayments the private sector was making against import letters of credit and the delays in completing a commercial bank financing package for the public sector. However, in that year the Central Bank was able to clean up the exchange system by honoring the exchange rate guarantees and thus to reverse its own quasi-fiscal position. The total cost was close to 5 percent of GDP, most of it falling due in 1989, the rest in 1990 and 1991. The bolivar depreciated by about 30 percent in real effective terms during 1989, facilitating the initiation of the trade liberalization program.

Overall, the new exchange rate system and the adjustment program adopted by the authorities in 1989 were successful in strengthening the balance of payments and reducing inflation, although the contraction in output was larger than expected. Measured average inflation for 1989 was much higher than in 1988, but in June 1989 the inflation rate began to decline significantly. The implementation of the flexible exchange rate system was successful despite the fact that coordination of exchange and credit policies was hampered during that year by the continuation of restrictions on interest rates, which were not liberalized until April 1990.

Gradual implementation of a flexible exchange rate policy continued until late 1990. But in mid-1990, the bolivar began appreciating in real terms due to an increase in inflationary pressures related to slippages in the authorities' fiscal program and to the oil price boom associated with the crisis in the Middle East. Only about half the oil revenue windfall was saved, and in general fiscal policy was relaxed in 1991. The Central Bank tightened credit and tried to avoid the real appreciation of the bolivar by limiting the effect of the oil revenue windfall on the foreign exchange market. In the event, the currency did appreciate in 1990 and 1991, as no progress was made in reducing inflation and there were large increases in net international reserves, facilitated in part by the government's privatization program.

During the first nine months of 1992, the authorities changed their exchange rate strategy and tried to reduce price pressures by stabilizing the exchange rate. However, a further weakening in public sector finances (associated with the decline in oil revenues, which credit policy could not offset fully) fueled pressure on prices. The Central Bank increased its average daily sales of foreign exchange from the level of the previous year—the level that would have been necessary at least to maintain international reserves unchanged during 1992. Under these circumstances, the exchange rate settled at about 65 bolivars to the dollar between March and September 1992. Large amounts of foreign exchange were sold in the interbank market during several episodes when political instability and increased uncertainty about economic policy put pressure on the bolivar. The Central Bank lost about US$1 billion in net international reserves, and the inflation rate edged up.

In early October 1992, the Central Bank reduced the amount of foreign exchange sold in the market in an effort to slow the loss of reserves and regain competitiveness. Unfortunately, this action coincided with renewed political and fiscal uncertainties, and there was a new attack on the bolivar. The Central Bank raised interest rates sharply but also increased its sales of foreign exchange; a further large decline in net international reserves occurred, and the currency depreciated significantly. By mid-November 1992, however, the Central Bank had succeeded in halting the loss of reserves and in stabilizing the currency.

III. Lessons from the Venezuelan Experience

The managed floating exchange rate system has contributed to Venezuela's fiscal adjustment in the face of external and domestic shocks and facilitated the implementation of an ambitious trade liberalization program. A flexible exchange rate system has allowed the country to cope with the effects of unstable oil export prices, changes in the direction of capital flows (by minimizing the effects of foreign interest rate disturbances on domestic demand), and shifts in the relative prices of tradable goods caused by the trade reform. It also can facilitate the use of a monetary anchor to help reduce inflation. As a side comment, it should be noted that the use of a fixed exchange rate as a nominal anchor does not appear to be a viable course as long as a fiscal problem persists. However, the implementation of the flexible exchange rate system in Venezuela has been uneven, with the exchange rate lagging inflation at times when fiscal and credit policies have been weak and inconsistent with the goal of a stable exchange rate. Short periods of relative exchange rate stability have been followed by rounds of sometimes large depreciations, with unsettling effects on markets.

The Venezuelan experience illustrates the crucial role that fiscal policy plays in determining how successful exchange rate policy is in achieving its aims. Intervention in the foreign exchange market to achieve a real depreciation of the currency cannot be effective when macroeconomic fundamentals are not right. Attempts to reduce exchange rate flexibility to lower inflation are likely to be short-lived, especially in a country with the degree of capital mobility that exists in Venezuela, where the monetary authority's reduced control over base money makes monetary policy less effective in reducing inflation.

It would appear that a successful program to reduce inflation, protect the balance of payments, and create sustainable conditions for economic growth must be based on a strong fiscal position as well as on suitable credit and wage policies. In the case of Venezuela, these policies might usefully be complemented by an oil stabilization fund that would help reduce the economy's vulnerability to oil shocks and smooth out government expenditures over the medium term. Hedging techniques for oil prices in future and options markets could also help to reduce the impact of oil price shocks.

Case Study of Mexico (1982–91)

Thomas Reichmann

Mexico is an interesting case, inasmuch as it provides examples of a number of different exchange regimes, some of which failed and some of which worked rather well. It is important to keep in mind, of course, that the exchange rate is but one of many elements in an economic program and that it is the whole program that matters. Also, each country has its own peculiarities, and some things worked in Mexico simply because of the nature of the country; they can hardly be replicated elsewhere.

The period of this case study dates from 1982 onward—that is, from the onset of the debt crisis up to 1992. Because some background is required to put this period into perspective, I will first briefly analyze developments in the years leading to the crisis.

I. The Period Leading to the Crisis

Mexico has long had a fixed exchange rate. In the years after the Great Depression and into the 1950s, the country had what was virtually a fixed rate. In the 22 years from 1954 until 1976—almost a whole generation—the value of the peso remained constant in U.S. dollar terms. We have to bear in mind, then, that we are dealing with a society that is very used to a fixed exchange rate.

As they were for many other economies, these years were also a period of inward-looking growth based on import substitution and high protective barriers. While it lasted, this strategy was quite successful in producing low inflation and high growth, but the inefficiencies of the model eventually caught up with it. The high cost of protectionist barriers and other distortions, together with the inefficiencies of growing with a small market, began to limit the possibilities for growth. By 1970, exports were almost stagnant, and the economy was in decline. When the Government stepped into the breach, growth resumed for a short period, but this time at the cost of an increasing fiscal deficit and rising inflation. By 1976, the financial situation had become unsustainable. The fixed exchange rate system had to be abandoned.

There was a large devaluation in 1976, with the peso dropping in value from Mex$12.50 to Mex$20 per U.S. dollar. The authorities also put in place a major adjustment program. However, the following

157

year large new petroleum reserves were discovered, and Mexico again became very creditworthy. As the country found itself swamped with offers of foreign loans, the urgency to adjust disappeared. Over the next five years, the Government managed not only to spend the new petroleum revenues but also to quadruple the foreign debt—from US$22 billion in 1976 to US$88 billion in 1981.

After the 1976 devaluation, a "fixed but adjustable" exchange rate system was initially put in place. The new system was intended to maintain a stable exchange rate, which would be moved only if necessary. Given the petroleum reserves and newly found riches, however, the system leaned more toward the fixed than the adjustable. While the fiscal deficit ballooned and inflation rose from 12 percent to the 20–30 percent per annum range, the exchange rate moved very little. By 1981, the rate had risen only to Mex$26 to the U.S. dollar, resulting in substantial appreciation in real effective terms—some 30–40 percent—under circumstances that included a large fiscal deficit of almost 17 percent of GDP and an external debt of US$88 billion. It required only the increase in world market interest rates in 1981 for expectations to turn around. Creditors recognized that the situation was unsustainable, capital started to flow outward, and Mexico entered the crisis that soon extended to all other debtor countries.

II. The Crisis and Early Adjustment

Thus begins the period I want to look at. In February 1982, when capital outflows began, the authorities tried to respond with another major devaluation of 40 percent. But it was not sufficient; capital continued to flow out, forcing the Government to suspend debt payments in August 1982. The authorities then started organizing a drastic adjustment program. The exchange rate was adjusted further (the cumulative depreciation was about 73 percent for 1982 as a whole), and, at the end of 1982, a dual exchange system was introduced. The dual system that was put in place comprised a rate for trade and debt transactions—the official rate—and a free rate, with which the official rate was supposed to converge. The official rate was arranged in terms of a crawling peg—basically a variant of the *tablita*—that would preannounce the path of future inflation.

But the new exchange arrangements were only part of the overall adjustment program, which was centered mainly around fiscal policy and was to achieve impressive results. From 1982 to 1983, the primary balance of the public sector—that is, the overall balance less interest payments—was adjusted by 10 percentage points of GDP, from a deficit of 5 percent to a surplus of 5 percent. Few countries have managed such an improvement. Much of the adjustment was accomplished by cutting expenditures and raising taxes, but a good part of it was the result of setting public prices at more realistic levels. But these adjustments, together with the massive devaluation—73 percent—made in 1982, pushed both the inflation and interest rates higher than had been expected. In the end, despite the 10-point improvement at the primary level, the overall deficit was cut by a little over 8 percentage points, declining from almost 17 percent of GDP in 1982 to 8.6 percent in 1983. Growth, however, was negative, with GDP dropping by almost 4 percent in 1983.

The new exchange rate regime worked relatively well. The current account responded immediately, moving into surplus. But, as it often does, the *tablita* had some unfortunate effects. A lot of wishful thinking was involved; in preannouncing the rate, the authorities always seemed to be signaling that inflation would be lower than anticipated—not only because there were expectations to massage, but because policymakers tend to be optimistic in such situations. The result was that the exchange rate lagged behind inflation, appreciating gradually during 1983–84 and into 1985. At the same time, after the significant fiscal adjustments of 1982 and early 1983, the fiscal position started to weaken slightly. The primary surplus declined from almost 5 percent in 1983 to 3 percent in 1985. The current account, which remained in surplus, also began to weaken. The situation was then compounded by two exogenous shocks: the earthquake of 1985, which involved substantial fiscal costs; and the drop in petroleum prices in 1986. From one year to the next, exports dropped by about US$8 billion—the equivalent of 40 percent of export proceeds—and 26 percent of public sector revenues vanished.

Mexico had to start the whole reform process over again. After three years of adjustment, most of what had been gained was lost. A new program was put in place, based—as the previous one had been—on fiscal and exchange rate adjustment. On the fiscal side, retrenchment measures worth about 3 percentage points of GDP were implemented. The primary balance was brought up to about 5 percent of GDP, while the depreciation of the peso was accelerated during 1985–86, for a cumulative 35 percent depreciation. Again, the balance of payments responded. By 1987, reserves were up, and the current account was showing a strong surplus; not surprisingly, however, inflation had climbed to 160 percent a year. Thus, when the world's stock markets crashed on "Black Thursday" in October 1987, Mexico was on the verge of hyperinflation. Within the country itself, the crash renewed mistrust in the currency. Capital started leaving the country, and by November 1987, the Banco de Mexico—the central bank—was forced to step out of the market and allow the rate to move freely. This situation caused some controversy in Mexico, given that the exchange rate crisis had occurred at a time when the country was gaining reserves and showing a current account surplus. The lesson the authorities drew from this situation was that as long as inflation existed, particularly triple-digit inflation, no exchange system would be stable. Stopping inflation had to be the priority.

III. Inflation and Devaluation

Twice—in 1982 and 1986—adjustments in the exchange rate brought about sharp increases in inflation in Mexico. In 1982, inflation climbed from the 20 percent range before the devaluation to the 50 percent range afterward. As we have seen, in 1986–87, it rose again, from 50–100 percent to 160 percent. In the context of Mexico in the 1980s, these increases were also manifestations of a more general problem: the resource transfer associated with the country's external debt. Because of the debt's size and its high real interest rates, the servicing costs were basically unsustainable and contributed heavily to inflation. We get an idea of the magnitude of the problem by looking at its history. Between 1970 and 1981, Mexico experienced an inward resource transfer; on average, during these years, the country could afford a trade deficit of about 1.3 percent of GDP per annum. Between 1982 and 1988—the six years after the crisis—this trend reversed itself. Mexico was transferring resources out of the country and running a trade surplus that averaged 6.3 percent of GDP annually. In the course of the debt crisis, a shift took place in the transfer of resources of close to 8 percentage points of GDP; in other words, the annual supply of goods in the Mexican economy declined an average of 8 percentage points of GDP. This phenomenon also had other dimensions. In the fiscal area, the Government had to resort to the "inflation tax" in order to service the debt, since the usual revenue sources were not sufficient to cover the added expense. In terms of competitiveness, restoring the external equilibrium required a large drop in real wages and, given the lag with which nominal wages adjust, inflation was the way to bring this about.

Despite the effects of the devaluations on prices, Mexico's overall inflationary inertia was less than in many other countries, and the exchange rate adjustments did result in improvements in the current account. Real wages dropped. In part, the reduced degree of inflationary inertia is explained by the fact that because Mexico had for generations lived with a fixed exchange rate, mechanisms of indexation were not that well established. Another factor, the cooperation of the labor unions, was the result of Mexico's particular political structure.

IV. Successful Stabilization: The 1987–88 Program

As we have seen, the exchange rate crisis in October 1987 convinced the authorities that as long as inflation existed, no exchange regime would be stable enough. A more comprehensive approach was needed to cope with the problems of inflation and growth in the Mexican economy.

A new program was devised in 1987, based on four planks[1]. The first and foremost of these was the fiscal effort. The second was the social pact—an agreement among business, labor, and Government aimed at breaking the inertia in the system. The third element involved finding a more permanent solution to the debt problem, while the fourth included a number of structural reforms.

The fiscal effort

A major new effort was made to improve public finances, and the primary surplus was increased by an additional 3 percentage points of GDP to a surplus of 8 percent, mostly by cutting expenditures and adjusting public prices.

The social pact

This agreement was something new in the overall strategy. It involved an initial drastic realignment of wages, public sector prices, and the exchange rate, which were then frozen at the new levels. This approach was not new; the same kind of package had been tried elsewhere. But what was singular in Mexico's case was that the freeze was for one quarter only, from November 1987 through February 1988. Mexico once again had a fixed exchange rate system, but this time one with a very short time horizon. The solution was a compromise between the desire to provide stability (a fixed rate) and credibility (a short horizon). With the country just coming out of 160 percent inflation, an indefinite freeze would not have been credible; on the contrary, it would have backfired, as it had elsewhere. But a three-month freeze had some credibility; most economic agents could believe it would hold for that long.

In February 1988, policymakers agreed that the freeze was working and decided to continue it for another three months. The freeze was renewed by mutual agreement every three months, so that the exchange rate and all other key prices remained frozen for the whole of 1988. By the end of 1988, fiscal adjustment and the freeze had

---

[1]See Claudio Loser and Eliot Kalter, *Mexico: The Strategy to Achieve Sustained Economic Growth*, IMF Occasional Paper 99 (Washington, D.C.: International Monetary Fund, 1992).

helped to turn expectations around. Inflation decelerated sharply, dropping from 160 percent in 1987 to 52 percent in 1988. The social pact was renewed for 1989 but was made more flexible: after a minor initial adjustment of the exchange rate, Mexico would move to an exchange regime with a preannounced peso slide. According to this system, the price of the U.S. dollar would be raised by one peso a day, the equivalent of about a 16 percent depreciation for 1989 as a whole. Mexico returned to a type of *tablita*. This system, with its preannounced slide, is the one that, by and large, continues to this day. It has been renewed every year, although with different rates of slide—first one peso a day, then 40 centavos a day, then 20 centavos, and once again 40 centavos.

The last change in the exchange regime was made in 1991, when the authorities decided to provide some more flexibility by creating a band within which the exchange rate could move. This decision was implemented by maintaining the November 1991 buying rate and applying the slide only to the selling rate, with the idea that by the end of 1992, the spread between the buying and selling points—the lower and upper intervention points—would be about 4 percent.

The reasoning behind this decision reflects the solution to a policy dilemma. On the one hand, to attract direct investment and long-term capital, it was imperative to have a more or less fixed rate system that would build confidence. On the other hand, the preannounced scheme, which made known how much the exchange rate would move each month, invited short-term speculative capital inflows. If speculators learn that a rate will move by half a percentage point during a certain month, and the interest rate is about 1 percent a month, they know that the best thing to do is to enter the market for a month and gain a free half point in interest. In such circumstances, it is necessary to introduce some risk into the system by creating the possibility of exchange losses, at the same time keeping the overall system more or less flexible. Thus Mexico established its band.

In late 1992, the agreement was renewed for 1993, with one slight difference: the band was widened further, from the initial 4 percent to 9 percent. To do this, the rate at which the upper intervention limit moves was increased from 20 centavos to 40 centavos a day. At present, with a band about 4 percentage points wide, and with the exchange rate moving close to the middle, there is the risk of a depreciation of up to 2 percent at any time—exactly what is needed in order to deter speculation.

Solving the debt problem

A comprehensive debt deal struck with the commercial banks in 1990 reduced the debt significantly. The bulk of what remained is now basically a fixed-interest loan with a 30-year maturity and guaranteed repayment of principal through zero-coupon bonds. This solution had two important repercussions. First—and most obvious—the annual transfer of debt service was cut by more than half, from 5.5 percent to 2.4 percent of GDP. But more important, uncertainty about servicing the debt was eliminated, greatly increasing confidence in Mexico's economic performance. This fact introduces an interesting consideration in terms of exchange rate policy. All through the 1980s, while Mexico had a huge debt overhang and an associated large debt service, expectations about the sustainability of the exchange rate could never really take hold. It was always feared that the next debt crisis would precipitate an exchange rate adjustment. Once the problem of the debt was put to rest (for 30 years at least), confidence in the sustainability of the rate rose substantially. This renewed confidence has also affected domestic interest rates, which came tumbling down.

Structural reforms

These reforms had actually been started during the very first program in 1983, particularly in the areas of privatization and trade. By 1985, Mexico had substantially reduced quantitative restrictions and lowered the maximum tariff from 100 percent to about 45 percent. In 1986, Mexico joined the General Agreement on Tariffs and Trade (GATT). Further progress was made with the 1988 program, which eliminated quantitative restrictions and further reduced the maximum tariff to 20 percent. Similarly, the 1988 program included a major liberalization of exchange restrictions, the unification of rates, and the formal reopening of the capital account, which had been closed at the time of the debt crisis. The privatization process accelerated after 1990: in 1991, enterprises worth about US$10 billion were privatized, representing close to 3 percent of GDP for that year.[2] Financial reform, including the liberalization of interest rates and the elimination of credit controls and reserve requirements, spurred financial reintermediation and lowered costs, particularly for the export sector. There have also been revisions to the foreign investment law and, in general, a number of initiatives to deregulate and reduce red tape.

V. Conclusion

In summing up, I would make two observations about the more recent features of Mexico's external position. Thus far, this four-pronged approach has been remarkably successful. Inflation is

---

[2]In 1992, about the same amount was privatized.

down,[3] economic growth has been quite acceptable in the last few years, and per capita GDP has been growing. However, after five years with a predetermined exchange rate, and given how slowly inflation has come down, the exchange rate has appreciated substantially. Mexico now faces a rather large current account deficit, raising the question of what caused this deficit to increase in an otherwise very successful inflation-fighting program. One possibility is a decline in private savings that has exerted pressure on the current account. From 1987 to 1991, private savings dropped by more than 4 percentage points of GDP, from 14 percent to 10 percent. At the same time, private investment moved up by some 3 percentage points of GDP, from 13.6 percent to 16.9 percent. Thus, the private sector's current account deteriorated by 7.6 percent of GDP. The relatively small deterioration in the overall current account during those years is attributable to the improvement in public sector performance.

Exactly why developments in the private sector can offset public sector adjustment is not clear. One explanation may be that at the same time an economy stabilizes and public finances improve, the inflation tax declines, permitting private sector consumption to expand. A related manifestation could be that as inflation declines and interest rates drop, the private sector receives fewer interest payments from the government. If the private sector treats these interest receipts as transitory income, the result is a corresponding decline in savings. Another possibility is a "wealth effect": stabilization could bring about large increases in stock market values or real estate, increasing private consumption and decreasing private savings. Whatever the explanation, the fact remains that in Mexico, as in a number of other countries, as the economy stabilizes and public finances improve, the private sector has an offsetting effect that tends to cause the current account to deteriorate and puts additional pressure on the exchange rate. On the other hand, as inflation settles down at a low rate, most of the factors just mentioned tend to disappear, private savings recover, and the current account deficit narrows again.

How have the structural reforms affected the equilibrium level of the exchange rate and competitiveness? Liberalization of the exchange system, reduced financial costs to exporters due to financial reform, reforms of the foreign investment code, and deregulation have all had definite, positive effects on competitiveness. The effect of trade liberalization on the exchange rate is more ambiguous, of course. On the one hand, there is a need to offset the impact on imports, but on the other hand, exporters' costs have been lowered, particularly for imported raw materials, and exportables have been

---

[3] At the end of 1993, inflation had dropped below 10 percent.

diverted from the previously protected domestic market (where they were bringing in high profits) to the open foreign market (where they attract lower profits). Considered in this light, liberalization has increased export possibilities. Over the last ten years, real wages have come down dramatically and have remained low, so that in terms of unit labor costs, the real effective exchange rate is still much lower than the rate based on relative prices. Eliminating the debt overhang has increased confidence in the peso and reduced the risk that the exchange regime may prove untenable. Considering all these factors, at the moment we cannot say for sure what the equilibrium level of Mexico's exchange rate should be. Only time and the evolution of the balance of payments will provide an answer.

Comment

Carlos Noriega

Mexico has been used as a case study partly because its relative success during the last few years has attracted interest. This interest is by no means entirely flattering—first, because success brings with it new problems, such as capital inflows, that are difficult to cope with; and second, because after ten years of struggling, we Mexican policymakers are by no means sure that our current policy has finally succeeded. Indeed, many internal elements indicate that something negative may still happen, and the external environment is, as always, uncertain. But it is useful in terms of exchange arrangements to study Mexico, since it has had both fixed and floating rates and single and multiple regimes—all with a certain degree of success for some time, and then with clear failures.

Because Thomas Reichmann and Claudio Loser have already given a clear chronological description of Mexico's exchange rate situation, I will talk only about six lessons that can be drawn from Mexico's experience. The first lesson is that it is often difficult for policymakers to see events clearly while the events are taking place. It is very easy today to look back over the last ten years and see where the mistakes were made. But during those years, we were coping with a potential crisis every day. We were never sure where we were heading or what the internal and external environments for our exchange rate policy would be in the future. So our policy was developed crisis by crisis, and short-term considerations very often overrode decisions that had been made from a long-term perspective. It is therefore not easy to talk about our "strategy," because we had to adjust our actions to the events taking place around us. We also faced very serious short-term demands. We had to service a very large foreign debt, for example, and did not have the resources to do so. If our exchange rate policy had a specific orientation, then, it was primarily to use very large devaluations to close the external gap generated by inflation.

The debt overhang is a good example of the kinds of problems we faced. In 1982, we were not even aware of the seriousness of this problem. The then Minister of Finance told the Congress that we were experiencing what he termed "a liquidity crisis," but then we were forced to suspend our debt service payments. It took a long time for Mexico to realize that the size of our debt was incompatible with growth and stability. Once we realized that, we had to convince the rest of the world—starting with the IMF—that we could not survive with the existing level of debt. The next step was to reach an agreement with creditor governments and banks. Settling our debt problem took almost seven years, from 1982 to 1989, when an agreement in principle was reached; the final agreement was not signed until February 1990, almost eight years after the debt crisis began. The uncertainty added to our problems. We were never really sure, for example, what level of external savings we could count on.

The second lesson involves the use of privatization to channel resources to the Government. In 1982, we understood that the Mexican Government was too large and had to be reduced. But it took time to set up the privatization of so many different public enterprises—including 18 banks, the enormous telephone monopoly, and many other large firms—in a way that would maximize Government revenues. Aside from the revenues, however, the process of privatization was important in itself because of the market-oriented signal it gave the economy.

We then had to decide what to do with the privatization revenues in a poor and underdeveloped country like Mexico. There were many demands on the money, and it took great courage for the President and ministers to decide that all of it would be used to amortize the domestic debt. It was a very difficult situation: peasants and workers were asking for a chunk of the country's resources, the Government was saying the country had no money, and at the same time the Government was paying back billions of dollars worth of domestic debt. In retrospect, however, I believe there was no other way the Government could have channeled resources from the private sector to our foreign creditors. We needed money and would not have been able to change our tax system quickly enough to generate more resources. Privatization thus played an important role in our efforts to reduce our debt and create a climate that would help stabilize our exchange rate.

The third lesson that can be drawn from the Mexican experience is that no matter how undervalued the real exchange rate is, it is still susceptible to a run against the currency. At the end of 1982, we had devalued by more than 40 percent—and in the short term it was mostly real devaluation—and yet there was a run against the Mexican peso. In 1987, we had even had a real exchange target for some time and had been devaluing at almost the same rate as inflation. Internal and external investors alike recognized that the rate was undervalued. But when the stock crisis developed in the United States in October 1987, the Mexican market was immediately contaminated, and investors fled. In the United States, the flight was out of the stock market into safer bonds, but in Mexico, despite the undervalued exchange rate and the fact that foreign reserves were at their highest level ever, there was an exchange rate crisis.

This crisis was particularly threatening because we had been told earlier that based on the experiences of other countries, we should reduce our domestic debt and increase real interest rates in our financial market. In fact, after several years of high inflation, our domestic public debt had been to a certain extent liquidated. For many years, we had had negative real interest rates, and the proportion of currency over GDP was only about one third of our historical level. By all measures, the financial market had contracted. And yet when faced with this lack of certainty from investors, the internal financial market was subject to a crisis that was reflected in our exchange rate market. We learned the hard way that an undervalued exchange rate does guarantee a firm base for planning everything else, because of the danger of a currency run.

The fourth lesson is that the external sector is extremely important. This lesson was also a painful one for Mexico, because we as a country have absolutely no authority or control over the external sector. One important determinant of the exchange rate is the terms of trade, and Mexico suffered deteriorations in its terms of trade in 1981, 1985, and 1986. As expected, our exchange market reflected these deteriorations.

There are other external determinants more subtle and difficult to identify and measure that are nevertheless important. Among them are the business cycles of larger economies, crises in foreign markets—like the recent problems with the European exchange rate mechanism—and factors such as the very weak recovery of the U.S. economy, which has led to a significant amount of dumping on the Mexican market. Because trade liberalization in Mexico was very orthodox, we did not pay enough attention to mechanisms that could legitimately have prevented such dumping. The result was a large inflow of capital and goods that caused the current account to deteriorate. It took us some time to realize that there was a problem, and more time to design a mechanism that would prevent dumping but not be overly protective.

Another important determinant of the exchange rate is tax arbitrage, especially in a country like Mexico, which is the base for many foreign companies. In order to maximize their profits worldwide, these companies register them in the country with the lowest marginal tax rate. As part of our structural adjustment, Mexico has decreased the average tax rate on corporations to a level that is very competitive vis-à-vis the U.S. market, so that taxes on corporations are lower in Mexico than in the United States. However, the automotive industry, which is in crisis in the United States, has not been making profits there recently and thus has an incentive to shift profits made elsewhere to their U.S. operations. Accordingly, the companies tend to overprice exports to their subsidiaries in Mexico, so that the profits are registered in the U.S., where the companies are not paying taxes. This behavior leads to a surge in the value of imports into Mexico and creates a signaling problem, because many observers interpret the increased import growth as a deterioration of the current account—when it may in fact be nothing more than a disguise for capital transfers.

The fifth lesson is that expectations cannot be ignored, and once again, Mexico offers a variety of examples of this fact. At the peak of speculation in 1962, Mexico had a floating regime, and the exchange rate went up from 22 pesos per dollar at the beginning of the year to 150 pesos per dollar—a depreciation of more than 80 percent. That exchange rate was not validated by any of the real factors, and yet the only way the central bank could improve the currency's credibility was to validate the rate. In fact, the Government chose to move from a multiple exchange rate regime to a dual exchange rate regime, leaving the higher exchange rate at 150 pesos per dollar. We understood that such an exchange rate was irrational, but once it had been reached, we found convincing the market that it was unreasonable very difficult. The same thing happened in 1987. After the U.S. stock market crashed, the Mexican floating rate rose to 2,200 pesos per dollar, and it was very difficult to convince the market that this rate was not sustainable. We actually had to prove that such a rate would lead to higher inflation.

The lesson here is that somehow the Government has to explain policy to the public, pointing out strengths and weaknesses, in order to avoid this type of irrational behavior, which is difficult to deal with after the fact. In Mexico, and probably in other countries, the exchange rate is a symbol of economic policy and must therefore be treated with care. It is not just another price that can be liberalized and left to move up and down as the market dictates. I am by no means saying that authorities should manipulate the market, but on the other hand, the exchange rate cannot just be ignored and the public left uninformed. It is difficult to judge whether our Government has had any success in this respect, for the fact that the exchange rate has not fluctuated strongly does not mean that our communication program has been successful. However, we have made a point of going to the public and describing what we are trying to do.

And, finally, the sixth lesson that can be drawn from our experience is that price stability is important per se because it affects the exchange rate. If the fundamentals are correct and price stability is sustained, then the exchange rate, whether fixed or floating, will also be stable. What is important is that economic policy be geared toward stability. We tried unsuccessfully in 1984–85 to stabilize through the exchange rate, and the result was an exchange rate crisis in 1985. Then, we reversed our policy almost completely, so that in 1986, when the price of oil was approaching its lowest level in many years, we tried first to devalue the exchange rate and then to establish a real exchange rate target. Although that target was successful in producing a current account surplus—despite the fact that our terms of trade had deteriorated dramatically—inflation did not come down. In fact, that year marked the beginning of a period of hyperinflation in Mexico; we had no anchor to help us in the important task of reducing inflation.

As a result, we gave the exchange rate a central role in our stabilization program of December 1987. From 1982 onward, we had been following an ongoing process of fiscal discipline that included cutting expenditures, privatizing, and completely revising the tax and public price structures. At the beginning of our stabilization program, most of what we call controllable prices were frozen in both the public and private sectors, and gradually private prices were liberalized. But it was difficult to liberalize the exchange rate immediately, so we took almost the opposite approach, setting a real exchange rate target supported by strong fiscal and monetary policy. This approach was responsible for our success in bringing down inflation.

We were able to stabilize the exchange rate only after achieving a certain degree of price stability. Each supported the other. Only very recently have we been able to allow more flexibility in the exchange rate, moving slowly from a fixed exchange rate or preannounced crawling peg to a system that allows the exchange rate to float within a band. The band has been expanded over time; the ceiling depreciates while the floor remains fixed.

We do not know what the future holds. The falling price of oil on the world market is an important concern for both our current account and public finances, because Mexico depends on oil revenues. Thus far in 1992, rains and floods have affected agricultural production. Because of developments like these, we know we will never be able to start with a clean slate when designing our policy. We must be prudent and leave ourselves enough margin to respond to potential internal and external crises. Despite our desire for a long-term strategy, we will have to go on "muddling through." Mexico's experience shows that instability is costly in terms of creating and sustaining long-run exchange rate policy. As I said earlier, Mexico's lack of a planning horizon was so painful and costly in terms of welfare, growth, and savings that I feel stability should be a goal in itself. Mexico is a vivid example of how important stability is in extending the planning horizon.

Summary of Discussion

In the discussion of issues relating to exchange rate systems, most participants agreed that the distinction between a freely floating regime and a managed float is not clear, especially if central banks do not make their targets or indicators clear. There was also agreement that capital account convertibility could be tolerated, depending on the exchange rate and interest rate regimes. For example, freely flexible interest rates serve as shock absorbers under fixed exchange rate regimes. Indonesia's fixed exchange rate regime had attributes of a crawling peg, with occasional devaluations that transferred what could have been exchange rate volatility to the interest rate.

In this connection, the relative merits of interbank foreign exchange markets and central bank auctions were discussed. The point was made that many countries—particularly those in which a large share of the foreign exchange earnings accrues to state enterprises—have foreign exchange surrender requirements, and in these countries the auction system not only works well but allows the government to pursue a managed float. In a number of developing countries, a managed float with supporting monetary and fiscal policies has contributed to external viability, diversification, low inflation, and economic growth.

Discussing Mexico, participants agreed that the country's open capital account had been a major factor in the authorities' decision to adopt a flexible rate system. Since the authorities felt that financial shocks would magnify exchange rate movements and send confusing signals to the real sector, the system Mexico adopted established a mechanism to stabilize the exchange rate but still provide flexibility. This combination of an exchange rate band and a flexible interest rate policy was designed to create a degree of uncertainty among speculators, thereby removing some of the pressure on the exchange rate.

Participants emphasized that foreign savings were attracted to Mexico and that the policy response to this inflow was either to allow foreign reserves to build up or to permit the current account to go into deficit. The capital inflows were judged to be a response to structural reforms and fiscal consolidation, as well as to potentially bright economic prospects (in part as a result of the North American Free Trade Agreement). A long-term current account deficit was therefore considered sustainable, and the exchange rate was allowed to appreciate.

Finally, it was agreed that the exchange rate had been a central instrument of Mexico's stabilization efforts but that the Government had also undertaken strong fiscal adjustment and followed a tight monetary policy. For this reason, exchange rate policy had not been misused, as the fact that the exchange rate had remained well within its band showed.

Exchange Rate Policy in a Monetary Union 7

Paul R. Masson

There have been many developments in the European Monetary System (EMS) recently, as well as debates over the eventual approval of the Maastricht Treaty agreed to in December 1991. But this paper will start from a somewhat more general perspective than just economic and monetary union (EMU) in Europe, first considering the reasons for a monetary union and the characteristics of a successful monetary union—that is, what makes the benefits of monetary union outweigh the costs of joining. Then the paper will move to some of the issues more specific to Europe, in particular the Maastricht Agreement and the transition to EMU.

I. Defining Monetary Union

What exactly is meant by "monetary union" or "common currency area"? The two should be distinguished, because, in principle, it is possible to have monetary union without replacing national currencies with a common currency. What is required in a monetary union is a common monetary policy, assuming the absence of various controls on capital flows or segmentation of financial markets. The very nature of a monetary union precludes separate monetary policies, and so, essentially, a monetary union has the characteristics of a common currency area, but no single circulating currency. Several currencies can coexist, provided their rates of exchange are fixed (and viewed as irrevocably fixed). This latter requirement can be a problem, as the turbulence in the EMS has demonstrated. Even though governments say that exchange rates or central parities are "irrevocably fixed," as long as there are different currencies, there will also be doubts about whether this remains true.

Monetary unions have historically taken several forms. A union could be the area in which the currency of, for instance, a dominant country circulates, because this currency is viewed as more stable or as having more of the characteristics of money than the currencies of smaller countries in the region; or it could involve setting up international institutions, and, of course, in Europe, that is the framework of the Maastricht Treaty. In Africa, as well, there are supranational institutions in the CFA franc zone.

Assessing benefits and costs

Clearly, such arrangements offer certain benefits: they permit a common currency to circulate in a large area, or they reduce transaction costs when several currencies circulate at a fixed rate (as opposed to flexible rates with higher transaction costs). More generally, such schemes reduce uncertainty by creating a single currency and a more stable basis for anchoring prices. But monetary unions also have their costs, primarily the loss of the exchange rate as an instrument for cushioning shocks. And this question of the costs of losing exchange rate flexibility has given rise to a large literature that is, perhaps misleadingly, characterized as covering "optimal currency areas," when in fact it attempts to assess the conditions under which the costs are reasonably small and hence outweighed by the benefits of a common currency.

Factor mobility

The initial insight of Robert Mundell was that factor mobility—and in particular labor mobility—reduces the costs of monetary union.[1] If one region of a currency area experiences an unfavorable shock—for instance, to the demand for the goods that it produces or to supply conditions—the exchange rate may help cushion that shock, making its goods cheaper and more salable abroad, thereby maintaining employment. In a common currency area, where the exchange rate cannot serve this purpose, labor mobility may substitute for exchange rate flexibility. Although there may be costs to those who actually have to move from one region to another, the overall cost to the economy is less if there is some degree of labor mobility.

Labor mobility is one issue that has been much discussed in the European context, because it is expected to help limit the dispersion of unemployment rates in different regions. Compared with the European Community (EC), the United States—and, to some extent, Canada—has much less dispersion of unemployment rates (Chart 1). There is less labor mobility in Europe than in North America, especially the United States. Other evidence on migration—for

---

[1]Robert A. Mundell, "A Theory of Optimum Currency Areas," *American Economic Review* 51 (September 1961): 657–65.

Chart 1. Dispersion of Unemployment Rates[1]

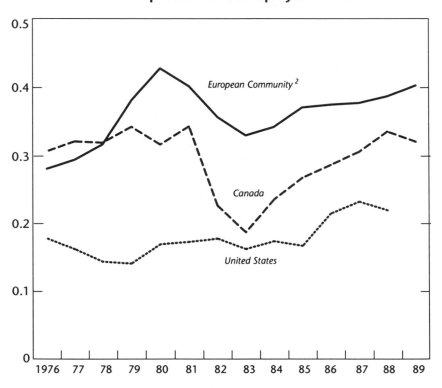

Source: International Monetary Fund, *World Economic Outlook* (various issues); and IMF staff calculations.

[1]Coefficients of variation, i.e., standard deviations of unemployment rates, scaled by the mean (components are weighted by population).

[2]Twelve current members, excluding Luxembourg, for which data were not available.

instance, between countries in the EC—clearly suggests that migration in Europe is much lower than in either Canada or the United States. There are a number of reasons for this: language differences and the fact that social benefits are not transportable are among them.

Interdependence

A second factor that may make the costs of monetary union less severe relative to the benefits is a high degree of interdependence among neighboring countries. This factor applies strongly to Europe, since the creation of the Single Market and the anticipation of even greater trade flows among EC countries have increased both the

Table 1. Selected Country Groupings: Intra-Area Trade as a Share of Total Trade

(Average, 1982–85)

	Percent of Exports	Percent of Imports	Percent of Total Trade
European Community			
EC 12[1]	54.3	51.4	52.8
ERM 10[2]	52.7	50.6	51.6
North America			
Canada and the United States	37.4	34.5	35.7
Canada, the United States, and Mexico	39.0	35.5	37.0
CFA Franc Zone			
CFA franc zone countries only[3]	6.6	10.7	8.6
CFA franc zone countries, including trade with France	27.9	38.6	37.8
CFA franc zone plus France	2.1	2.4	2.3

Source: International Monetary Fund, *Direction of Trade Statistics*, various issues; and IMF staff calculations.
[1] Belgium, Denmark, France, Germany, Greece, Ireland, Italy, Luxembourg, Netherlands, Portugal, Spain and the United Kingdom. Data for Belgium and Luxembourg are consolidated.
[2] EC 12 minus Greece and Portugal.
[3] Benin, Burkina Faso, Côte d'Ivoire, Mali, Niger, Senegal, Togo, Cameroon, Central African Republic, Chad, Congo, Gabon, and Equatorial Guinea.

importance of transaction costs in exchanging currencies and the advantages of moving to a single currency. However, not all common currency areas have extensive interregional trade (Table 1). Clearly, the amount of trade among EC countries is quite high—higher, for instance, than trade between Canada and the United States, which is itself extensive in comparison with trade among other countries. The countries in the CFA franc zone, for instance—another example of a monetary union—have very little common trade. Including their trade with France, the ratio to total trade is quite substantial. Adding France's trade to the denominator, however, makes the rate quite low. Interdependence need not be the primary criterion for deciding whether a currency union is appropriate.

Sectoral diversification

A third criterion, which is important in minimizing the unfavorable effects of shocks to countries in a currency union, is a high degree of sectoral diversification of each of the country's economies. The more similar the countries are in industrial structure, the less likely they are to be hit by shocks that affect their economies

Table 2. Industrial Countries: Shares of Production, 1986[1]

(*In percent*)

	Agriculture[2]	Construction	Energy and Mining[3]	Manufacturing	Services[4]
Canada	4.0	7.6	9.0	23.4	56.0
United States	2.3	5.5	5.8	22.2	64.2
Japan	3.1	8.1	4.2	31.4	53.3
France	4.7	6.6	3.8	27.8	57.0
Germany	2.1	6.1	4.2	38.3	49.4
Italy	5.0	6.7	5.7	27.2	55.5
United Kingdom	2.1	6.7	7.8	27.6	55.9
Belgium	2.5	5.8	4.1	25.4	62.2
Denmark	6.6	8.3	3.0	24.6	57.5
Greece	17.3	7.4	5.1	21.1	49.1
Netherlands	5.2	6.3	9.1	23.4	56.0
Portugal	8.6	6.4	3.6	33.8	47.5
Spain	6.1	7.5	3.4	21.2	51.8

Source: Organization for Economic Cooperation and Development, National Accounts data base.
[1]GDP at current prices. Shares are scaled to sum to 100.
[2]Including hunting, fishing, and forestry.
[3]Mining and quarrying (including petroleum and natural gas production), plus electricity generation and gas and water distribution.
[4]Excluding government services.

differently—and against which exchange rate flexibility is often the best protection. For instance, because of its dependence on relatively few primary commodities and agriculture, Australia may be hit by terms of trade shocks that make exchange rate flexibility important. In contrast, European economies are very diversified; though Table 2 gives only a very broad breakdown, it shows that the relative importance of primary commodities in Europe is small. Only Greece has a large output share for agriculture. Energy production is also not very important for European economies: the Netherlands and the United Kingdom have somewhat higher ratios than other EC countries, but no higher than Canada, for instance.

Wage and price flexibility

Clearly the decision to participate in a common currency area constrains a country's monetary policy by fixing the exchange rate, and the degree of wage and price flexibility is crucial to the impact of such a nominal exchange rate choice. In the limiting case of perfectly flexible wages and prices, then the nominal exchange rate chosen is itself arbitrary and does not have consequences for the real economy. For Europe, a more relevant polar case is real wage inflexibility; if there is real wage inflexibility, the choice of exchange rate also will not affect the real economy, but, in fact, adjustment will have to occur—with potentially large costs—through unemployment.

Econometric models

These criteria are useful for considering currency unions; however, because there are several of them, econometric models that include the various linkages are essential in making an overall assessment of the potential impact of a fixed exchange rate or monetary union on an economy. The EC Commission undertook such an exercise in the context of a 1990 study that considered what the transition to a common currency might imply for the variability of inflation and output (Chart 2).[2] The experiments, conducted using the IMF's Multimod model, suggested that the EMS, in its early period—from 1979 until about the mid-1980s—had produced somewhat more output variability, but less inflation variability. The increasing rigidity of the exchange rate mechanism (ERM) was, the study suggested, reducing both output and inflation variability, and this perceived improvement would continue as Europe moved closer to the goal of monetary union—a monetary union with a monetary policy determined symmetrically by monetary conditions throughout Europe. This future was perceived as offering better results than the EMS accompanied by fixed exchange rates—elsewhere it has been called an asymmetric EMU—with the Bundesbank basically setting monetary policy for Europe. In all, the study is a fairly reassuring view of the benefits of monetary union in Europe.

The IMF has also looked at the question of output and inflation variability in the context of shocks hitting Europe under different monetary regimes. The results are summarized in the box in Chart 3 that considers outcomes for all of Europe. One finding indicates that when countries target either their money supplies or a European money supply, a symmetric EMU with a European monetary target seems to give the lowest output and inflation variability. However, the other alternatives seem to be ranked differently from those of the EC Commission. The IMF has also done other experiments, assuming a nominal income target as opposed to a monetary target, and the outcomes were fairly sensitive to this assumption. On the basis of these results, the case for EMU may be somewhat less strong than the EC has argued.

---

[2]European Commission, "One Market, One Money: An evaluation of the potential benefits and costs of forming an economic and monetary union," *European Economy* 44 (October 1990): 3–347.

Chart 2. Macroeconomic Stability of EMU

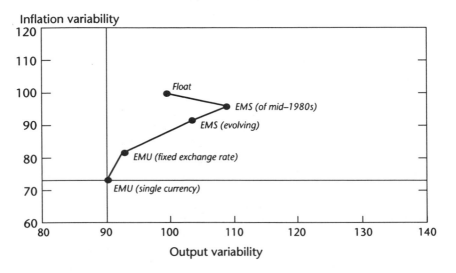

This graph plots the combinations of variability of output (GDP) and infla-tion for the EC average in index form, as resulting from the stochastic simula-tions. The position of each of the four regimes ('free float,' 'EMS,' 'asymmetric EMU,' and EMU) corresponds to an intersection between a regime-dependent output-inflation trade-off curve and a shifting preference curve.

Source: Stochastic simulations with the Multimod model of the IMF under the responsibility of the European Commission services. GDP is measured as a percentage deviation from its baseline value; inflation is measured in per-centage point differences with respect to baseline inflation rates. The indices used in the graph are obtained by first averaging the squares of the devia-tions for 43 simulations over the period 1990–99 and then taking the square root. Dividing by the root mean-squared deviations for the free float regime and multiplication by 100 then gives the indices.

Monetary and fiscal policies

The Delors Report and the subsequent Maastricht Treaty have con-sidered the interaction between monetary and fiscal policies in some detail. The general argument is that it is not sufficient to create a common monetary policy, even when the central bank is formally separated from the fiscal authorities. There must be some con-straints on fiscal policies, or these policies will interfere with mone-tary policy and may eventually force the central bank to monetize debt or bail out governments that would otherwise default on their debts. There is also the issue of the spillovers of different fiscal policies within a currency union; for instance, a country operating a

Chart 3. Floating Exchange Rates vs. the EMS and Symmetric or Asymmetric EMU, with Money Exogenous

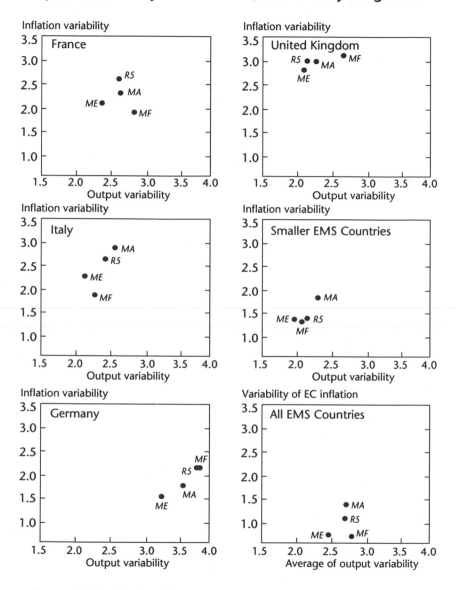

Source: IMF staff calculations.
MF = Floating rates.
R5 = EMS with realignment triggered by real exchange rate.
ME = Symmetric EMU, European money target.
MA = Asymmetric EMU, German money target.

very expansionary fiscal policy will clearly affect conditions in other countries in a different way than it would if the countries had separate currencies. In particular, an expansionary fiscal policy may, for a time at least, cause the exchange rate of all the countries in the union to appreciate against other countries. This argument suggests a need to coordinate fiscal policies within a monetary union.

Market forces

An important part of the debate concerns the question of whether markets will discipline fiscal authorities. Here again existing monetary unions with different types of fiscal authorities, such as the states of the United States or the Canadian provinces, become important reference points. The evidence suggests some degree of discipline, indicating that, in general, borrowing costs reflect objective criteria that make borrowing more difficult and expensive as debt increases. Of course, there have been times when the market has not anticipated problems soon enough. In the United States, for instance, the city of New York was unable to service its debt during the 1975 fiscal crisis; internationally, the Latin American debt problems of the 1980s were not reflected promptly in interest rates or in restrictions on lending.

Federal fiscal Policy

A final issue concerning fiscal policies in a currency union is the degree to which federal fiscal policy or transfers among regions are important. The argument in favor of transfers suggests that shocks affect regions or countries in the currency area differently; with no mechanism for adjusting to or cushioning those shocks that replaces the exchange rate instrument—such as a high degree of labor mobility—there must be a system of taxation and transfer payments to bring about compensating regional flows. In particular, the affected regions would pay less in taxes and receive higher transfer payments than the others in a federal fiscal system. A well-known study by Sala-i-Martin and Sachs[3] argues strongly that the U.S. federal fiscal system plays a large role in cushioning shocks; in particular, the authors estimate that perhaps 40 cents of each dollar of the costs of an unfavorable shock in a region are recovered through lower taxes and higher transfers. The study points out that the absence in Europe of a federal fiscal system with this magnitude of flows between countries may create serious problems for monetary union.

[3] Xavier Sala-i-Martin and Jeffrey Sachs, "Federal Fiscal Policy and Optimum Currency Areas," in *Establishing a Central Bank: Issues in Europe and Lessons from the U.S.*, edited by Matthew Canzoneri, Vittorio Grilli, and Paul R. Masson (Cambridge: Cambridge University Press, 1992), pp. 195–220.

It is important to distinguish between redistribution among regions—that is, poor regions receiving favorable fiscal treatment on a more or less permanent basis—and the stabilization role of fiscal policy. Is the issue shocks that produce temporary losses of output and hence can be cushioned, or is it the need for long-term development assistance to poorer areas? Chart 4 plots the variation across U.S. states or Canadian provinces of pretax income and income net of taxes and including transfers. A large degree of compensation through the federal fiscal system would produce a very flat slope, since redistribution would compensate for any large variations before the fiscal flows, and there would be rather little variation in the net incomes of the cross-section. The chart shows some flattening, but it is barely perceptible. Tamim Bayoumi and I found much more redistribution in Canada than in the United States, but no more than 20 cents or so out of the dollar.[4]

In the EC, at least under existing structural funds and a proposed cohesion fund, the amount of redistribution would also be fairly modest, perhaps on the order of a few percent. Still, there is a considerable difference between the North American countries and the EC. We found a somewhat greater stabilization role for the federal system in the United States than in Canada; the EC has no such system. As mentioned earlier, this lack may present a problem for the EC. However, the counterargument to this need to link monetary union with fiscal federalism would be that national governments currently perform stabilization in Europe and would continue to do so under EMU, reducing the need for stabilization at the federal level. The issue of redistribution, which is potentially more serious, is related to convergence.

Convergence

Convergence is an issue because it has generated one of the major debates leading up to the Maastricht Treaty and remains a topical question in Europe. To what extent is convergence, both real and nominal, a precondition for monetary union or, conversely, a consequence of union? In a monetary union, members adopt a common monetary policy, and in the long run, inflation converges. The need for convergence of inflation before monetary union is questionable.

There is no need to guarantee that regions in a monetary union will have the same real per capita income or any other measure of real convergence. In Europe, for example, there is clearly much less convergence of real per capita income than in the United States,

[4] Tamim Bayoumi and Paul R. Masson, "Fiscal Flows in the United States and Canada: Lessons for Monetary Union in Europe," *European Economic Review* (forthcoming).

Chart 4. Federal Fiscal Flows and Personal Income

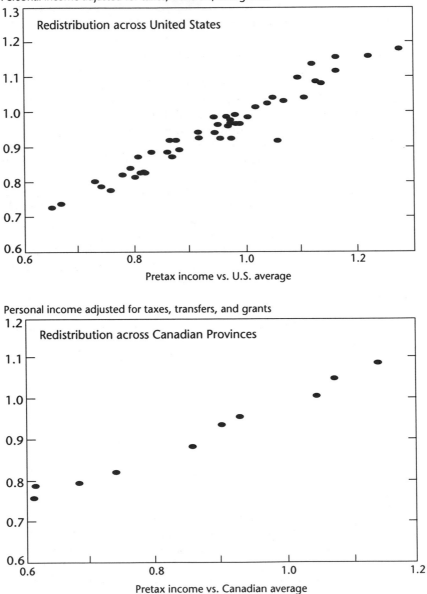

Personal income adjusted for taxes, transfers, and grants

Redistribution across United States

Pretax income vs. U.S. average

Personal income adjusted for taxes, transfers, and grants

Redistribution across Canadian Provinces

Pretax income vs. Canadian average

Source: Tamim Bayoumi and Paul R. Masson, "Fiscal Flows in the United States and Canada," *European Economic Review* (forthcoming).

Chart 5. Dispersion of Real Per Capita Output[1]

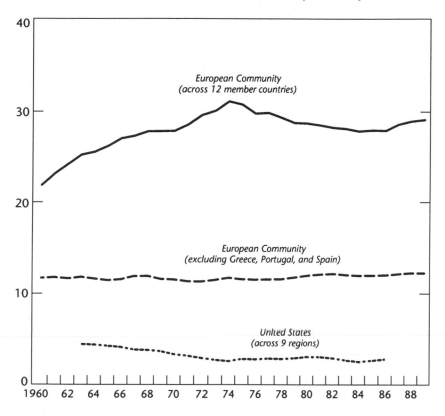

Source: International Monetary Fund, *International Financial Statistics* (various issues); and IMF staff calculations.

[1]Coefficients of variation, i.e. standard deviations of real per capita output, scaled by the mean (components are weighted by population).

where the regional variation is really quite modest—less than 5 percent in terms of the standard deviation of real per capita income (Chart 5). The regions comprise several states and may include quite poor states—West Virginia, for instance—but the nine census regions are comparable to the European countries in average size. For the 12 EC countries, the variation is much greater—on the order of 30 percent—and excluding the 3 poorer members of the EC (Greece, Portugal, and Spain) still leaves a substantial variation. Apparently, real convergence has not occurred in Europe. However, the evidence from the United States could be used as an encouraging sign that monetary union may encourage real convergence; in fact, a much longer run of data on the United States suggests that there has been considerable convergence over the past century.

II. The Maastricht Treaty

The Maastricht Treaty includes four convergence criteria as preconditions for proceeding to Stage III of monetary union and an eventual single currency. The fiscal aspects are given some emphasis. There is a ceiling of 3 percent on deficits as a ratio to GDP and 60 percent on gross government debt—with some qualifications that leave considerable room for discretion in deciding which countries actually qualify. Countries may exceed the 3 percent deficit temporarily and must prove only that they are well on the way to reaching the 60 percent debt ratio, not that they have achieved it. Even so, the fiscal criteria are potentially constraining, given the current situation of a number of countries. And the existence of such criteria clearly reflects the view that fiscal policy can interfere very seriously with the operation of monetary policy and should be used to prevent countries with unsustainable fiscal policies from entering EMU and interfering with its operation.

Other criteria state that the inflation rates of entering countries must not exceed that of the three countries with the lowest inflation rates by more than $1^1/_2$ percentage points and that, using a similar measure, long-term rates may be only 2 percentage points higher. In addition, the countries must not have initiated any realignments in the two preceding years.

While these rules may be open to interpretation in some special cases, the treaty takes a quite strong line on the various preconditions needed to proceed to monetary union and establishes a timetable that is also potentially constraining. The treaty calls for setting up an EC central bank, creating a supranational institution that would, in essence, run monetary policy. Countries would not compete to set monetary policy, but clearly the treaty makes no provision for developing EC fiscal powers on the scale of fiscal federalism in, for instance, the United States or Canada.

According to 1992 data, only France, Denmark, and Luxembourg satisfied all the criteria. Several countries, in particular Italy, Greece, and Portugal, needed substantial fiscal and inflation adjustment in order to meet the criteria (and more recent data makes this true of a wider set of countries). For instance, in Italy, the general government balance in 1992 was a little over 10 percent of GDP, the debt ratio was 110 percent of GDP, and the inflation rate was about $5^1/_2$ percent for the year. The Maastricht criteria suggest that inflation should have been no more than about 4 percent. Also, long-term interest rates were much higher in Italy than the treaty permits. Of course, since the timetable calls for a move to Stage III on January 1, 1997 at the earliest, the 1992 data are not immediately relevant, but they do show the need at least for substantial fiscal adjustment. Other countries—including Belgium, France, Germany, Spain, and the United Kingdom—have less severe fiscal problems but also demonstrate a clear need to lower deficits in order to qualify for EMU.

How has individual countries' ability to reach these convergence criteria been affected by the recent realignments in the EMS? As long as the inflation consequent on devaluation can be kept from producing a spiral of wages and prices, and given the fairly depressed economies, it is reasonable to be somewhat optimistic about the effects of the realignments, which have probably helped to create a more sustainable path toward monetary union. They have not solved any fiscal problems, but perhaps they have underlined the need for quick action on fiscal matters in, for instance, Italy, and the market has signaled that the countries must take the criteria seriously and be seen to do so early on.

The costs of Maastricht

In general, these deficit reduction policies should have a contractionary effect on the European economies, at least temporarily. How severe will the costs be? The problem with answering this question is that there are also costs to nonadjusting: clearly unsustainable fiscal policies could eventually lead to a financial collapse that would produce high interest rates or even to a drastic reversal that would have very negative effects on output. In short, continuing with unsustainable policies entails high costs, but these are hard to quantify. The nature of the comparison is a false one, in that unless the costs of not adjusting are accurately estimated, there is no baseline against which to make the comparison.

However, the IMF has done a limited exercise in examining the output effects of reducing the fiscal deficits to levels that would permit meeting the Maastricht criteria by the end of 1996. Even without taking into account the favorable effects on confidence of putting a halt to a clearly unsustainable fiscal policy, the output declines are relatively modest—certainly important in the case of Italy, but at the EC-wide level, rather small, as are the international impacts. There seems to be no cause for the concern sometimes expressed that meeting the Maastricht criteria will produce a deflationary bias not only to European economies but to the world economy. Moreover, after a few years of slower growth in output, the effects on output should become positive.

Speculative attacks and other issues

The issue of speculative attacks is very much in the minds of people who are looking ahead both to the treaty's ratification and to the transition to Stage III.[5] In this context, the issue is how quickly transition to monetary union should be made. The treaty clearly balances several considerations. The advantage of swift action would presumably be to minimize the time available for such speculative attacks. But establishing institutions—particularly the European central bank—will take time. In this regard, the treaty has established a fairly long period for the move to monetary union; thus, this issue is likely to receive some attention in the next few years.

There are also long-term issues, assuming that EMU is established. How wide should the ultimate membership be? Potentially, there are many other candidates for not only EC but also EMU membership. Will an expanding membership lead to the European currency unit (ECU) eventually becoming a dominant world currency? The issue of labor mobility—how will that evolve over time in the EC? Will increased labor mobility be necessary if a monetary union is created, especially if an EC-wide fiscal system is not created? These are some of the questions that can be answered only over time—and after the EC has moved closer to EMU than it has thus far.

[5] Ratification has been achieved; the treaty went into force on November 1, 1993.

A Primer on the CFA Franc Zone 8

Saleh M. Nsouli

Interest in the two monetary unions in Africa, which have served their member countries well for the last 40 years, has surged recently. This upsurge in interest has been stimulated by the emerging monetary union in Europe and the disintegration of the ruble area in the former Soviet republics.

This paper provides a brief overview of Africa's monetary unions, addressing three questions. First, what are the institutional arrangements in the West African Monetary Union and the Central African Monetary Area? Second, what are the economic and financial policy implications of these arrangements? Third, what has been the economic performance of the member countries of these unions, particularly in the last decade?

This paper will not examine whether these unions constitute optimum currency areas.[1] In a recent study, James M. Boughton concluded that, based on the usual criteria for a successful monetary union, the CFA franc zone would not "appear to be a natural candidate for a common currency area." However, he pointed out that these countries "have gained a measure of financial stability that has proved elusive elsewhere in the region by trading away the exchange rate as an instrument for external adjustment. Whether this trade-off will reap dividends in the long run is one of the key questions facing Africa in the 1990s."[2]

I. Institutional Arrangements

The two unions, often referred to as the CFA franc zone, currently consist of 13 fairly diverse countries.[3] The West African Monetary

Note: I am grateful to E. A. Calamitsis, A. D. Bida-Kolika, J. Bungay, L. K. Doe, S. Eken, A. Jbili, M. Lazare, K. Nashashibi, P. Youm, and M. de Zamaroczy for useful comments and suggestions, as well as to I. M. Fayad for excellent research assistance. The views expressed are those of the author and do not necessarily reflect those of the IMF staff.

[1] See Nsouli (1981), McLenaghan, Nsouli, and Riechel (1982), and Boughton (1991 and 1992) for discussions of the issues involved.

[2] Boughton (1992).

[3] The Islamic Republic of Comoros is also technically part of the franc zone, but not a member of the two unions. The reference in this paper to the CFA franc zone is confined to the two unions.

Union comprises Benin, Burkina Faso, Côte d'Ivoire, Mali, Niger, Senegal, and Togo. The Central African Monetary Area includes Cameroon, the Central African Republic, Chad, the Congo, Equatorial Guinea, and Gabon.

Six key elements characterize these unions.[4]

- Each union has its own supranational central bank, which in turn has agencies in each member country.
- Each union has its own currency, designated as the CFA franc. However, within each region the CFA franc denotes a separate currency. For the West African Monetary Union, it is the franc de la Communauté Financière d'Afrique; for the Central African Monetary Area, the franc de la Coopération Financière en Afrique Centrale.
- The CFA franc for each of the two unions has been pegged since 1948 to the French franc at a fixed exchange rate of CFAF 50 = F 1.
- The CFA franc is fully convertible into the French franc and, with some exchange restrictions, into other currencies. Convertibility is guaranteed through an agreement with the French Government.[5] Under this agreement, the reserves of the countries are pooled together in an "operations account" at the French Treasury, and, in case of need, an overdraft facility is provided at market-related interest rates.
- Under the monetary arrangements, there is a statutory ceiling—equivalent to 20 percent of the borrowing country's tax receipts for the previous years—on government borrowing from the banking system for all member countries.
- Credit to the private sector is limited on an annual basis in member countries, consistent with the national objectives of achieving or maintaining domestic and external financial balances, as well as with the overall objectives of each union.

II. Policy Implications

The implications for economic and financial policymaking for the countries in the two unions derive from the fact that the exchange rate serves as a nominal anchor, having been fixed to the French

---

[4] For a more detailed review of institutional arrangements, see Bhatia (1985), Bloch-Lainé and others (1956), Bourdin (1980), Guillaumont and Guillaumont (1984), and Guillaumont, Guillaumont, and Plane (1988).

[5] Although the transportation of bank notes out of the unions has recently been prohibited, this restriction does not in principle affect the convertibility of the currency through bank transactions.

franc at an unchanged parity since 1948. As a result, these countries must rely on other policy instruments in their adjustment efforts. In particular, fiscal and credit policies are used more intensively than they are in countries where the exchange rate is also available as a policy instrument.[6] Price and wage flexibility is likewise important. Although considerable progress has been made in liberalizing the economies of CFA franc countries, wages remain relatively high and recent attempts at reducing public sector pay have met with stiff resistance. Further, producer prices for a number of agricultural products have been maintained at levels above world prices.

Many of the countries in the two unions are currently experiencing serious economic and financial problems that stem from both policy weaknesses and exogenous shocks. Four key reasons for these problems can be singled out.

First, most of these countries pursued highly expansionary fiscal policies in the late 1970s and the 1980s. The zone's restrictions on government borrowing from the domestic banking system translated into excessive external borrowing and, in a number of cases, into accumulated domestic and external payments arrears.

Second, the monetary authorities attempted to compensate for the expansionary fiscal stance (particularly in the second half of the 1980s), in part by limiting credit to the private sector, effectively crowding out private sector needs.

Third, the extensive public enterprise sector in these countries resorted to heavy bank borrowing. As the financial position of many public enterprises continued to weaken, nonperforming bank loans accumulated and contributed to serious liquidity problems in the banking system.

Fourth, most of the countries in the zone suffered from sharp deteriorations in their terms of trade—starting in the late 1970s and early 1980s—although the intensity and pattern of the deterioration have varied from country to country.

During the 1980s, many of the CFA franc countries implemented adjustment programs supported by IMF resources. However, fiscal policy—the main policy instrument in the adjustment arsenal of these countries—proved unwieldy, and efforts to reduce budgetary imbalances met with only limited success. Although there are differences across countries, the average overall fiscal deficit of the 13 franc zone countries, on a commitment basis and excluding

---

[6]See Connolly (1985), Crockett and Nsouli (1977), Deverajan and de Melo (1987 a and b), Devarajan and Rodrik (1991), Macedo (1985), and McLenaghan, Nsouli, and Riechel (1982).

190   Saleh M. Nsouli

Chart 1. Sub-Saharan African Countries:
Central Government Fiscal Deficit
(As percent of GDP)

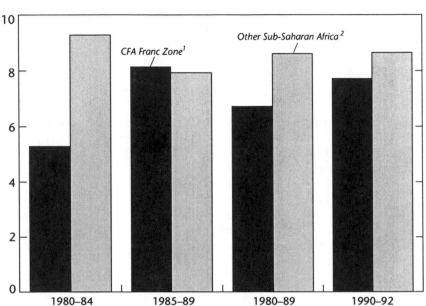

Source: International Monetary Fund, World Economic Outlook data base.
[1]Benin, Burkina Faso, Cameroon, Central African Republic, Chad, Congo, Côte d'Ivoire, Equatorial Guinea, Gabon, Mali, Niger, Senegal, and Togo.
[2]Botswana, Burundi, Cape Verde, Comoros, Djibouti, Ethiopia, Ghana, Guinea, Guinea-Bissau, Kenya, Lesotho, Liberia, Madagascar, Malawi, Mauritania, Mauritius, Mozambique, Nigeria, Rwanda, Sao Tome and Principe, Seychelles, Sierra Leone, Somalia, Sudan, Swaziland, Tanzania, Uganda, Zaïre, Zambia, and Zimbabwe.

grants, was reduced markedly in the first half of the 1980s to below the average deficit for the other sub-Saharan African countries. It gradually widened in the second half, rising above the average for the other sub-Saharan African countries, reflecting declines in the ratio of government revenue to GDP and an inability to compress current expenditure (Chart 1). These developments reflected not only a further weakening in the terms of trade of the franc zone countries, but also expanding informal sector activities, the financial problems confronting public enterprises, the spillover effects of the banking system's growing illiquidity, changes in the tax system that at times did not yield the expected revenue, and weaknesses in tax policy and administration. Reducing the ratio of current expenditure to GDP substantially proved difficult, given the large share of the government wage bill in current expenditure and the rising interest obligations on both domestic and external debt. Nonetheless, some progress appears to have been made during 1990–92, when the average deficit for the zone was narrowed to below the average for the other sub-Saharan African countries.

Some analysts have argued that the fixed exchange rate and lack of exchange restrictions means that excess demand pressures in the monetary unions spills over (primarily into the external sector), affecting inflation less severely. These analysts consider that other African countries using the exchange rate as a policy instrument have experienced higher inflation rates, which have contributed to an expanded nominal tax base and helped reduce real wages and other expenditures. In addition, the appreciation of the nominal effective exchange rate in the second half of the 1980s lowered revenues from international trade transactions. Accordingly, these analysts argue that fiscal adjustment in the CFA franc zone, with its anchored currency, has not been helped along as much as in other African countries through the effects of exchange rate adjustments and inflation. This argument underscores the trade-offs that exist when a currency is anchored over a long period of time. But while the relation between exchange rate and fiscal policy cannot be overemphasized, the fiscal problems confronting these countries stem from the factors previously mentioned and need to be tackled directly.[7]

In contrast, the record of credit policy has been better. Although credit policy was fairly expansionary until around the mid-1980s, it was brought under control in the second half of the 1980s and further tightened in 1990–92 in an attempt to contain the growing external imbalances (Chart 2). To this end, real interest rates were significantly raised in the second half of the 1980s. Overall, the ratio of domestic credit to GDP has remained well below that for the other sub-Saharan African countries.

III. Economic Performance

The debate about the West African Monetary Union and the Central African Monetary Area has often centered on whether or not these unions have benefited their member countries. One way of answering this question is by evaluating the countries' performance in terms of inflation, economic growth, and the balance of payments relative to other sub-Saharan African countries, with the caveat that

---

[7]See Nashashibi and Bazzoni (1993) and Touré (1991) for a discussion of the issues involved in fiscal adjustment in the CFA franc zone.

Chart 2. Sub-Saharan African Countries: Domestic Credit
(As percent of GDP)

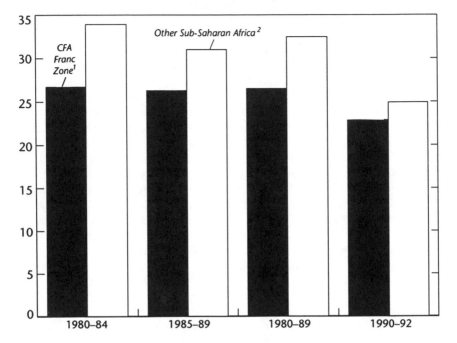

Source: International Monetary Fund, World Economic Outlook data base.
[1]Benin, Burkina Faso, Cameroon, Central African Republic, Chad, Congo, Côte d'Ivoire, Equatorial Guinea, Gabon, Mali, Niger, Senegal, and Togo.
[2]Botswana, Burundi, Cape Verde, Comoros, Djibouti, Ethiopia, Ghana, Guinea, Guinea-Bissau, Kenya, Lesotho, Liberia, Madagascar, Malawi, Mauritania, Mauritius, Mozambique, Nigeria, Rwanda, Sao Tome and Principe, Seychelles, Sierra Leone, Somalia, Sudan, Swaziland, Tanzania, Uganda, Zaïre, Zambia, and Zimbabwe.

numerous factors apart from the monetary arrangements affect these variables.

Inflation

There is a consensus that the countries in the unions have performed well in terms of inflation. During the 1980s, the average annual inflation rate for the zone was about 7 percent, compared with an average of some 25 percent for other sub-Saharan African countries. It is noteworthy that the annual average rate of inflation declined sharply in the zone in the second half of the 1980s, to less than 3 percent, and even further in 1990–92, to less than 1 percent,

Chart 3. Sub-Saharan African Countries: Consumer Prices
(Annual percent change)

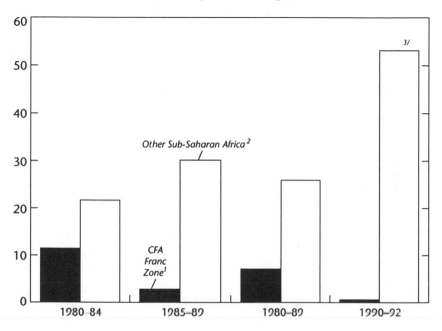

Source: International Monetary Fund, World Economic Outlook data base.
[1]Benin, Burkina Faso, Cameroon, Central African Republic, Chad, Congo, Côte d'Ivoire, Equatorial Guinea, Gabon, Mali, Niger, Senegal, and Togo.
[2]Botswana, Burundi, Cape Verde, Comoros, Djibouti, Ethiopia, Ghana, Guinea, Guinea-Bissau, Kenya, Lesotho, Liberia, Madagascar, Malawi, Mauritania, Mauritius, Mozambique, Nigeria, Rwanda, Sao Tome and Principe, Seychelles, Sierra Leone, Somalia, Sudan, Swaziland, Tanzania, Uganda, Zaïre, Zambia, and Zimbabwe.
[3]Countries listed in footnote 2 except Zaïre in 1992.

while inflation picked up substantially in the rest of sub-Saharan Africa, averaging some 30 percent per year during 1985–89 and exceeding 50 percent during 1990–92 (Chart 3).

Economic growth

The annual growth rate for the CFA franc countries averaged 2.8 percent during the 1980s, about the same as for other sub-Saharan African countries (Chart 4). But although the growth rate of these countries was nearly twice that of other sub-Saharan African countries in the first half of the 1980s, it started to fall behind substantially in the second half of the decade. Accordingly, while these countries

Chart 4. Sub-Saharan African Countries: Real GDP
(Annual percent change)

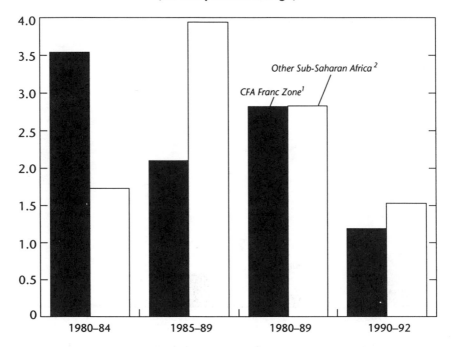

Source: International Monetary Fund, World Economic Outlook data base.
  [1]Benin, Burkina Faso, Cameroon, Central African Republic, Chad, Congo, Côte d'Ivoire, Equatorial Guinea, Gabon, Mali, Niger, Senegal, and Togo.
  [2]Botswana, Burundi, Cape Verde, Comoros, Djibouti, Ethiopia, Ghana, Guinea, Guinea-Bissau, Kenya, Lesotho, Liberia, Madagascar, Malawi, Mauritania, Mauritius, Mozambique, Nigeria, Rwanda, Sao Tome and Principe, Seychelles, Sierra Leone, Somalia, Sudan, Swaziland, Tanzania, Uganda, Zaïre, Zambia, and Zimbabwe.

were growing well in the mid-1980s, their more recent experience raises serious questions. Nonetheless, it is interesting to note that the average annual growth rates of the zone and the other sub-Saharan African countries dropped during 1990–92 to 1.2 percent and 1.5 percent, respectively, and thus were close to each other.

External current account

The combined external current account deficit, excluding official transfers, widened in the latter part of the 1970s, peaking at nearly 20 percent of GDP during 1980–82. It then narrowed briefly in 1983–84 but deteriorated again in the late 1980s. During 1985–89, the

Chart 5. Sub-Saharan African Countries:
Current Account Deficit, Excluding Net Official Transfers
(As percent of GDP)

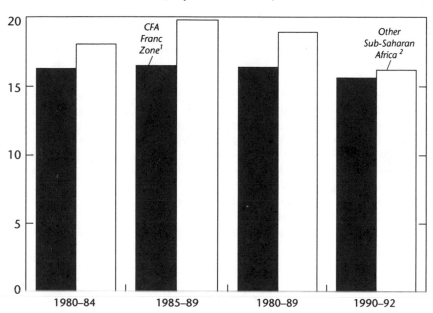

Source: International Monetary Fund, World Economic Outlook data base.
[1]Benin, Burkina Faso, Cameroon, Central African Republic, Chad, Congo, Côte d'Ivoire, Equatorial Guinea, Gabon, Mali, Niger, Senegal, and Togo.
[2]Botswana, Burundi, Cape Verde, Comoros, Djibouti, Ethiopia, Ghana, Guinea, Guinea-Bissau, Kenya, Lesotho, Liberia, Madagascar, Malawi, Mauritania, Mauritius, Mozambique, Nigeria, Rwanda, Sao Tome and Principe, Seychelles, Sierra Leone, Somalia, Sudan, Swaziland, Tanzania, Uganda, Zaïre, Zambia, and Zimbabwe.

zone's deficit averaged 16.5 percent of GDP, whereas those of other Saharan African countries averaged some 20 percent (Chart 5). In 1990–92, the average deficit in the zone dropped to 15.6 percent of GDP, close to the 16.2 percent deficit of the other sub-Saharan African countries. During 1980–92, the average deficit for the zone as a ratio to GDP remained below that of the rest of the region, but the relative deterioration of the zone's external position can be gauged by the average deficit, which was about 9 percent of GDP during 1970–74, compared with close to 40 percent for the rest of sub-Saharan Africa. In subsequent years, the external current account position of the zone widened, while that of other sub-Saharan countries narrowed, with the two groups' average deficits as ratios to GDP virtually converging in 1990–92.

Some analysts have attributed the relative deterioration in the zone's external position to an erosion of competitiveness. The movements in the index of the real effective exchange rate and the terms of trade are indicators of changes in competitiveness (Chart 6).[8] For the zone as a whole, the real effective exchange rate index declined by some 17 percent between 1980 and 1992. In contrast, the index for the other sub-Saharan African countries declined by some 32 percent over the same period. Did the other sub-Saharan African countries improve their competitiveness faster than the CFA franc countries? In fact, the zone's position may have reflected France's hard currency policy of the mid-1980s, which translated into a hard CFA franc policy. In addition, the terms of trade of CFA franc zone countries fell on average by close to 25 percent during 1980–92, while those of the other sub-Saharan African countries declined by only some 11 percent. The movements in the indexes and terms of trade should be interpreted with caution, however, and more country-specific studies are needed to determine whether or not there has been a loss of competitiveness.

IV. Conclusion

The overall performance of the countries in the two monetary unions suggests that belonging to the franc zone was definitely beneficial in limiting inflation. In addition, the average growth rate for these countries during 1980–92 was close to that of the other sub-Saharan African countries. These results reflect primarily the relatively restrained monetary policies the unions pursued, the stability of the exchange rate, and the openness of the economies. The CFA zone countries are almost the only ones in Africa that have a virtually fully convertible currency. As a result, internal disequilibria have not resulted in shortages of foreign exchange; the private sector has had access to foreign exchange, and imports have not been constrained by the lack of foreign currency.

Nonetheless, the CFA franc zone faces several challenges today: the general sluggishness of economic activity; the large fiscal deficits in a number of countries, which have caused the accumulation of substantial domestic and external payments arrears; and the relative deterioration in the average external current account position of the zone.

---

[8]See Faes (1993) and Godeau (1993) for a discussion of issues relating to the peg of the CFA franc.

Chart 6. Sub-Saharan African Countries: Terms of Trade and Real and Nominal Effective Exchange Rates
(1980=100)

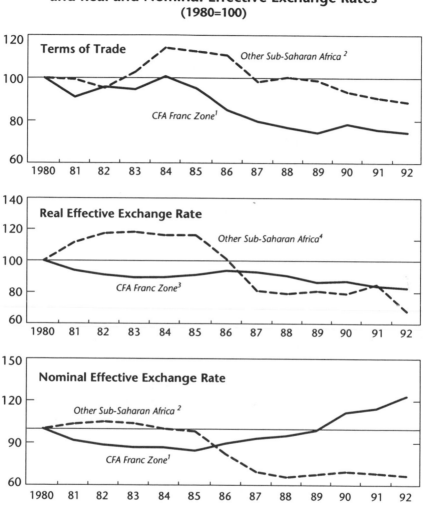

Source: International Monetary Fund, World Economic Outlook data base.
[1]Benin, Burkina Faso, Cameroon, Central African Republic, Chad, Congo, Côte d'Ivoire, Equatorial Guinea, Gabon, Mali, Niger, Senegal, and Togo.
[2]Botswana, Burundi, Cape Verde, Comoros, Djibouti, Ethiopia, Ghana, Guinea, Guinea-Bissau, Kenya, Lesotho, Liberia, Madagascar, Malawi, Mauritania, Mauritius, Mozambique, Nigeria, Rwanda, Sao Tome and Principe, Seychelles, Sierra Leone, Somalia, Sudan, Swaziland, Tanzania, Uganda, Zaïre, Zambia, and Zimbabwe.
[3]Countries listed in footnote 1 except Benin and Equatorial Guinea.
[4]Countries listed in footnote 2 except Comoros, Djibouti, Guinea, Guinea-Bissau, Liberia, Sao Tome and Principe, and Somalia.

An important issue for the CFA franc zone today is achieving a sustainable level of economic growth with a viable external position. Can these countries reduce consumption and improve competitiveness with structural reforms and policies that manage domestic demand alone, or will they need the price-switching and money-illusion effects that an exchange rate change can bring about? This issue came to a head recently in a debate in July 1992 among the presidents of the franc zone countries. They came to the conclusion—outlined in their statement of July 31, 1992—that they wanted to maintain the anchor to the French franc and to reinforce their internal adjustment efforts. Whether these internal adjustment efforts will succeed remains to be seen.[9]

References

Bhatia, Rattan J. 1985. "The West African Monetary Union: An Analytical Review." IMF Occasional Paper 35. Washington, D.C.: The International Monetary Fund.

Bloch-Lainé, François, and others. 1956. *La Zone Franc*. Paris: Presses Universitaires de France.

Boughton, James M. 1991. "The CFA Franc Zone: Currency Union and Monetary Standard." IMF Working Paper 91/133. Washington, D.C.: International Monetary Fund.

——. 1992. "The CFA Franc Zone: Zone of Fragile Stability in Africa." *Finance and Development* 29 (December), pp. 34–46.

Bourdin, Joel. 1980. *Monnaie et Politique Monétaire dans le Pays Africains de la Zone Franc*. Dakar: Nouvelles Edition Africaines.

Connolly, Michael. 1985. "On the Optimal Currency Peg for Developing Countries." *Journal of Development Economics* 18 (August), pp. 555–59.

Crockett, Andrew P., and Saleh M. Nsouli. 1977. "Exchange Rate Policies for Developing Countries." *The Journal of Development Studies* 13 (January), pp. 125–43.

Devarajan, Shantayanan, and Jaime de Melo. 1987a. "Adjustment with a Fixed Exchange Rate: Cameroon, Côte d'Ivoire, and Senegal." *The World Bank Economic Review* 1 (May), pp. 447–87.

——.1987b. "Evaluating Participation in African Monetary Unions: A Statistical Analysis of the CFA Zones." *World Development* 15 (April), pp. 483–96.

Devarajan, Shantayanan, and Dani Rodrick. 1991. "Do the Benefits of Fixed Exchange Rates Outweigh Their Costs? The Franc Zone in Africa." NBER Working Paper No. 3727. Cambridge, Mass.: National Bureau of Economic Research.

[9]Subsequent to the presentation of this paper, the CFA franc in the two monetary unions was devalued, effective January 12, 1994, to CFAF 100 = F 1.

Faes, Géraldine. 1993. "Franc CFA: Comment Eviter l'Inévitable." *Jeune Afrique* 1701–2 (12–15 August), pp. 47–50.

Godeau, Rémi. 1993. "La Dévaluation en Douze Questions." *Jeune Afrique* 1701–2 (12–15 August), pp. 50–57.

Guillaumont, Patrick, and Sylviane Guillaumont. 1984. *Zone Franc et Développement Africain*. Paris: Economica.

Guillaumont, Patrick, Sylviane Guillaumont, and Patrick Plane. 1988. "Participating in African Monetary Unions: An Alternative Evaluation." *World Development* 16 (May), pp. 569–76.

Macedo, Jorge Draga de. 1985. "Collective Pegging to a Single Currency: The West African Monetary Union." NBER Working Paper No. 1574. Cambridge, Mass.: National Bureau of Economic Research.

McLenaghan, John B., Saleh M. Nsouli, and Klaud-Walter Riechel. 1982. "Currency Convertibility in the Economic Community of West African States." IMF Occasional Paper 13. Washington, D.C.: International Monetary Fund.

Nashashibi, Karim, and Stefania Bazzoni. 1993. "Alternative Exchange Rate Strategies and Fiscal Performance in Sub-Saharan Africa." IMF Working Paper 93/68. Washington, D.C.: International Monetary Fund.

Nsouli, Saleh M. 1981. "Monetary Integration in Developing Countries." *Finance and Development* (December), pp. 41–44.

Touré, Mamadou. 1991. Statement to seminar on Fiscal Policy Issues in the CFA Franc Zone Countries, March 6, at the International Monetary Fund, Washington, D.C.

Comment

John Odling-Smee

One thing Paul Masson did not emphasize was the debate that took place in Western Europe on the question of whether economic and monetary union would be better for the general level of inflation than a continuation of the existing European monetary system. One side in this debate held that as long as there was scope to adjust exchange rates, as there is in the existing system, some countries would be able to have higher inflation rates. Fixing exchange rates and, ultimately, creating a single currency would remove that scope, and the high-inflation countries would be forced to accept inflation closer to the center, lowering the average inflation rate. The counter view was that the average inflation rate depended on the behavior of the dominant monetary authority. With a single currency, the dominant authority would be the new European central bank, perhaps with some involvement from governments; with the existing European monetary system, this bank was, in essence, the Bundesbank.

It is not possible to resolve this debate a priori, but it is quite possible that involving more authorities in the governance of the new European central bank would result in a somewhat more inflationary outcome, on average, than what would occur if the Bundesbank alone were in charge. This outcome would hold true if the high-inflation countries no longer had high inflation, because with a single currency they would have to lower their inflation rates. A cynic might argue that the only reason why many countries want to have a European central bank rather than the European monetary system is because they want to have a somewhat easier overall inflationary position.

This topic serves as an introductory point and a transition to what I want to say about the ruble area, because one of the more interesting features of developments in the ruble area over the last year has been the way the incentives within the system have created a clear inflationary bias. The absence of monetary coordination has provided an incentive for all countries to try to inflate as quickly as possible, stimulating inflation throughout the whole region. For this reason, the question of finding the monetary arrangement that best controls inflation or brings about monetary stability in a currency region is something that West Europeans look at from a slightly different point of view in terms of the ruble area.

Another introductory point is again in contrast with what Mr. Masson has been saying. I shall be less concerned with what in some sense ought to be done in the ruble area, in terms of economic objectives, than with what can be done. In terms of the countries, the question is one of political feasibility, since the issue has become rather politicized. In considering economic policy for the region, therefore, it is necessary to be very conscious of the political constraints.

I shall start with a few words about the current situation in the former Soviet Union and then draw attention to the main problems in the ruble area arising from the currency question, discussing possible solutions. The countries of the former Soviet Union have tried to establish working monetary relations between themselves. Although they once used the same currency—the ruble—some of them have already introduced their own currencies. Exactly how to make their system work has become a topic of much debate.

The current situation in the 15 countries of the former Soviet Union has evolved quite quickly since the beginning of 1992, when they were all using the ruble, the currency of the former USSR. During the second half of 1992, first Estonia, then Latvia, and finally Lithuania introduced their own currencies. Estonia pegged the kroon at eight to the Deutsche mark. Latvia and Lithuania floated their currencies—the Latvian ruble and the talonas—which the authorities say are temporary. In November, Ukraine also left the ruble area and introduced its own temporary currency, the karbovanets, which is also floating. The three countries that have temporary currencies—Latvia, Lithuania, and Ukraine—intend to introduce what they regard as their own permanent currencies at some stage in the future, although none has announced a date.[1] They do not want to introduce a permanent currency until the financial situation is under control, because they do not want a new currency associated with the very difficult monetary situations they now face, perhaps compromising its prestige. They are therefore waiting for a moment when they can introduce the new currencies successfully, with a reasonable amount of monetary stability. To an economist, this change from a temporary to a permanent currency is a purely technical one, although it has real political significance for the countries involved. Thus, it is possible to talk about these four countries as though they already have their own currencies.

Of the other 11 countries, 2 or 3 have already announced their intention to introduce their own currencies in the relatively near

---

[1]In mid-1993 Latvia and Lithuania introduced permanent national currencies; Ukraine has not yet done so.

future. Azerbaijan, in particular, has mentioned February 1, 1993,[2] and one or two others have said they will take action fairly soon. Other countries have introduced what are called coupons, or surrogate rubles. These trade, one for one, with the ruble and really exist only in cash—not in noncash (i.e., deposit)—form. They were introduced owing to a shortage of cash rubles early in 1992 that has now ended.

Russia continues to issue the ruble and remains the dominant country in the ruble area. Its GDP is over 60 percent of the GDP of the total territory of the former USSR. Now that Ukraine, which had between 15 and 20 percent of total GDP, has left the ruble area, Russia's share of ruble area GDP is about 75 percent. It controls the only supply of ruble bank notes, since all the printing presses for ruble bank notes are on Russian territory. It also has large balance of payments surpluses with nearly all the other member countries of the ruble area because of the traditional structure of trade. Russia is an exporter of raw materials, especially energy, while the other former republics export manufactured and agricultural goods.

The ruble area as it functions now is defined by the fact that monetary policy among the countries involved is not coordinated. Each central bank extends credit to its government and to commercial banks independently, sets reserve requirements independently, and determines interest rates independently. Although there may be some local control from a government or parliament, there is no effective coordination. The maneuverability of ruble area central banks outside Russia was limited in early 1992 by the Central Bank of Russia's position as sole issuer of ruble currency, but these central banks were able to finance different rates of credit expansion by borrowing from the Central Bank of Russia, by creating bank reserves, and, in some cases, by issuing coupons or parallel national currencies.

In attempting to isolate themselves from the relatively tight credit policy of the Central Bank of Russia in the early months of 1992, some of these central banks adopted divergent credit and interest rate policies. Some, however, continued to pursue a restrained monetary policy, but once one or two—especially the larger ones—began expanding domestic credit at a rapid rate, others realized that this policy constituted a "free ride." They could expand domestic credit and create strong inflationary pressures throughout the ruble area as a whole, but these pressures would be shared by all the area's countries, reducing the risk to individual economies. In fact, it was in the interests of individual countries to expand credit in the absence

---

[2] In December 1993, the Azerbaijan authorities issued a decree stating that the manat would become the sole national currency January 1, 1994.

of any centralized controls or agreements. This was the source of the inflationary bias that I mentioned before. Of course, all the strong inflationary pressures in the former Soviet Union cannot be attributed to the lack of coordination. The policies of Russia itself were very inflationary, and almost certainly they account for the larger part of the overall inflationary pressures in the ruble area.

Until the end of June 1992, Russia automatically financed payments imbalances with the other countries of the former Soviet Union through correspondent accounts the other central banks held with the Central Bank of Russia. At the beginning of the year, Russia was uncertain how the ruble area would operate and did not want to impose too many restrictions on the system. The correspondent account balances were allowed to grow. After the first two or three months, the other countries began to accumulate debts to the Central Bank of Russia—a result of growing payments imbalances.

With effect from the first of July 1992, Russia changed its policy, and, in order to control the growth of interstate credit through these correspondent accounts, the Central Bank of Russia instructed its main branches to centralize all interstate payments through one Moscow office. The Central Bank created a new system of bilateral correspondent accounts, under which payments from another state could not be processed until that state was either running a payment surplus with Russia—not a very common event—or had negotiated a technical credit with Russia to finance a payments deficit ("technical credit" was the name given to explicit credit of a certain amount). In essence, these countries were told that from the first of July they could not borrow from the Central Bank of Russia unless they negotiated an explicit amount. Open-ended credit was stopped. This new system rather quickly led to the blocking of payments from those states that had exhausted their credit limits—as a number of them quite quickly did. This development in turn affected not only payments for trade, but trade itself. One problem was that traders learned their payments had been blocked only after goods had actually been shipped; a Ukrainian exporter, for example, would sell goods to Russia, but the Central Bank of Russia would block the payment, leaving the Russian importer unable to pay the Ukrainian exporter. Huge arrears therefore developed in both directions, but mostly it was Russian enterprises that accumulated arrears with enterprises in other states of the former Soviet Union.

These arrears were not the only consequence of the new system. The aim of the new system was to control credit expansion to the other states, but it did not succeed. Whenever states ran up against their credit ceilings, they applied strong political pressure on Russia to ease the ceilings. In most cases the ceilings were raised, especially after July, when the Central Bank of Russia's new management showed a greater willingness to extend credit not only to other states but within Russia itself. As a result, the new policy did not restrict the inflationary pressures created by the systemic problem of lack of coordinated monetary policy within the ruble area.

One further consequence of the new arrangements has been that the rubles used in different ruble area states are no longer worth the same amount. Of course, the notes are worth the same amount, because they can be smuggled across borders and exchanged, but the noncash rubles—the deposit money—cannot always be used equivalently. A number of states have introduced restrictions on deposit rubles domestic enterprises earn by exporting to Russia, barring the conversion of Russian deposit rubles into domestic rubles. Other forms of restriction have also grown up. The result is that these deposit rubles are now being exchanged at exchange rates that differ from par, giving rise to a de facto segmentation of the market for deposit rubles within the ruble area.

For example, the primary market for deposit rubles is in Latvia, which, interestingly enough, is outside the ruble area. On November 30, 1992, selling rates quoted by the Bank of Latvia were 0.22 Latvian ruble for each Kazakhstan ruble; 0.24 Latvian ruble for each Ukrainian ruble; 0.35 Latvian ruble for each Belarussian ruble; and 0.4 Latvian ruble for each Russian ruble. These rates are less than one because the Latvian ruble has appreciated: Latvia has been pursuing a tighter monetary policy than other countries in the ruble area since breaking free from the ruble. The differences among those rates are the consequence of the restrictions in the ruble area.

In sum, the lack of a coordinated monetary policy has created a serious inflationary bias in the system and generated issues concerning "free rider" countries. For example, one or two very senior policymakers in some of the smaller ruble area countries have indicated to the IMF their understanding of what the IMF has been saying to them since the beginning of 1992 about the importance of coordinating monetary policy. They have tried very hard to adhere to the rough guidelines that have several times been agreed to about growth in credit. But when some of their bigger neighbors allow credit to grow very rapidly, these policymakers are unable to restrain their politicians from insisting that the smaller countries should follow suit. These countries are clearly under great pressure.

Another point to be made here is that a single currency area can be broken up not by the formal introduction of separate currencies—although obviously that will cause disintegration—but by the imposition of restrictions on payments and capital flows, which generate de facto separate currencies.

In terms of solutions, the situation in late 1992 is clearly very unsatisfactory. The restrictions that countries feel they must introduce in order to try to make the ruble work in some way are seriously damaging trade and payments. All the countries suffer under this arrangement. Clearly a cooperative solution is the right sort of response to this situation. The IMF's advice is that these countries make a clear choice between two alternatives and act on it: either remain in a single currency area with a common monetary policy or introduce a separate currency.

Under the first option, the countries would have to agree on clearly defined mechanisms for the pursuit of a common monetary policy with only one currency circulating throughout the area. Cash and deposits would need to be interchangeable throughout the area. Credit emission would be determined by a single authority. An alternative system in which separate monetary authorities are responsible for credit emission might be possible, but the authorities would agree on the total amount of credit and its allocation. (This solution was discussed earlier in 1992 but was not then politically feasible.)

In the absence of coordinated but separate monetary policies, it is necessary to have a single monetary policy. There are two ways of organizing such a policy. One is to have an interstate monetary institution of the sort the West Europeans have been discussing and incorporating in the Maastricht Treaty. The second is to have a single central bank, presumably the Central Bank of Russia, coordinate monetary policy for all countries in the ruble area. The choice between the two is a political matter that must be decided by the states themselves. What we can say as economic advisors is that it is essential for the survival of a single currency area that responsibility for the common monetary policy be placed squarely in the hands of a single authority. This authority should be responsible for providing adequate information to all the central banks in the area on important decisions regarding monetary, credit, and exchange rate policy and for harmonizing foreign exchange systems, central bank finance rates, and commercial bank reserve requirements.

Under the second option, in which countries introduce their own currencies, plans would have to be made to ensure that the new currencies were introduced, rubles withdrawn in an orderly way, and disruptions minimized. Governments would need to devote much time and energy to creating the institutions and acquiring the expertise needed to conduct independent monetary and exchange rate policies and manage international reserves. Decisions would have to be made on monetary policy under the new currency, including which exchange rate regime to use. Whatever exchange rate arrangements were adopted, the authorities would need to implement rules and procedures necessary for the conduct of an anti-inflationary monetary policy.

It is absolutely clear that a choice must be made between these two options. Moreover, it is doubtful whether in practice the political situation is such that the first option is feasible. The surrender of sovereignty required to accept a single monetary authority is not

likely to be forthcoming in a period when newly independent nations are being built. Most of these countries will find that the only
viable solution is to introduce their own currencies. This is politically
feasible, though not necessarily economically desirable. I am not
drawing on the four considerations that Mr. Masson mentioned at
the beginning of his talk—factor mobility, the amount of interdependence between these economies, the degree of congruence, and wage
and price flexibility—to decide on optimal currency areas. These
issues, of course, could well point in another direction that would
lead to a different sort of debate. But in the current situation, political
considerations are paramount, and economic policymakers have to
take them into account.

Finally, the solution to the current difficulties requires a direct approach to the balance of payments financing problem. What has
happened, essentially, is that balance of payments financing from
Russia, which has been made available to the other countries
through credits on the correspondent accounts, has not led to appropriate policy adjustments in the recipient countries. These countries
have opted for financing without adjusting; in fact, the incentive
structure is such that they have not been aware of the need for
adjustment. Their willingness to adjust would be enhanced if interstate credit arrangements were formalized and separated from payment arrangements, making the balance of payments financing constraint more transparent.

One of the problems with the existing system is that the terms of
the credit lines currently provided by the Central Bank of Russia
through the correspondent accounts are poorly defined and constantly changing. Interest rates were initially set at the same rate as
the Central Bank of Russia's refinancing rate. They were subsequently reduced to zero. Repayment dates have been set and reset on
an ad hoc basis. Credit limits have been increased frequently, in some
cases on political grounds. Thus, there is great uncertainty about how
much credit is available and how to get it. This situation does not
inspire the countries running deficits to try to manage their affairs
well, cut down on borrowing to avoid running into credit limits, or
adjust appropriately in advance. It is important that procedures be
developed for extending credit to meet chronic balance of payments
deficits through channels other than the payment systems, so that
systems are not overburdened with financing and payments and
trade is not arbitrarily disrupted.

Summary of Discussion

Participants agreed that if the states of the former Soviet Union
(FSU) were to adopt separate convertible currencies, a payments

union would not be necessary because the commercial banks could handle all clearing and settlement operations. A multilateral clearing operation would be required only if some of the currencies were not convertible. However, any clearing mechanism should avoid extending credit beyond a maximum of one week—a much shorter period than was embodied in the European Payments Union (EPU) mechanism.

The discussion then turned to the future of the European Monetary System (EMS). It was pointed out that even if the commitment to existing parities under the EMS was strengthened, the system was not a substitute for full monetary union. To avoid the possibility of speculative attacks under the EMS, the market would have to be convinced that all participating countries were pursuing the same monetary policy. In fact, the market would have to be convinced that one currency was as good as another in terms of existing parities. This weakness suggests that the transition within the EMS from flexible to more fixed rates might not be as smooth as anticipated. However, the EMS was generally perceived as an "in-between" system that has worked reasonably well, unlike the in-between system of the FSU, which has not worked well, especially given the existing constraints.

Participants believed that in recent years the CFA franc countries had suffered a serious loss of competitiveness due to their failure to undertake adequate measures to strengthen the internal adjustment process. At the same time, political pressures had prevented currency devaluations, even though neighboring non-CFA zone countries had devalued. The internal adjustment process had been hindered by institutional rigidities—including strong labor unions that had forced wages up to uncompetitive levels—and an unwillingness to take the necessary fiscal actions. There was also agreement that the magnitude of the problems facing the CFA zone economies had been partially hidden by a buildup of arrears. If these arrears had been paid, the operations account with the French Treasury would have shown a more negative position. The consensus was that the exchange rate would have to be moved unless CFA zone governments substantially strengthened their domestic adjustment policies.

Multiple Exchange Rate Systems: The Case of Argentina 9

Steven B. Kamin

There is an extensive literature focusing on the conduct of exchange rate policy in developing countries. Much of this literature, particularly in previous years, assumed that developing countries had the same unified exchange markets and unitary exchange rates that prevailed in most industrial countries. More recently, analysts have begun to acknowledge the highly segmented nature of exchange markets in many developing countries. In some of these countries, the monetary authority may peg the exchange rate for commercial transactions but allow a second exchange rate for international financial transactions to float freely. In other countries, exchange controls intended to ration scarce international reserves have given rise to black markets for foreign exchange.

Regardless of whether multiple exchange rate systems are legal or illegal, they have important implications for economic performance and policy. At the macroeconomic level, multiple exchange markets may complicate the process of stabilization, altering the effects of exchange rate and monetary policies relative to what would be expected with a unified exchange market. At the microeconomic level, multiple exchange markets may alter patterns of resource allocation and encourage rent-seeking, smuggling, and other activities for which no incentives would exist in a deregulated market environment.

The discussion that follows is divided into two parts. To begin with, I define multiple exchange rate systems more closely and discuss, at a general level, various issues regarding the operation and consequences of multiple exchange rate systems. These issues include, first, the distinction between legal and illegal multiple rate systems; second, the rationales for these systems; third, the reasons why governments follow policies that give rise to multiple exchange markets; fourth, the economic roles multiple rate systems play in different countries and the consequences of those roles for economic

Note: This paper represents the views of the author and should not be interpreted as reflecting those of the Board of Governors of the Federal Reserve System or other members of its staff.

welfare; and finally, the unification of multiple rate systems. Many of the conclusions described in this section are based on a recent World Bank study of multiple rate systems in various countries (Argentina, Ghana, Mexico, Sudan, Tanzania, Turkey, Venezuela and Zambia).[1]

As it turns out, the exchange rate systems of these countries fit loosely into two categories with different characteristics. The first comprises the Latin American countries, where exchange controls were prompted by macroeconomic crises and where the primary effects took place at the macroeconomic level. The second group comprises Turkey and the African countries, where exchange controls were a response to cumulative deteriorations in competitiveness and where these controls led to profound distortions in resource allocation at the microeconomic level. Today, it is especially interesting to consider how the transition economies of Eastern Europe and the former Soviet Union might fit into this framework.

In the second part of my discussion, I summarize my case study of Argentina, which was written as part of the broader World Bank study described above.[2] Argentina's experience with exchange controls and multiple exchange markets in the 1980s is particularly interesting, for a number of reasons. First, this period was an extremely turbulent one in Argentina's macroeconomic history, culminating in inflation rates that exceeded 100 percent per month. Second, exchange controls and exchange rate policy represented an important part of the Government's efforts to control inflation and stabilize the economy. Finally, the widespread evasion of exchange controls that took place in Argentina in the 1980s typifies the types of problems governments face in trying to insulate their economies from market forces.

I. Multiple Exchange Rate Regimes

What exactly is meant by multiple exchange rate practices? In principle, a multiple exchange rate regime is any exchange rate regime that applies two or more exchange rates to the same currency. Many developing countries have applied separate, fixed exchange rates to different types of transactions, but this practice is, in essence, equivalent to a single exchange rate coupled with different taxes or subsidies (depending on the transaction). In the following discussion,

---

[1]Miguel A. Kiguel and Stephen A. O'Connell, "Parallel Exchange Rates in Developing Countries: Lessons from Case Studies," Policy Research Working Paper 1265 (Washington, D.C.: World Bank, 1994).

[2]Steven B. Kamin, "Argentina's Experience with Parallel Exchange Markets: 1981–1990," International Finance Discussion Papers No. 407 (Washington, D.C.: Board of Governors of the Federal Reserve System, 1991).

a multiple exchange rate system will refer to a system involving one or more fixed exchange rates for current account transactions and one or more floating or market-driven rates for capital transactions. This type of system presents policymakers with numerous difficulties, because the separate exchange rates involved may react in very different ways to the same shocks or policy actions. As an example, an increase in the money supply that drives up domestic prices is likely to lead to the real appreciation of a fixed nominal exchange rate but may cause a real depreciation of any floating, market-driven rate. Models and theories devised to deal only with single, fixed exchange rates may break down in the context of multiple rates of this kind.

Legal and illegal systems

The first distinguishing characteristic of exchange rate regimes is their legality (or lack of it). Legal multiple rate systems are often referred to as dual exchange rate systems, and the Belgian example, which persisted until very recently, was perhaps a prototype of this. Most current account transactions took place at a pegged official rate, while most capital account transactions occurred in the free market, which determined their rates.

Such systems are no different in economic principle from many "illegal" systems, particularly in developing countries where official and black or "parallel" markets exist side by side. In illegal systems, transactions are often conducted much as they are in "legal" systems: trade takes place at the official fixed rate, and capital flows occur at the illegal floating rate. Legal and illegal systems are also similar in their effects on the rest of the economy. For this reason, the World Bank study addresses them jointly.

Trade barriers, quantitative restrictions, or high tariffs alone are not in themselves sufficient to generate a black market for foreign exchange, however. For a parallel exchange market to develop, there must be some restriction on transactions in foreign exchange at the official price, as well as an excess demand for or supply of official foreign exchange at that price. Only under these conditions will people go to a black market to buy or sell foreign currency.

Rationales for multiple rate systems

There is only one legitimate rationale for having a multiple rate system that routes current account transactions through a pegged rate and capital account transactions through a floating rate: to insulate domestic prices and activity from exchange rate fluctuations deriving from transitory shocks in the financial market. Such a policy, if it is to succeed, requires properly managing the official exchange rate to ensure that it remains competitive. That done, the market-driven rate for capital transactions should fluctuate around the official pegged rate, which presumably would represent the mean of those fluctuations. In fact, in developing countries, the parallel market rate is rarely more appreciated than the official rate—although there are certain exceptions. And the fact that the parallel market rate is usually more depreciated than the official rate points to one of the key dangers of adopting a multiple rate system: there is a great temptation not to adjust the official exchange rate when it needs to be adjusted, allowing it to become increasingly overvalued and the economy decreasingly competitive.

A second and related problem with multiple exchange rate systems—especially if the rate becomes overvalued—is that it is very difficult to prevent leakages of transactions from one market into the other. A typical example, which will be discussed in the context of Argentina, involves exporters who are required to surrender their foreign exchange receipts to the central bank at the official rate, but who instead hide some of those receipts and sell them on the black market at a more depreciated rate. This common practice can lead to the breakdown of a multiple rate system.

Finally (and this is a somewhat more speculative but, I think, a legitimate criticism of multiple rate systems), to the extent that they create incentives for cheating, multiple exchange rate systems can blur the line between legal and illegal activities. Illegal behavior tends to spill into other areas of economic regulation, particularly tax enforcement. When exporters hide their receipts from the government in order to sell them on the black market, they probably are also hiding their income from the tax authorities. In Argentina, there was a simultaneous breakdown of the multiple exchange rate and tax collection systems. Such occurrences do tend to be interwoven, and they underscore the principle of good governance that would avoid having laws on the books that cannot be enforced.

Aside from the one legitimate rationale for parallel systems—to allow a fluctuating capital account rate to buffer the economy from the effects of transitory shocks while maintaining a correctly valued official rate—most other purported rationales for multiple rate systems depend on the systematic overvaluation of the official rate. For this reason, it is difficult to make a case for these rationales based on considerations of efficiency. One good example is the argument that some governments—especially those with net foreign currency obligations to the rest of the world—can gain implicit tax revenues through a multiple rate system. Governments can set the official rate at an overvalued level, force exporters to turn over their receipts at the overvalued rate, and then use this cheap currency to pay off foreign currency obligations. It is true that this scheme confers a fiscal benefit on the government, but it is a highly distortionary benefit that hurts exporters while helping those importers who may have preferred access to official foreign exchange. Undoubtedly, such a benefit is inferior in terms of welfare to a more broad-based system of taxation.

Why governments really choose multiple rates

Regardless of the purported rationales behind multiple exchange rate systems, historically the choice of such regimes has tended to be motivated by more direct, practical considerations. Usually, multiple rate systems are the result of severe balance of payments difficulties. In order to protect their international reserves and avoid a substantial devaluation, governments may choose to limit the range of transactions for which they will provide foreign exchange. The World Bank study found that this process tends to differ somewhat among countries. In Latin America, the initiating problems tended to be severe balance of payments crises associated with large capital outflows.

Chart 1 indicates the path of the real parallel market exchange rate (RPER, in local currency per dollar) and the parallel market premium (the percent difference between the parallel and official exchange rates) in three Latin American countries after exchange controls were initiated. In all three countries, parallel exchange rates depreciated sharply following the imposition of exchange controls and then appreciated as the situation stabilized. Hence, at the onset of balance of payments crises, the parallel market rates tended to overshoot the level at which they would eventually stabilize, more so in Argentina and Mexico than in Venezuela.

To the extent that such overshooting is typical, it creates a rationale, at least at the onset of a severe balance of payments crisis, to impose a dual exchange market. As long as the initial steep depreciation of a market-based exchange rate is reversed soon afterwards, it makes sense to insulate domestic prices from those fluctuations by maintaining a more stable pegged exchange rate for commercial transactions. Ideally, this pegged rate would be adjusted, so that once the payments crisis was past, the rate would be close to the market rate for financial transactions. Then the exchange controls could be removed and the exchange market unified.

However, after imposing exchange controls, the authorities do not always remove them when the crisis subsides. This was the case in Argentina, Mexico, and Venezuela. Dual markets developed in each country following the establishment of exchange controls, and the authorities continued to rely on the controls to prop up somewhat overvalued exchange rates, neglecting more fundamental fiscal and

Chart 1. Parallel Exchange Rate (PER)

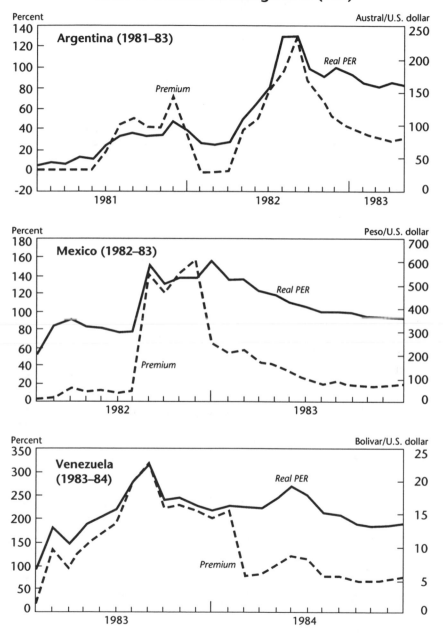

Sources: International Monetary Fund, *International Financial Statistics* (various years); and *World Currency Yearbook*.

monetary adjustments. Thus, in principle there may be a role for dual exchange markets, but in practice they often are not used appropriately.

In the case of Turkey and various African countries, which were also covered in the World Bank study, the process of tightening controls in the face of balance of payments deterioration was somewhat more gradual. It was also more closely linked to the deterioration in the current accounts that resulted from the overvaluation of official exchange rates than to speculative surges in capital outflows. In the absence of speculative crises and the overshooting associated with them, these countries probably had fewer justifications for multiple rate practices than Latin American countries.

The economic roles of multiple rate systems

There were also differences in the economic functions of the parallel exchange markets in Latin American and African countries. In Latin America, most current account transactions took place at the official rates, and sufficient foreign exchange usually was available to meet the needs of importers at that rate, since demands for foreign exchange for trade were not excessive. The primary role of the parallel market in Latin American countries was to finance capital inflows and outflows. Sometimes the premium of the parallel market rate relative to the official rate grew very large in Latin America, but this development usually reflected a macroeconomic crisis that gave rise to capital outflows and not a severe misalignment of the exchange rate itself.

In consequence, the multiple rate system probably did not have severe distortionary impacts on the real side of the economy in Latin America. The real problem for Argentina and other Latin American countries lay in the difficulties the multiple rate system caused for macroeconomic management. In the African countries, by contrast, exchange rates became much more severely overvalued and foreign exchange was more stringently rationed in the official market. Thus, the parallel markets played a more important role in supplying foreign exchange for importation, with very distortionary consequences. Importers with preferred access to foreign exchange enjoyed huge subsidies, whereas both importers lacking this access and exporters paid very high implicit taxes. For example, in the early 1980s much of Ghana's economy moved underground when the official exchange rate become so severely overvalued as to be irrelevant to most prices and transactions in the private sector.

Unification of multiple rate systems

A substantial amount of the literature on exchange rate policy in developing countries is devoted to the desirability, timing, and manner of implementing exchange market unification—that is, the combining of multiple rates into a single, unified rate. To a large extent, questions of the optimality of exchange market unification and the best means of achieving unification are somewhat academic.

In Latin America, multiple exchange rate systems were often abandoned not because they were no longer needed or because they were viewed as undesirable, but because they were no longer sustainable in a macroeconomic crisis. Moreover, the most important factor in determining whether unifying exchange rates will give rise to a favorable outcome is not the method used to implement the unification, but the associated macroeconomic policies. In the late 1980s, Mexico combined unification with fiscal restraints and structural reforms, and the country's stabilization program took hold relatively quickly. By contrast, Argentina, which unified its exchange market in December of 1989, experienced another round of hyperinflation (with inflation rates of nearly 100 percent per month) before it was able to stabilize. In essence, macroeconomic policies are far more important than exchange rate policies in ensuring stable prices, output, and financial systems.

II. The Case of Argentina

My paper on Argentina addresses the following questions: first, what motivated Argentine policymakers to impose the exchange controls that gave rise to a parallel market in 1981; second, how effective these controls were in achieving their intermediate objective, which was to allow the authorities to set the official exchange rate with some degree of independence from financial market developments; and third, how effective the exchange controls were in helping the authorities achieve their ultimate policy objective of stability combined with growth.

In talking about the evolution of Argentina's exchange control regime, I cover approximately 12 years of Argentina's history, from 1978 through 1990. This period can be divided into four phases (Chart 2). During the first of these, from the late 1970s through the early 1980s, no exchange controls existed. The policies of this initial phase set the stage for the balance of payments crisis and the experience with exchange controls that were to follow. Exchange controls were imposed in 1981, and the short time characterized by a spike in the parallel market rates—the second phase—represented a transition for Argentina. Once certain problems were resolved during this transitional phase, Argentina had a long period—the third phase— during which economic policy was geared toward fighting inflation. At the end of this phase, exchange rate pressures became so great that the Government had to remove the exchange controls and unify

Chart 2. Macroeconomic Developments in Argentina

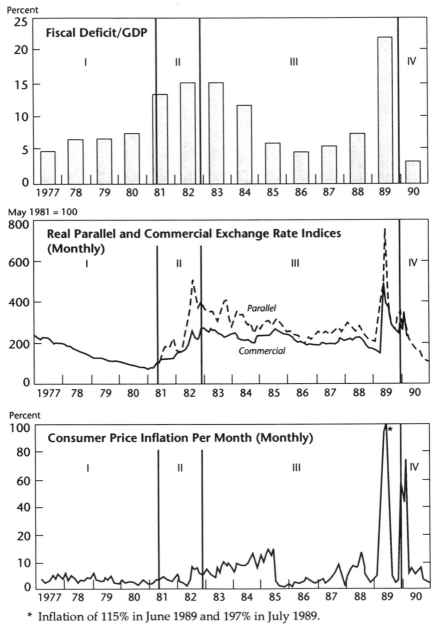

* Inflation of 115% in June 1989 and 197% in July 1989.

Sources: Carlos A. Rodriguez, *The Macroeconomics of the Public Sector Deficit: The Case of Argentina* (World Bank PPR Working Paper Series 632, March 1991); Foundation for Latin American Research (FIEL) data base; and IMF staff calculations.

and float the exchange rate. The subsequent phase, which is shown only up to the first part of 1990, is the post-exchange control phase.

The no-exchange control phase

The policies of the first no-exchange control phase ultimately gave rise to exchange controls and parallel markets. The depreciation of the official exchange rate (which was unified at that time) at a rate lower than the rate of inflation in order to bring inflation down was particularly significant in this regard. Chart 2 shows that this policy had some success, although inflation remained quite high by international standards. But because the exchange rate was being depreciated at a rate lower than the inflation rate, the real exchange rate appreciated steadily. As a result, the current account deficit grew substantially toward the end of this period. A severe recession developed in the tradable goods sector, and both private and public indebtedness ballooned, in large part because the Government was borrowing money from abroad to finance the deficit. Toward the end of this phase, investors began to realize that a devaluation was inevitable and began sending their capital overseas, prompting the Government to borrow further to support the exchange rate. These actions forced a series of devaluations that started in early 1981.

The transitional phase

By mid-1981, the Government faced four crucial and seemingly insoluble problems. First, there were severe balance of payments outflows in response to perceptions of macroeconomic breakdown; second, the private sector was deeply indebted; third, the economy had slid into recession; and, finally, inflation, prompted in part by the recent devaluations, had accelerated. The problem for the Government was that policies intended to address problems in one area tended to exacerbate problems in another area. For example, a steep devaluation would help curtail balance of payments outflows, but it would also raise inflation, deepen the contraction in the real sector, and hurt those with a high degree of external indebtedness. Conversely, monetary contraction would help the balance of payments and reduce inflation but create severe ramifications for both debtors and economic activity.

In order to reconcile these competing problems, the Government adopted the following strategy. First, it instituted a dual exchange market with a fixed commercial exchange rate and a floating rate for financial transactions—which later became, in essence, an illegal parallel market rate, also for financial transactions. Second, it depreciated the real official exchange rate substantially. Third, in order to curtail pressure on the real black market rate, which was depreciating rapidly, it imposed controls on capital outflows and effectively nationalized private external debt. To help private debtors still further, interest rate ceilings were imposed on deposits and loans; combined with inflation rates exceeding those ceilings, this tactic had the effect of inflating away most of the real value of the debt in the economy in 1982.

The results of these policies were a huge run-up in the real value of the parallel market rate, an acceleration of inflation, and an intensification of the Government's foreign debt problems. On the other hand, what at that time was considered to be the key problem—the indebtedness of the private sector—was largely eliminated. In consequence, by the end of the transitional phase, various of the imbalances of the previous years had been corrected. The real official exchange rate was now at a relatively depreciated level, the balance of payments crisis had eased, and private debt had been largely eliminated.

Fighting inflation

The key priority for Argentina's Government during the third phase was reducing inflation. To this end, a series of anti-inflation programs was launched that included wage and price controls, a fixed exchange rate, and some degree of fiscal adjustment. Initially, these programs succeeded in reducing inflation. During the first, the 1985 Austral Plan, inflation dropped radically. During the second, the "Plan Primavera," inflation also fell significantly. Then, after the hyperinflation at the end of the Alfonsin period, the so-called "Plan Bunge y Born" reduced inflation again. But these successes were always temporary, because there was no sustained fiscal adjustment.

Absent a sufficient reduction of the fiscal deficit, monetary growth continued, causing not only further deterioration of the trade account but capital outflows that drove up the parallel exchange rate. In turn, foreign exchange began leaking from the official to the parallel market, forcing the Government to devalue the peso and abandon the stabilization program. Without the correct macroeconomic policies, the fixed exchange rate programs could not function, even when bolstered by exchange controls. By December 1989, evasion of exchange controls had become so rampant that the Government, faced with a ballooning public debt, rising inflation, and ongoing capital outflows, realized it could no longer control the prevailing exchange rate, and so floated the currency. That action ended Argentina's most recent experiment with exchange controls.

The post-exchange control phase

After the exchange controls were removed and the exchange rate floated, Argentina had another bout with hyperinflation in March of

1990. This experience demonstrates that unifying an exchange market is not, by itself, a magical cure for a country's macroeconomic problems; unification must be bolstered with the right fiscal and monetary programs. That said, Argentina did gain certain benefits from unifying the market and floating the fixed exchange rate. First, by abandoning exchange controls and the fixed exchange rate, the Government was better able to focus on its primary consideration, reducing the fiscal deficit. Second, floating the exchange rate in essence disciplined Argentine policymakers, who understood in 1990 that the smallest degree of monetary emission would result in a steep plunge in the value of the currency and another bout of hyperinflation.

The effectiveness of exchange controls

Gauging the effectiveness of exchange controls requires determining whether they allow the Government to segment the official and parallel exchange markets, thus permitting the official rate to be set independently of the financial rate. I will present data showing that Argentine exchange controls were not effective in this sense. At times, changes in the parallel market rate forced the Government to adjust its official rate, because whenever the parallel rate depreciated too much relative to the official rate, strong incentives were created for exporters to hide their export receipts and sell them on the black market instead.

Table 1 indicates the results of a simple econometric regression designed to explain movements in the level of Argentina's exports, based on the movements of certain other variables: the real exchange rate, the parallel market premium, Argentina's output, and output in the rest of the world. As expected, the coefficient on the real exchange rate is positive, indicating that a depreciation (increase) in the real exchange rate generally led to increases in Argentine exports. And as hypothesized, the coefficient on the parallel market premium is negative, indicating that increases in the gap between the parallel market exchange rate and the official rate tended to reduce the level of exports in the economy. The coefficient is fairly large at .27, indicating that during the periods when the gap was largest, Argentine exports may have been depressed by as much as 10–40 percent.

It may also be true that when the parallel exchange rate rises relative to the official rate, officially reported imports also rise. Increases in the parallel premium provide an incentive for importers to report as many imports as possible, acquire the corresponding sum of foreign currency at the official exchange rate, and then sell the money on the parallel market. To test this hypothesis, another equation was estimated that relates the level of imports to various explanatory variables, including the real exchange rate and the parallel

Table 1. Merchandise Export Equation
Quarterly Data: 1978/IV–1988/II

Dependent Variable: Log (Real exports)

	(OLS)	(IV)
Constant	−6.06 (−1.16)	−1.10 (−.17)
Log (real exchange rate)	.28 (2.60)	.23 (1.74)
Parallel premium	−.27 (−1.99)	−.39 (−2.06)
Log (real GDP)	−.38 (−.65)	−1.24 (−1.46)
Log (real foreign GDP)	.57 (1.67)	.78 (1.97)
DUMQ2	.27 (5.68)	.29 (5.66)
DUMQ3	.20 (3.85)	.22 (3.84)
DUMQ4	−.08 (−1.30)	−.02 (−.25)
Standard error of regression	.10	.10
$\bar{R}_2$	.74	.72
Durbin-Watson statistic	1.91	1.88

(t–statistics in parentheses)

premium (Table 2). As expected, the coefficient on the real exchange rate is negative, indicating that real depreciations tended to depress imports. However, the parallel market premium apparently did not affect the level of imports; other factors appear to have been more important in determining imports than the value of the premium, as other researchers have found in other countries. Importers may have been more interested in evading tariffs than in boosting their reported imports in order to obtain foreign exchange.

Whenever the gap between the parallel and official rates became too large in Argentina, the balance of payments deteriorated, forcing the Government to depreciate the official exchange rate. Therefore, the official rate was never fully independent of the parallel rate. A third regression (Table 3) estimates the Argentine Government's exchange rate "reaction function," relating the month-by-month rate of depreciation of the official exchange rate to the level of the real official exchange rate, the Argentine-U.S. inflation differential, and the

Table 2. Merchandise Import Equation
Quarterly Data: 1978/IV–1988/II

Dependent Variable: Log (Real imports)

	(OLS)	(IV)
Constant	−4.28	−7.73
	(−.87)	(−1.14)
Log (Real exchange rate)	−.48	−.40
	(−3.40)	(−2.35)
Parallel premium	.04	.01
	(.31)	(.09)
Log (real GDP)	1.07	1.36
	(2.33)	(2.16)
Tarif rate	.15	.02
	(.36)	(.05)
Index of nontariff barriers	−.13	−.12
	(−1.27)	(−1.26)
Log (lagged real imports)	.42	.46
	(3.96)	(3.93)
DUMQ2	.13	.12
	(2.90)	(2.74)
DUMQ3	.19	.19
	(4.19)	(4.02)
DUMQ4	−.10	.08
	(1.90)	(1.34)
Standard error of regression	.09	.09
$\overline{R}_2$	.92	.92
Durbin-Watson statistic	2.12	2.20

(t-statistics in parentheses)

parallel premium. As expected, a higher (more depreciated) real exchange rate tended to be associated with a lower rate of depreciation. Also as expected, when inflation in Argentina was higher than inflation in the United States, the Government had to depreciate its official exchange rate more rapidly. Finally, all else being equal, increases in the parallel market premium tended to induce the Government to increase the rate of depreciation of the official exchange rate. Basically, then, the Government could not pursue official exchange rate policies that differed markedly from the dictates of the market.

Of course, the pursuit of official exchange rate policies insulated from market forces was merely an intermediate goal for Argentine policymakers. Ultimately, what governments care about—and

Table 3. Commercial Exchange Rate Determination
May 1982 – July 1988

Dependent Variable: Official Depreciation

	Monthly	Quarterly
Constant	1.89	6.87
	(3.04)	(3.01)
Log (Real exchange rate)	−.21	−.76
	(3.05)	(3.02)
Inflation differential	.89	.85
	(7.19)	(5.29)
Parallel premium	.12	.58
	(2.36)	(3.27)
Standard error of regression	.06	.12
$\bar{R}_2$	.50	.67
Durbin-Watson statistic	2.20	1.79

(*t*-statistics in parentheses)

Argentina was no exception—is not the exchange rate, but economic stability and growth. And so I arrive at my final question: did the parallel exchange rate system help Argentina achieve its ultimate objectives of reduced inflation and stable economic growth?

To some degree, this is a purely academic question, since the Argentine economy exploded into extreme hyperinflation by the end of the exchange control period. But it is possible to ask whether exchange controls had a positive, marginal impact on the economic situation. The answer is essentially the same one I gave earlier in reference to the Latin American countries in general—that during the transitional period of the early 1980s, there may have been a case for having a dual exchange market system. Had the authorities floated the exchange rate at that time, it probably would have followed a path similar to the one the parallel market rate pursued over that period. Inflation would have accelerated even more than it did, and real incomes and real activity probably would have contracted more than they did, as well. Such a development would have been unfortunate, because the parallel rate appreciated a fair amount subsequent to the crisis, meaning that the economy would have experienced an unnecessary degree of turbulence and volatility.

Ideally, the authorities should have implemented a dual exchange market system—while simultaneously following proper macroeconomic policies—in order to stabilize the economy by the beginning of 1983. Then they could have abolished the dual exchange rate system and unified the exchange rate markets. Combined with appropriate fiscal adjustment and monetary restraints, these actions might have resulted in much better economic performance in the 1980s than in fact took place. Instead, the authorities retained the exchange controls, relying on them as a poor substitute for proper monetary and fiscal policies. The resulting sequence of cumulative policy mistakes erupted in the hyperinflation of 1989, when the controls had to be abandoned. In retrospect, therefore, the possibility exists that early on in Argentina's experience, the country could have benefited from exchange controls, but these controls certainly should not have been sustained.

Comments

Mohamed A. El-Erian

My objective in commenting on Steven Kamin's discussion is two-fold: first, to explore in a selective manner his approach and findings; and second, to complement his analysis with a brief overview of the experience with multiple exchange rate (MER) regimes in Middle Eastern countries. These comments are intended to provide a more comprehensive basis for discussing related issues affecting developing countries.

Mr. Kamin provides a useful discussion of Argentina's exchange rate policy in the 1980s, in the context of an analysis of the key factors affecting the supply of and demand for foreign exchange. After noting the main determinants of the parallel exchange rate and the channels for interaction with the "official" rate, he examines some of the policy implications for the real economy, inflation, and external capital flows.

Mr. Kamin's analysis gives the MER policy approach a mixed report card. On the positive side, it notes that Argentina's MER regime helped minimize the disruptive impact of financial market uncertainties in the early 1980s. On the negative side, the regime outlived its usefulness, but the associated unfavorable impact was reduced by market-related arbitrage operations.

The analysis raises several issues, especially when considered in light of the experience of other countries. Among these issues, four in particular stand out.

- First, the analysis could have examined in more detail the welfare losses associated with the imposition of multiple exchange rates and controls beyond the initial period, as well as how these could have been mitigated by a more liberal exchange regime. Among the interesting points to be examined are the impact on consumption and tradeable production and the implications for segmentation of domestic financial markets.
- Second, to what extent did the parallel market premium provide an adequate benchmark for determining the commercial exchange rate? Specifically, did distorting interactions between the two markets contribute to an effective exchange rate that differed substantially from the underlying equilibrium rate?
- Third, to what extent were developments affected by exogenous factors beyond those analyzed in the paper (e.g., changes in U.S. dollar LIBOR rates)? Moreover, did changes in the international

debt strategy—and associated prospects for improving relations with commercial creditors and limiting adverse externality effects on trade-related financing—play an important role in the interaction between the parallel and official markets?

• Finally, Mr. Kamin treats the period as uniform in terms of the structure of the exchange regime. Yet the period was characterized by numerous changes, including some in the legal status of the parallel market. Could these "structural changes" have affected the estimated parameters of the equations?

The discussion's overall framework is particularly pertinent to my second objective—to provide a brief overview of experience with MERs in Middle Eastern countries. Such an overview complements Mr. Kamin's analysis by introducing countries that differ from Argentina in one important respect—the extent of the integration of their financial markets with those in industrial countries.

Multiple exchange rate regimes, which basically take a cost-management approach to foreign exchange, have been implemented in several Middle Eastern countries in the last 20 years, including Algeria, Egypt, Iran, Morocco, Sudan, Syria, and Yemen. In other countries in the region, with the exception of the Gulf Cooperation Council (GCC) countries, the authorities have at times resorted to direct quantitative controls without MERs. The fact that GCC countries are excepted is related in large part to the fact that the governments of those countries have direct access to the bulk of foreign exchange earnings from oil exports.

Within the countries that implemented MERs, it is possible to distinguish two broad approaches. Algeria and Morocco adopted relatively simple regimes, basically setting a premium for specific transactions. In Egypt, Iran, Sudan, and Syria, MERs tended to evolve into complex and fragmented systems of foreign exchange pricing. As a result, these systems were characterized by separate exchange rates for some capital, invisibles, and merchandise trade transactions; in some cases the same transaction was subject to different rates, depending on whether it involved the public or private sector. These MERs were supported by a relatively complex system of controls over international transactions and foreign exchange surrender requirements.

In contrast to the Argentine experience, the Middle Eastern authorities' main motivation in choosing MERs was not to isolate the real economy from what were perceived as disruptive capital flows but to provide incentives for certain current account transactions. Specifically, the objectives were to promote the export of certain goods and services (such as workers' remittances and tourism receipts) and to curtail specific foreign exchange expenditures, with the aim of directly reducing the balance of payments deficit and influencing its composition.

The use of MERs also reflected policymakers' concern that a comprehensive exchange rate adjustment would put upward pressure on the prices of certain "sensitive" imports. The MER was seen as providing relatively favorable exchange rates for "essential" items and more depreciated rates for others. In some countries, fiscal considerations also came into play, as policymakers were able to contain the budgetary cost of essential expenditures by providing foreign exchange at more favorable rates. Budgetary gains from the reduced expenditures were offset, however, either by central bank losses (i.e., no net quasi-fiscal gain) or by implicit taxes on private sector foreign exchange activities.

MERs tended to remain in place for a considerable period of time, though not without changes. In fact, policy attempts to tinker with the MERs—with a view to rationalizing the system—sometimes had an opposite effect. For example, during the transition to a market-based unified rate, some countries experimented with the idea of using new exchange rates as a means of implementing a partial effective devaluation. However, continued large financial imbalances often meant that a new rate became fixed and limited in scope, requiring a yet larger number of exchange rates. Similarly, attempts to influence the rate in the parallel market in order to limit the depreciation of the "official rate" were often frustrated by the emergence of another informal market, sometimes outside the country.

In recent years, Middle Eastern countries have made significant progress toward unifying their exchange rates. Previous tentative policy steps involving shifts of products among exchange markets and a resulting depreciation of the effective exchange rate have given way to bolder efforts. These stronger steps have been taken as part of comprehensive macroeconomic adjustment and structural reform policy efforts aimed at increasing the overall responsiveness of the region's economies and reducing domestic and external financial imbalances.

Some general conclusions may be drawn from an analysis of Middle Eastern countries' experiences with MER regimes.

- Middle Eastern countries used MERs to influence certain types of current account transactions and reduce budgetary outlays. The underlying reason for implementing these regimes was the authorities' inability to correct the domestic financial policy imbalances that were weakening the external position, among other things.

- Two related factors in particular increased the attractiveness of MERs to policymakers: (i) the severity of foreign exchange shortages in the official sector; and (ii) the relative importance of sources of foreign exchange receipts the authorities could not easily control with quantitative restrictions.
- As in Argentina, MERs did not prove to be a temporary policy response. In some countries, their prolonged use was accompanied by increased complexity in foreign exchange pricing, which contributed to growing economic and financial distortions, misallocation of production and consumption resources, and, in some cases, currency substitution. In fact, rather than helping to resolve the underlying problems, the MERs tended to introduce a host of additional policy complications. The distortionary effects made medium-term external viability and sustained economic growth more difficult to achieve. Exchange rate policies were sometimes overloaded with numerous and conflicting objectives, often without adequate support from other macroeconomic policies.
- MERs were associated with an inward-based economic system dominated by the public sector. The public sector, which generally had access to the appreciated exchange rate for its imports, benefited from an important subsidy at the expense of exporters and private sector importers. Private sector activities were effectively relegated to a residual role in many areas. As a result, these economies proved less adaptable than others to changes in international economic and financial conditions.
- The implementation of complex MERs involved considerable administrative costs, including those associated with surrender requirements, over-invoicing of imports and under-invoicing of exports, separating transactions, and processing license requests, among others. Nevertheless, there were indications of considerable leakages between markets in some countries. Effective separation of exchange markets proved difficult, as it involved maintaining close control over the underlying transactions. While such leakages may have in some cases improved the allocation of foreign exchange, the disorderly and fragmented process also involved considerable allocative inefficiencies and equity losses.
- Recognition of the economic costs of MERs led to repeated attempts to simplify the exchange system, with a view to moving toward a unified market-related rate. Until recently, many of these attempts were frustrated by the inertia and large subsidies that had developed because of the MERs. Financial imbalances also frustrated the policy effort in two important ways. First, the larger the imbalances, the greater the spreads between the prevailing average exchange rate and its underlying market value,

and the greater the challenge the authorities faced in taking bold policy actions that altered the associated implicit taxes and subsidies. Second, partial policy moves (particularly moving commodities between markets) had a very limited overall impact but involved costly sector-based disruptions. The recent success that some Middle Eastern countries have had in unifying rates has much to do with the up-front adoption of a realistic market-based rate and appropriate supporting domestic economic and financial policies.

Peter J. Quirk

Steven Kamin has gone over in some detail, and with much refinement, the case of a specific country that has maintained a multiple exchange rate system. What I intend to do, in a hopefully complementary way, is to go over some of the historical and background material relating to the IMF's involvement in the area of multiple exchange rates and to try to give a broad view of trends and remaining practices.

The IMF is involved in this area because Article VIII of its Articles of Agreement specifically calls on members not to have multiple exchange rates. That being said, there are transitional arrangements under Article XIV that do in fact permit countries to maintain multiple exchange rates for a transitional period. In some cases the practices have been sustained for a very long period, but in recent years there has been something of a watershed in the use of multiple rates. Major differentials among multiple exchange rates have virtually disappeared from the IMF member countries, and we do not usually hear arguments these days in favor of sustaining multiple exchange rates.

Among *industrial countries*, Belgium in particular had a long-standing dual exchange rate system that was finally unified in 1990. Chart 1 suggests some of the reasons why this practice was finally abandoned. As earlier speakers have noted, a major argument for multiple rates in the literature was that a dual rate for capital could insulate the real economy from short-run financial shocks. However, the exchange rate differential between the two Belgian markets was very limited, and thus the degree of insulation from the overall swings in the exchange rate was not a major consideration in dismantling the dual exchange market. There was another important consideration, however: the system's administrative cost. In Belgium, that cost was considerable, because the system was changed frequently to take into account various types of transactions

Chart 1. Exchange Rates in Multiple Markets

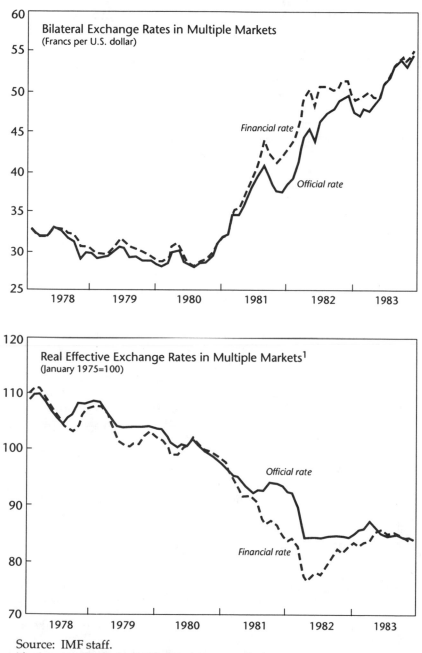

Source: IMF staff.
[1]An increase in the index denotes an appreciation.

that had become virtually uncontrollable and therefore had been reclassified from one dual market to the other.

A few similar systems existed in other industrial countries, but these did not involve a specific exchange rate. Until recent years, France had a practice called the *devise titre*, which was a self-contained market for foreign securities. At an earlier stage, the Netherlands also had a separate market—the O-guilder market—for foreign securities. The United Kingdom had an investment currency market that was abandoned in the late 1970s. But to a degree, these markets ran into the same problem: they could not be effectively enforced, and thus a substantive differential from the official market could not be sustained. At present no industrial country has a multiple exchange rate system.

In the group of *developing countries*, performance with respect to the obligations under Article VIII of the Fund's Articles of Agreement was very much affected by the debt crisis of the 1980s. Many of the official unitary exchange rates in place at the outset of the debt crisis were unsustainable, but for political or social reasons the authorities did not change them completely. Instead, the authorities split the exchange rate in various ways, maintaining the old rate for certain transactions and introducing more depreciated exchange rates for others. Long-term trends reflect these practices. Some 38 percent of world trade took place under multiple rates in 1971—which, along with the 1950s, was a peak period in the use of multiple rate regimes. However, the proportion of world trade currently subject to multiple rates fell steadily throughout the 1980s, to well below 10 percent. Moreover, the types of multiple currency practices IMF members maintain now are generally characterized by very narrow spreads between rates that apply to relatively small groups of transactions.[1]

In addition to multiple exchange rates, other practices can give rise to effectively different exchange rates, including taxes, subsidies, and related arrangements that are applied to exchange transactions. An important example of such a practice involves the forward foreign exchange market. In a number of developing countries, credits are available, but local borrowers are unwilling to assume the exchange rate risk connected with servicing foreign borrowing. In these countries, the central banks have sometimes taken upon themselves the role of guarantor for exchange rate risk. However, this practice has proved extremely dangerous. A 1988 IMF survey of these practices

---

[1]For a listing of multiple exchange regimes as of end-1992, see *Exchange Arrangements and Exchange Restrictions, Annual Report 1993* (Washington, D.C.: International Monetary Fund, 1993). Since December 1990, there have been further unifications and narrowing of the differentials between dual markets. For example, Angola, Bulgaria, China, Costa Rica, Dominican Republic, Ghana, Guyana, Haiti, Honduras, Hungary, Mexico, Sudan, and Viet Nam have unified multiple exchange rate systems.

emphasized the consequent very large fiscal losses.[2] For instance, by 1983 the Philippines had accumulated losses equivalent to 6 percent of GDP, adding significantly to the fiscal deficit. Indonesia at one time had guaranteed swaps that caused major budget difficulties. In all cases where an indirect tax subsidy is embedded in either a forward exchange rate, some form of interest rate subsidy connected with an exchange transaction, or direct exchange taxes on subsidies on foreign exchange transactions, the IMF investigates the practice, which in effect constitutes a separate exchange rate.

In more basic terms, it is by now generally accepted that the exchange rate is a key price for the economy. On a microeconomic level, a multiple exchange rate is similar to the separate consumer prices that would be charged for an item if one person were given a 10 percent discount and another assessed a 20 percent premium. But multiple exchange rates differentiate all goods an economy produces and therefore clearly undermine not only the core of the price system but the signals emanating from that system. However, as I stated at the outset, these arguments are quite widely accepted, and only a very small number of countries continue actively to pursue multiple rate practices.

One rationale for such systems that has been encountered recently occurs in connection with the countries of the *former Soviet Union*. The argument holds that the very large depreciation of the ruble raises the question of whether foreigners investing in domestic assets are paying enough. In other words, the argument maintains that with the ruble depreciating rapidly (to about 400 per dollar), the economy's real domestic assets are greatly undervalued. This argument may be true in some instances (e.g., the cost of meals for tourists), but the difficulty is that without investment in foreign technology to update the productive base, the transition economies will never be integrated fully into world markets. The productive apparatus is there, but investment clearly has to play a strong role before the quality and acceptability of the goods can improve. In some states of the former Soviet Union where the ruble trades at around 400 per dollar, rates for direct investment have been as low as 50 and even 20 per dollar. At such rates, the exchange rate functions as a huge disincentive for inward investment. On the other hand, nonproductive investments (such as real estate that can be acquired at low prices) or mobile factors of capital (such as plants and equipment that can be removed from the country) may need protection. In this respect, a number of countries maintain direct controls on the tapes of investment or disinvestment countries find acceptable,

---

[2]See Peter J. Quirk, Graham Hacche, Viktor Schoofs, and Lothar Weniger, *Policies for Developing Forward Foreign Exchange Markets,* IMF Occasional Paper 60 (Washington, D.C.: International Monetary Fund, 1988).

rather than on foreign currency itself. However, such impediments on investment must also be carefully weighed, because they can slow the development process considerably.

Finally, as I have noted, there has been remarkable progress in this area recently, and 45 years after the original Bretton Woods agreement, we are finally seeing one practice that goes against the spirit of the IMF's Articles of Agreement becoming obsolete.

Summary of Discussion

Participants discussed the advantages and drawbacks of multiple exchange rates. The point was made that countries with balance of payments deficits were often forced to choose between adopting multiple rates or exchange controls. Most participants agreed that the effects of a multiple exchange rate system on an economy were similar to the effects of restrictions on current payments, as the latter were likely to lead to the development of a black market for restricted transactions—or, effectively, to a multiple rate system. However, a multiple rate system was thought to be preferable, for several reasons. First, its costs can be explicitly identified. Second, it can protect export profitability when separate rates exist for current and capital transactions. Once a country's financial system is liberalized and the economy becomes increasingly attractive to foreign investors, capital inflows may increase, causing the currency to appreciate and discouraging exports. A separate rate for capital transactions, however, could allow the parallel market to accommodate a wider variance in the exchange rate, while keeping the official rate for current transactions fairly stable.

On the other hand, participants expressed the view that with a dual rate system, capital inflows could enter a country disguised as export receipts (or vice versa) to take advantage of the higher rate. In Chile, the variance of the legal parallel market rate for capital transactions was much higher than the variance of the official rate for current account transactions. The official rate was considered to be properly aligned, as evidenced by the satisfactory current account outturn over the last several years.

The general consensus was that there are circumstances in which a properly managed dual rate system could have advantages. An important drawback, however, is the added difficulty a dual rate system presents, since under this system the authorities would not be aware of the market signals needed to set the appropriate official rate. Moreover, experience with multiple rate systems has shown that these systems are often subject to abuse and that political factors have influenced rate setting.

PART **IV**

Exchange Regimes and Transition Economies

Exchange Rate Policies in Economies in Transition **10**

Rüdiger Dornbusch

Exchange rates, which are central to good economic performance, have much to do with credibility and are vastly underrated as economic instruments that can have a pervasive influence on macroeconomic stability, static competitiveness, and the dynamics of an economy's evolution. Inappropriate exchange rates will come under severe pressure and, ultimately, will have to change, possibly resulting in a political and economic crisis. Because of their importance, exchange rates are a central topic in economic management. Unfortunately, there is a solid body of prejudice concerning them, even within the IMF; everybody has a different idea about what they should be. Many of these prejudices have been tested and eliminated, so that the only way to make additional headway on the subject is through discussion, not by using a textbook.

The first point I want to make is that no country's situation is unique. Many economists maintain that the same rules apply to all countries and that therefore broad generalizations are the only way to proceed. (Of course, another school of thought, to which Tip O'Neil would have belonged, maintains that everything is in the details.) With exchange rate issues, it is necessary to determine whether a country's situation is so unique that no other experience is relevant, or whether one country's experience resembles that of any other in the principal points and therefore can be subject to the same conclusions.

In the context of transition, which is my more narrow topic, this question is particularly important, because it is tempting to suggest that command economies, with their 99 percent state ownership, are unique and that what characterizes Mexico, for example, cannot have any relevance to Belarus. Such thinking is unproductive, because it overlooks the many lessons that can be learned from years of exchange rate failures and successes.

I. A Historical Comparison

In making a case for using other countries' experiences as a starting point in examining specific exchange rate issues, I would like to spend a moment discussing the end of the Austro-Hungarian empire. The collapse of the empire is more than distantly related to the collapse of the former Soviet Union—in fact, I would argue that the two events were very similar. When the last Austro-Hungarian emperor, Charles I, fell from power in 1918, many independent republics rapidly emerged from the previous empire, very much under the influence of U.S. President Woodrow Wilson's declaration in support of nationalities. From one day to the next, new countries were created: Poland was one, Czechoslovakia another. Many territories were ceded to Italy, Poland, Yugoslavia, and Romania, until finally nothing remained of the former Austrian empire except Vienna, which was left with the public debt and the bureaucrats. In everybody's pocket, on the day of separation, were Austrian crowns, because they were the money of yesterday and a replacement currency could not be created overnight.

Of course, one of the first priorities of an independent country is to print a lot of its own money to pay the bills. In this case, the result was that Austria and Hungary had hyperinflation, and Czechoslovakia did not. It is interesting to learn why not all of the new countries experienced hyperinflation and to follow the Austrian crowns through the transition from a single empire to nation-states. Czechoslovakia tried for a short time to run a joint central bank with Austria. It was agreed that the Vienna-located central bank would not print money to finance the Austrian Government and that a bank commissioner would supervise all activities. Predictably, the bank did nothing other than finance the Government by printing money 24 hours a day, and the bank's board met when the Czech commissioner was out of town. Obviously, this situation did not last very long: after three months, the strict Czech Finance Minister, Alois Rasin, closed the Czech borders for a week, had all the currency the residents held stamped, and required residents to surrender 50 percent as a "wealth tax" that was expected, by reducing the amount of money in circulation, to push prices back to their prewar level. Of course, not everyone was totally honest; despite heavy penalties, unstamped notes found their way to Vienna and helped fuel the hyperinflation there. The value of the stamped Austrian crowns, which had become Czech money, immediately rose, and the crowns were soon commanding a high premium in Zurich. For months, stamping occurred in every region, but the efforts were not coordinated: new monies emerged in parallel with the stamped crowns, and hyperinflation developed that would last for three years.

It took around four years for hyperinflation to take hold in Austria; Russia has had only two years. So while Russia is well positioned to achieve hyperinflation, it is not yet there. In the end, how was stabilization achieved in Austria? It had been politically impossible to balance the budget, because food subsidies could not be removed, but keeping them in order to maintain social peace also helped fuel hyperinflation. Finally, the League of Nations intervened with a substantial stabilization loan—5 percent of GNP—with some conditions. The Parliament had to pass a law giving the Government the right to do anything necessary to balance the budget over the next two years. In addition, the League of Nations required an independent central bank, a fixed exchange rate, and a League of Nations commissioner in Vienna. The commissioner would submit monthly reports on the situation, and, if things did not go well, the loan would be suspended. Even before these arrangements were made public, the exchange rate stopped deteriorating. Price stability came within a week, and prosperity within two.

Here is a story with all the earmarks of something that could be happening today between the Ukraine and Russia: competitive money creation, the stamping of monies, the groping for a central bank arrangement, the attempt to balance the budget—all of these things are very much the same, because of a number of common factors. The first is that the transition from an empire to a democracy invariably involves very unstable politics. Everybody is in agreement about throwing out those in charge, be they emperors or Communists. The moment those in power are toppled, the broad coalition breaks up, and suddenly everybody has a separate agenda. Because there is a very active democracy, balancing the budget is the one thing that is impossible, and so huge budget deficits develop. Without external financing and a domestic capital market, huge budget deficits mean money creation—and that soon means inflation and, ultimately, hyperinflation.

The second common factor is nationalism. The Austro-Hungarian empire had fiercely suppressed nationalism. The entire senior civil service was Austrian; Austrian or Hungarian had to be learned in school, even in areas where Czech was the mother tongue. The moment the republics became independent, their single preoccupation was to turn their backs on everything in the past, imposing tariffs and quotas and creating their own money. Of course, the integrated trade arrangements that had existed before became obsolete immediately, and that loss had a terrible effect on output and trade patterns.

Another factor involves the diminishing interest of the West. As it became accustomed to famines in Austria, the West lost interest. The Allied Supreme Council as much as blamed the problem solely on Austria's budget deficits. The Austrians reacted in a somewhat extreme manner: the Jesuit Chancellor of Austria traveled to Italy to ask the Italians to annex his country. The neighboring countries were deeply disturbed by this development, fearing that if the Italians annexed Austria, Hungary and Czechoslovakia would be next, so a group of countries asked the Allied Supreme Council for assistance for Austria. The equivalent of this episode today is the Ukraine's reluctance to give up its nuclear missiles, provoking the West to react with greater involvement.

This example supports my case that in terms of exchange rates, parallels can be drawn from many earlier experiences and brought to bear on current situations. At some stage, however, it is necessary to decide which of the details that could influence potential outcomes ought to be given special consideration.

II. Why Are Exchange Rates Important?

One of the striking features of transition economies is that all relative prices seem too low. How can this problem be remedied? Perhaps the best method is to use free trade and an exchange rate system to create, in a stable, predictable, and transparent fashion, a pricing system that will accurately reflect world prices. A country very badly needs the right set of prices; otherwise, whatever is positive and useful in the country is underpriced and underused. It is important to utilize assets and resources constructively. The fact that the structure of prices can be so wrong makes a strong case for paying attention to the exchange rate as one of the primary ingredients in improving a country's economic structure. I think the exchange rate is even more relevant in a transition economy than it would be in basically capitalistic economies that are closed, very closely managed, or mismanaged and in need of modernizing.

For example, Mexico before Presidents Miguel De La Madrid and Carlos Salinas was a closed economy with high tariffs and quotas on top of the tariffs. Licenses were often required, and they were difficult to get. As a result, Mexican prices differed greatly from U.S. and world prices. In addition, a very rich Government was living off oil, keeping low-income people happy through a system of subsidies. In that economy, there was still a connection to the rest of the world, because although domestic capital goods were extremely expensive, import licenses were available, and profits were an issue, even in some state enterprises. In this description, does Mexico differ qualitatively from, for example, Ukraine today? True, Mexico had far more connection with the rest of the world in its pricing system than Ukraine currently has in its: Mexico may have been closed, but its people could see enough of the rest of the world to understand which types of goods should be smuggled. But both Mexico and Ukraine demonstrate that the only way to have the right price structure is through a relatively open trade system and a well-focused exchange rate system. This is one of the arguments for a special role for the exchange rate system.

A second argument is economic organization. In a command economy, or an economy that is somewhere between command and the market, it is important to have trade with and direct investment from the rest of the world. Luring such investment requires a well-focused exchange rate system. Economic modernization proceeds best if, rather than being legislated, it is nurtured by cross-border fertilization and allowed to spread to the rest of the economy. Mexico again provides an example. After six years of a relatively open economy, modernization is spreading rapidly, in large part because of external support and contacts with the rest of the world. If a country's exchange rate system functions poorly, such interaction will eventually stop. This idea, incidentally, is nineteenth-century thinking about the advantages of trade for economic development, and I highlight here that a sensible exchange rate system is an essential ingredient to enjoying this modernizing influence free of charge.

A third argument involves linkages. The former Soviet Union was heavily integrated across borders with other command economies, but it has now defined a new trading pattern. We are seeing that the exchange rate systems in this region are too poorly managed to accommodate the new trade. Either there is exchange control, no exchange rate system, or a very unstable exchange rate. These problems do not help the new trading system, which recognizes the advantages of trading with the West but does not see maintaining trade with the former empire as taboo. I take that to be a strong case for a European Payments Union style arrangement, something I will discuss later.

Lastly, there is the issue of corruption. In certain countries, it is extremely easy to manipulate a foreign exchange system in order to win a special rate. This behavior has an extraordinarily negative influence on the economy. It is also true that because the exchange rate is so visible, a single price can become more important than the price of bread. It can become a highly politicized price, and if there is no professional competence to act as a counterweight, the exchange rate—and, ultimately, the economy—may become a victim of politics. Ignorance is also often very powerfully at work when it comes to exchange rates. For instance, some may believe that imports have to be cheap so people can buy them. But the truth is that if people cannot afford imports, they ought not to buy imports—and that truth is not popular.

As I have tried to show, there are a number of considerations that make exchange rates a particularly important topic for the transition economies, especially in light of the new and relatively widespread interest in these economies. There has always been an exchange rate, but it was an unrealistic one; now it is necessary to move to some level of realism. Of course, there are black market rates, which may be two, three, or even four times the official rate. In the former Soviet Union, for instance, one ruble to the dollar was the price of foreign exchange for state enterprises, which bought foreign exchange and foreign goods at this rate despite any economic considerations. The absence of a link between the exchange rate and economic considerations in the minds of economic agents highlights an important factor in thinking about exchange rates: economic transactors must recognize the exchange rate's effects on economic decisions.

III. Choosing the Right Regime

What are the primary considerations in searching for an exchange rate regime? There are really three. The first is the degree of convertibility. Is there to be strict exchange control, current account convertibility, or full convertibility? The second is the relationship between the central bank and the foreign exchange market. At one extreme, we might have the equivalent of a gold standard; at the other, a complete separation between the two, although the central bank would have a powerful influence. The third consideration is the relationship between the trade and exchange rate regimes, which must be considered together. A trade regime may be liberal, for instance, but its potentially positive effects may be suppressed by the exchange rate regime. It does not make any difference where a tariff is collected, for instance. An explicit 50 percent tariff on certain imports and a special exchange rate for certain imports are equivalent tariffs in a protective structure. And multiple exchange rates simply do in the foreign exchange market what is not done for one reason or another—perhaps administrative—in the port.

What are the possible exchange rate arrangements? Exchange rate regimes are generally classified according to whether or not the rate moves. But I would suggest that the very best monetary arrangement for a transition economy is the adoption of another currency, such as the deutsche mark. The deutsche mark is a solid currency—probably the most solid—followed by the Dutch guilder, which would be an equally good choice. It is a travesty to believe that an underdeveloped country without any management experience, financial expertise, or real background in the world ought to create money. Yet the countries least able to manage money are those that most want their own. Even during hyperinflation, these countries are proud of their money and will not admit that it is a disgrace. But, by printing it, they may be financing a deficit—another good reason not to have a national currency.

In Western Europe, the race is on to abolish national monies, because some countries, including Italy and France, have had trouble with theirs. Again, the deutsche mark is the most stable currency, and other countries would like to emulate its stability. The experience of a number of countries suggests that a country with no appropriate institutional or political setting should not suddenly adopt its own variant of the ruble and pay a lot of money to a firm in Canada to get it printed. As I have said, hyperinflation will be the result. To those people tempted to put forward a national currency as a way to symbolically honor national heroes, I would say that the national heroes can be put elsewhere—on monuments, for instance. In reality, in these situations a national money is just an extravagance.

Currency boards

What about currency boards? Currency boards are a way to demonstrate that the national currency is sound, through 100 percent backing for the existing stock or at least at the margin. There is a big difference between these two situations, because starting at the margin with a large existing stock means that the slightest run can wipe out available reserves. This type of backing is really nothing more than a marginal gold standard. But 100 percent backing for the entire money supply is the equivalent of being pegged to the deutsche mark or the dollar until further notice. "Further notice" is that time when the need for 100 percent backing is called into question—and, starting from 100 percent, the need can be questioned all the way down to zero. Somewhere on the way, it will be convenient to start printing money.

Argentina, in the aftermath of many hyperinflationary episodes, has a monetary arrangement of 100 percent marginal and average backing. But even with that arrangement—one to one against the dollar—they are having a run on their currency. How is that possible? It is possible because people do not believe that Argentina really has a currency board. The country has had 45 percent inflation in the last 18 months, despite the dollar backing and fixed rate. Nobody believes the currency will hold, because for 100 years Argentina has had a currency crisis just before Christmas, and the crisis is occurring again. But currency boards are nonetheless attractive, because they foster credibility in the exchange rate system.

With a currency board, it is important to choose the right currency for the peg. If a country closely tied to countries in the European monetary system (EMS) pegs to the U.S. dollar, for instance, the fluctuations of the dollar relative to Europe—up to 50 percent—could result in extraordinary real instability. So the choice for a country like Estonia, with its newly founded currency board, really is between the deutsche mark or a basket. The argument for a basket is that the currencies are weighted against each other—dollars, lira, and so on—but again, my view is that one currency is preferable. With a single peg, people can say their currency is as good as (for example) the deutsche mark; further, when something happens in the EMS, an extraneous problem will not suddenly develop. Credibility is also an issue here: people want to be able to bite into a coin and feel that it is real. In essence, then, a currency board ought to be a very thin national veneer above an underlying reputable currency. Anything else will become a problem for financial markets—including a basket, which can become inconvenient, because the standard is discretionary. In this regard, Estonia was very right to go to a deutsche mark peg, and if inflation develops and the currency board attempts to move to a basket, people should criticize the currency board.

On my shopping list for transition economies, I go further, to fixed exchange rates. If a currency board has 100 percent marginal reserves, foreign exchange that flows in through balance of payments surpluses is bought up by the central bank, which then issues one-for-one local currency. But when foreign exchange flows out, it is as if there were a gold standard: the money supply is reduced, there is a credit squeeze, and interest rates go through the roof. Funneling foreign exchange through a central bank at a fixed rate is an automatic mechanism for stabilization. No discretion is involved; one person can run the central bank and oversee foreign exchange operations. A fixed exchange rate provides the critical link that gives the rate credibility—namely, the fact that the money supply is geared to foreign exchange movements. It is clear that the currency is being managed according to a strict criterion. If the fixed exchange rate becomes a problem, interest rates can be raised to defend it; if it is not defended, a crisis and devaluation ensue. Fixed exchange rates are noninstitutionalized currency arrangements, useful at the beginning, but they soon wear out if the central bank is not following appropriate policies and the institutional setting is weak. The bank will continue to hand out money, and the fixed exchange rate will collapse because of the lack of institutional support. Currency boards, on the other hand, have a lot of institutional support.

Multiple exchange rates

A country may feel that it needs a number of economic policy instruments to meet its objectives. For instance, a poor country may want to keep food prices low and make luxuries very expensive. On the export side, because primary commodity industries do not respond to exchange rates on account of the long gestation lags for their investments, a country may choose to give these industries a bad rate. At the same time, it may want to give nontraditional industries, which have no lags at all, much better exchange rates, because these industries are viewed as the entrepreneurs that build a modern economy. This kind of thinking can result in up to 50 different exchange rates.

Multiple rates encourage bureaucracy and corruption: the civil service administers the multiple exchange rate system, opening itself to bribes. It is essential to come out against this sort of system immediately, because even two exchange rates may be too many. Multiple rate systems result from the conjunction of people with a feeling for the structure of industry and politicians who have a feeling for what is necessary for the next election. When these two types of people meet, the result is a really awful exchange rate system. So a system of multiple exchange rates is to be avoided, even during a transition. One exchange rate should suffice, because its essence is that, at the margin, the costs and benefits of foreign exchange are equalized.

Subsidies and the tax system can be used to offer industries special treatment, but a country going this route will soon find out just how much it costs. The foreign exchange market should not be used to obscure priorities, and governments should not make the mistake of thinking that just because something has a gestation lag, it ought to have a bad exchange rate. In five years, an industry offered a poor rate will disappear, because, with such an unfavorable rate, businesses have no choice but to take their equipment out of the country and sell it.

Dual exchange rates

If multiple exchange rates are out, how does a country gain some leeway in its exchange system? One way is to have two rates: a fixed rate for current account transactions and a flexible rate for the capital account. The fixed rate for current account transactions provides some macroeconomic stability for countries wishing to avoid a wildly fluctuating rate that upsets the price level, then wages, social peace, the budget, the money supply, and again the exchange rate. An anchor is necessary, and countries that are comfortable intellectually or politically with controlling the money supply can use the exchange rate on the current account.

Of course, such an anchor can create a problem with capital flows. Capital flows begin the very day the system begins to open. Someone has a cousin in Chicago, for instance, who wants to send a thousand dollars into the country—a transaction that is certainly not going to be made through the central bank. Capital flows exist, and the only question is how to manage them. One way is by channeling them all through the central bank at a fixed exchange rate on the way out, but this method is unpopular. The alternative is to create a market system for them, divorcing the central bank from capital account transactions and allowing the banking system and people on the street corners to deal freely in foreign exchange. At the same time, the central bank can maintain a fixed rate for approved commercial transactions. Any volatility in policies that leads to volatility in capital flows will then affect the flexible capital account rate as if it were a black market rate, leaving the price level unaffected and reducing the risk of macroeconomic instability.

While there is a lot to this argument, there are two problems with it. The first is that some sort of exchange control is clearly necessary in order to license the people receiving foreign exchange for import transactions. However, the moment a good rate is established for import transactions, people will start inventing transactions, importing used equipment described as "new," for example, or rare drugs that turn out to be aspirin. There is also the business of import inspection, which requires that people be employed to check boxes to ascertain whether the imports are actually there. So dual rates are an attractive concept, but they require a bureaucracy that inspects effectively, and if a country is institutionally weak or democracy has reduced the bureaucracy too much, they are probably the wrong answer.

The second argument against dual rates is that they require isolating the price level from the capital account. The following example illustrates the problem: if the capital account rate has a 100 percent premium over the fixed rate for current account transactions, every exporter will want the capital account rate. The exporters then "under-invoice" their exports and pay what they save into a Swiss bank account. The value of Latin American exports to the United States in Latin American statistics is 30 percent less than the value of U.S. imports from Latin America in U.S. statistics—a discrepancy that reflects export invoicing. But the moment exports are under-invoiced to take advantage of the depreciated rate for capital account transactions, a feedback is created to the domestic price level, and the prices of domestic exportables at home rise. Then, because people have the alternative of getting these goods from outside the country, imports increase and pressure on prices is reduced.

One rule for dual exchange rate systems, then, is that the rate for capital account transactions must diverge greatly from the current account rate. It can fluctuate, but there has to be a limit. What would the limit be? Above 20 percent, it is impossible to stop commercial transactions from getting the capital account rate, but 15 percent is probably an even better rule. Either the current account rate or monetary policy needs to be flexible enough to keep the rates in line. Mexico had a dual exchange rate system from 1982 until around 1987 and very carefully watched the divergences. As a result, there are few horror stories about that experience with a dual system. If there is little divergence, however, there may not be enough leeway. A rate that can move a bit may serve as a shock absorber; if a 10 percent depreciation of the capital account rate will not affect the price level, this flexibility is an advantage. But again, a whole bureaucracy is required to run such a system, and in an institutionally weak setting, this need for oversight is a very strong reason not to choose this path.

The alternatives are to have one fixed rate, to allow total flexibility, or to "forget about" the capital account. This last is an attempt to avoid the convertibility question by wishing away capital flows. The prejudice here is the dichotomy "current account transactions are good, capital account transactions are bad." I think this distinction between current and capital accounts is overdone, however. The capital account does not have to do only with speculation and making money, and the current account does not have to do only with food, exports, and other "good" things. Everybody recognizes that unless foreign companies can remit their profits, investment will be low. If businesses have to keep extensive records and account for every penny, an unfriendly environment develops. And if firms have to argue with bureaucrats about whether certain remittances of profits are capital outflows or not, the environment becomes hostile. My suggestion would be, in the absence of an effective bureaucracy, to have unified rates and convertibility on both current and capital accounts.

A country may argue that by adding extra personnel, it can manage a multiple rate system. This argument does not hold up, however, because the costs are too high, as the country following this route will soon discover. The bureaucrat who controls foreign exchange has absolute power over it, and in the end, the businesspeople needing licenses will have to bribe someone. It is more efficient to forget about distinguishing between the transactions, to establish full convertibility, and to learn to live with it. In a market-oriented economy with a democratic, accountable government, many things are possible. But for a country just coming out of a repressive experience, the worst thing has to be perpetuating that repression at the foreign exchange desk, where people know only too well how to stop others from doing good business.

Fixed and flexible rates; crawling pegs

Once multiple or dual rates are eliminated, the choice is between fixed and flexible rates. Fixed rates are a problem, because inflation makes them unsustainable. Interest rates go up to defend them, balance sheet problems arise, and recessions develop, because these rates are often not defensible. In the end, there may be a collapse that is invariably blamed on speculators and "foreign professors." On the other hand, flexible rates fluctuate, creating macroeconomic and political problems. A better option is a crawling peg, which can be very powerful. The crawling peg is designed to adjust the exchange rate when domestic inflation exceeds international inflation by depreciating domestic price levels in a way that does not invite speculation. The depreciation should take place at a steady pace, in increments so small that nobody is willing to speculate and everybody understands what is going on. Interest rates will then reflect the anticipated pace of depreciation, and competitiveness will not be lost. Brazil has used a crawling peg with extraordinary success, and since that experience the crawl has become routine in countries that do not want to fight inflation at the expense of competitiveness. A crawling peg is the right answer when a country wants to avoid having its exchange rate misused in the fight against inflation. When the exchange rate is misused, a barrier of protection often develops, and the rate becomes misaligned.

The crawling peg is not popular with central bankers. Central bankers—the new generation—are all hard money men. They want a firm anchor to fight inflation and therefore advocate a completely fixed exchange rate. Their type of thinking has influenced Europe for the last two years, and what has happened since October 1992 is the complete collapse of the arrangement they advocated. Exchange rates have become overvalued either because countries have too much inflation—as in Spain, Italy, and Great Britain—or because their competitiveness has suffered on account of a loss of markets, a terms of trade shock, or a domestic financial crisis. Instead of allowing a substantial depreciation, these countries held on to their fixed rates, maintaining that the markets would ultimately come to believe in these rates. A crawling peg could be a strong answer to inflation problems of this type, which are not going to be resolved soon and which can affect a country's competitiveness. However, the crawl does not actually solve the inflation problem; rather, it validates the inflation and tells the foreign exchange market that the exchange rate cannot bring inflation down. Incomes policy, monetary policy, or both must be used to reduce inflation, but not the foreign exchange market. Countries with strong and sustained economic performance and significant inflation always have a crawling peg. Chile has used one with extraordinary success in the last ten years, ever since an episode of brutal overvaluation with a terrible collapse in 1982. Chile, incidentally, is currently the only Latin American country with Asian-style growth.

If fixed rates are a problem in inflationary economies, it is possible to use totally flexible rates. The primary concern with totally flexible rates is the absence of a nominal anchor. Monetary policy is a potential nominal anchor, but in an economy that is just developing a financial structure, the demand for money is unknown, and the money supply cannot be closely controlled. As a result, the exchange rate can fluctuate widely, especially if it is affected by a capital account driven by expectations about monetary policy, and if the central bank does not really know where things are headed. For these reasons, flexible exchange rates are difficult to use properly in a rapidly changing economy. For example, during the financial innovations of the 1980s in the United States, the dollar went up by 50 percent because people were watching the various measures of monetary aggregates, which were reflecting primarily those financial innovations. This kind of movement is often an issue in a transition economy, where the entire economic structure is evolving and predicting money demand is almost impossible. Even in industrialized countries, money demand equations are often difficult to use well, although econometricians have tried for 20 years to make them work. Finding a money demand equation in a transition economy is a heroic undertaking, because the data do not exist. For this reason, I am skeptical of flexible exchange rates in these situations.

Again, a crawling peg is probably the right answer, because it sets up the exchange rate as the single priority to preserve competitiveness. I see competitiveness, rather than financial stability, as the most important function of an exchange rate, more so in a transition economy than in an industrial one, because competitiveness is an essential ingredient of modernization, reform, and an open economy.

A crawling peg exchange rate system has two variants: a preannounced crawl (perhaps tied to the daily rate) and a crawl geared to the difference between the domestic and external inflation rates. The preannounced crawl contains inflation at the margin, because the preset exchange rate path allows for some inflation but does not automatically accommodate full inflation. I think this system is a good one for a country that has a predictable inflation rate and that wants some nonaccommodation. After first using a crawling peg, Mexico moved to preannounced mini-devaluations, which at 2 percent turned out to be too small, given the 15 percent inflation rate. The rate dropped to 7 percent, which was tolerable for a while, but such a rate ultimately has serious consequences, as Mexico found out. Over the last few years, Mexico's wholesale prices have increased 40 percent in dollar terms, compared with the United States, where wholesale prices have increased by 5–6 percent. The result has been a sharp drop in competitiveness, a gigantic trade deficit, a loss of confidence, and soaring interest rates. What will happen next? There will be a speculative attack—maybe not tomorrow, but someday. Mexico needs to accelerate its crawl in order to improve competitiveness.

I mention Mexico because it is an economy that has undergone extensive modernization and runs a budget surplus. In fact, Mexico has managed to get everything right except the exchange rate. And the faulty exchange rate now means that interest rates are 16–17 percent in real terms, that the budget is being further tightened to cut the trade deficit and defend the exchange rate, and that economic growth is 2 percent less than population growth. The next two years—1993 and 1994—will be the same, if the crisis has not occurred by then. Even in exceptionally well-managed economies, then, the exchange rate can go wrong in the end, as it did in Chile in 1979, at the tail end of modernization and an "economic miracle." There was a large overvaluation, a terrible collapse, and then five years of up to 30 percent unemployment. Since that episode, Chile has never again misused its exchange rate the way Mexico is misusing its. It is simply not enough to do everything right if the exchange rate is not in order, because the exchange rate is a central link once capital mobility has been established—and capital mobility always happens, particularly if the exchange rate is in the wrong place. If it is, it can eliminate accumulated successes and cause macroeconomic instability with high interest rates and low growth. And in the end, external events will be the determining factor. The vote on Maastricht broke Italy, and the U.S. Congress's vote on the North American Free Trade Agreement could adversely affect Mexico. Certainly, Mexico does not want an overvalued rate as that vote takes place.

Again, if a country lacks stability and cannot predict its money supply, it cannot manage a flexible rate. It can try a fixed rate, but a fixed rate will not adjust for inflation. In such a case, a country should let the rate crawl, although without preannouncements, which tend to encourage mismanagement. Brazil used to depreciate by the difference between the local consumer price index and foreign wholesale prices, a differential to which a margin was added to provide an extra 1–2 percent real depreciation every year. This system was extraordinarily good for competitiveness, allowing the country to develop a substantial trade sector as well as a rule that was followed long enough to become virtually tamper-proof. The rest of the system bore the entire burden of living with indexation. However, a complete indexation in the foreign exchange market puts pressure on the budget, the central bank, and incomes policy to manage inflation. As currency prices in Europe show, managing inflation from the foreign exchange market is very successful for three years. But by the fourth year, it results in huge bills.

IV. A Payments Union?

Whatever Estonia does will have relatively little effect on the world. But what Russia does has implications for all the states of the former Soviet Union and for the East European countries. If each of these economies adopts a different system of exchange control, there is a real possibility that trade will contract. Each country will be defensive about allocating foreign exchange for imports, because there are so few exports. The current trade collapse in the former Soviet Union is in part the result of foreign exchange controls. Of course, there is also a strong dose of nationalism involved. The outside observer—the IMF, for example—must realize that full convertibility with a crawling peg may not happen. Countries undergoing difficult restructuring are unlikely to have clean foreign exchange markets, and sooner or later foreign exchange is going to have to be administered. Most exchange rates have a tendency to be overvalued, so foreign exchange is always scarce, trade is repressed, and production falls. This scenario developed in the former Soviet Union and in

East European countries that belonged to the Council of Mutual Economic Assistance (CMEA). Trade with Russia has fallen by a factor of 20–30 percent or more, and all the former CMEA members are paying for it. The region's disorganized exchange rate systems are not the only reason for this collapse, but they are one significant factor.

What is to be done? The answer lies in something like the European Payments Union (EPU), which was organized by the United States in 1950 as part of the Marshall Plan in an effort to create an economically prosperous region that would act as an antidote to communism. In 1947, trade had come to a virtual standstill among the European countries. Everyone wanted dollars, because dollars would buy food, raw materials, machines—things countries could not buy with other currencies. Countries defended the few exports they had in order to turn them into dollars. The EPU was developed as a type of a clearing union that would allow the European countries to trade with one another without using dollars. Bilateral clearing was the first round, but this system proved too primitive, and trade surpluses developed. A surplus with one country could be used to pay a third, so multilateral clearing was the next logical step. The U.S. authorities organized the clearing system so that it could function without forcing countries to offset exports with imports daily: accounts were cleared monthly, and each country could draw on an interest-bearing balance in the EPU. Even countries like Switzerland, which had a fully convertible currency, were members, because they wanted to trade with countries that lacked hard currencies. Within ten years, Europe had moved to full convertibility and full liberalization of trade, and the EPU ended in 1958.

CMEA countries need this type of system to encourage the kind of trade among themselves that is not now taking place, because these countries are so set on earning dollars and, as a result, are ignoring some other potentially useful trade. Because there are no hard monies, a payments union is essential as a way of settling balances without using rubles, coupons, or the like. The issue is not just Poland or the Czech Republic—certainly not the Czech Republic, which is financially stable, has a convertible currency and substantially free trade, and is virtually merging with southern Germany. The problem is the countries that are not making it—and will not be for ten years—but that do have interesting trade that could be beneficial to all parties. I conclude that an important part of thinking about exchange rates is considering a payments system that can function even when currencies are mismanaged (as some of those in the transition economies are likely to be) and that will not destroy trade. The EPU is a perfect economic model and a good political model, because an EPU-style arrangement for the countries of the former Soviet Union could dampen many of the enthusiasms that are slowly pushing the countries of that region closer to civil war.

Comments

Thomas A. Wolf

In mid-1992, many observers were advocating a fixed exchange rate for Russia, in line with the other elements of the stabilization program that the Government and Central Bank had committed themselves to with the support of the first credit tranche arrangement with the IMF. Since there is so much support for either a fixed exchange rate or a crawling peg for most transitional economies, why did the Russian authorities ultimately *not* select one of these two regimes?

The first—and perhaps most salient—reason is that the country had only negligible reserves, an important consideration in this kind of situation. Second, limits existed on the extent to which other countries felt themselves able, due to their own budgetary problems, to provide direct balance of payments financing to help support a fixed exchange rate. The reluctance of these governments to provide balance of payments support above and beyond what was already being provided may also have been due to perceptions that Russia was highly unstable, both politically and economically. The lack of a coordinated monetary policy within the ruble area meant, simply, that the Russian authorities did not have full control over their money supply or inflation rate. And there were certainly doubts about the authorities' ability to carry out appropriately tight financial policies and coordinate them adequately between the Government and Central Bank. These perceptions have been borne out somewhat by the experience since August 1992. The idea now is to try to defend the liberalization of the foreign trade and exchange rate systems and not to compromise the reform effort by trying to defend a fixed exchange rate that, as I will try to explain, is at best arbitrary.

It would have been difficult to determine which exchange rate could have been defended in Russia in the second half of 1992. Even with additional resources from abroad, the Russian authorities had very little information or experience to go by, especially in comparison with some of the East European countries. Russia's interbank market for foreign exchange was quite thin at that time, and the authorities lacked very basic data on the extent of implicit subsidization of foreign trade. Some of the East European countries, on the other hand, had been able to draw on a great deal of information in this area, so they had some sense of the exchange rate equivalent of various explicit or implicit export subsidies, for example. Finally, the

Russians had no track record of maintaining solid financial policies, and, as I said before, there were real questions about the Government's ability to carry out coordinated, tight fiscal and monetary policies.

Russia's situation differed somewhat from Poland's at the end of 1989 or the former Czechoslovakia's at the end of 1990, because major price liberalization had already occurred in Russia at the beginning of 1992. It was generally agreed that Russia no longer had an immense overhang of money, but some key prices were still controlled, especially for energy, and the impact of increases in those prices on the overall price level had not been determined. The impact would have depended on the demand for money and the downward flexibility of other prices, among other things, and there was very little solid evidence on these variables in Russia at that time.

What would have been the appropriate range within which to fix the exchange rate? As others have said, the precise level at which the exchange rate is set is probably not terribly important in the transitional economies. The objective should be to get the rate in roughly the right range, and it is key that the currency not start out overvalued. In Poland in late 1989, for example, despite a substantial track record of currency auctions and a data series that permitted calculations of the exchange rate equivalent of export subsidies, it was extremely difficult to determine an appropriate exchange rate. In other words, there was little agreement on the precise rate that would provide a trade balance strong enough to help build up reserves and, at the same time, prevent unnecessary inflation and a decline in real wages (which might not have been socially acceptable). Expert estimates for the correct zloty rate varied anywhere from about zl 6,500 per dollar to about zl 13,000 per dollar—a considerable range. The rate that was finally selected was around zl 9,500 per dollar. Even in this situation, therefore, the uncertainties were tremendous, but they pale in comparison with the circumstances in Russia.

The purchasing power parity-based exchange rate mentioned for the Russian ruble in the second half of 1992 was in the range of rub 20 to rub 30 per dollar. The current rate—rub 418 per dollar (appreciated somewhat from the 450 that Rüdiger Dornbusch mentioned)—is far from that rate. In mid-1992, not only were there numerous purchasing power parity calculations, there was a very recent record of strong Central Bank intervention in the interbank market. As a result, the exchange rate in that market had appreciated in nominal terms to around rub 130 to the dollar—five to six times the purchasing power parity rate. There were also calculations based on an assumed dollar wage in Russia—once stabilization had more or less succeeded—similar to the average dollar wage in Eastern Europe in the year or two following macrostabilization. Estimating inflation and nominal wage growth in Russia under a stabilization program, it was possible effectively to solve for the exchange rate that would provide the dollar-equivalent wage (the calculations suggested an exchange rate even more depreciated than rub 130 to the dollar). These examples illustrate the very broad range within which the monetary authorities had to work.

It is important not to focus on purchasing power parity, however, especially during a period of transition when relative prices, production, and consumption are undergoing tremendous changes and inflation is high. Purchasing power parity calculations in such circumstances do not mean very much, except perhaps for tourists or businesspeople making everyday expenditures, and do not tell us which short- or even medium-term exchange rate would clear the foreign exchange market. Why might this be particularly true in Russia, and why is it important to be so careful about assuming that the appropriate exchange rate should be close to some purchasing power parity rate? A classic reason is that a fairly predictable relationship exists between official exchange rates and purchasing power parity rates, and for a country at a relatively low level of development, the differential between these two rates will be considerable.[1] This logic suggests that if Russia had already achieved some degree of stabilization, the market exchange rate would have been considerably more depreciated than the purchasing power parity rate.

With a few exceptions, Russia had almost completely liberalized imports in early 1992. In theory, exports had also been liberalized, but the major exportables (oil, gas, many precious metals, other metals, and timber, among others) were still subject to export quotas. It was an unusual situation with liberalized imports but not liberalized exports. Holding everything else constant, then, a much more depreciated market clearing exchange rate could have been expected than what a purchasing power parity calculation suggested, simply because exports were artificially constrained. Furthermore, it is generally recognized that at least with respect to most manufactured products, especially finished manufactures, many Russian producers are simply not competitive in world markets. This fact suggests that a purchasing power parity calculation—which typically would be based primarily on food or a household consumption basket—may not contain many of these potentially tradable manufactured products and may actually understate the true purchasing power parity rate (or at least the rate relevant to foreign trade). The same kind of problem exists with imports. As many Russians know, many of their

[1]See, for example, Irving B. Kravis, Alan Heston, and Robert Summers, *World Product and Income* (Baltimore: The Johns Hopkins University Press, 1982).

imports are really complementary imports, or nonsubstitutes. There is a tremendous pent-up demand for many products that simply are not produced in Russia or, if they are, do not meet the standards of quality found on world markets. Once again, the implication is that an adjusted purchasing power parity calculation would provide a rate somewhat more depreciated than one based on a market basket heavily loaded with fresh vegetables and various consumer staples.

Finally, those exportables that make up the lion's share of Russian exports to the world—namely energy products—must be taken into account. Here the Russians have been faced with a continuing decline in production not entirely unrelated to economic policy. In the very short run, however, the drop in petroleum output and the stagnation—even slight decline—in natural gas production is, most experts agree, relatively unaffected by policies. Over the medium run, with the right investments, pricing policies, and other factors, a tremendous scope exists for expansion of output and exports. But in the short run, production and exports—because of inadequate policies to curb consumption—have been falling.

Taken together, these factors make clear the difficulty of using anything close to a purchasing power parity rate for Russia as a fixed exchange rate that could be defended with very scarce financial resources (a low level of reserves or money borrowed, or perhaps given, by the rest of the world). And what should that exchange rate have been? No one knows, and in this case there were so many uncertainties and questions about the stance of economic policy and the ability of the authorities—regardless of their commitments—to carry through these policies that it would have been a mistake to try to fix the exchange rate in mid–1992. Indeed, experience with economic policy in the second half of 1992 suggests that the correct decision was not to try to peg the rate at that time.

Gérard Bélanger

Since we really do not have very solid evidence that one exchange rate system is better than another, a number of circumstances need to be taken into account in deciding which system is preferable for a given country. Thus, I would like to organize my comments around four sets of issues: one dealing with convertibility, the second with the role of the exchange rate in planned versus transition economies, the third with the experience of countries in Central and Eastern Europe, and the last with the interpretation of various indexes of real effective exchange rates.

Convertibility

I very much agree with the approach to convertibility taken in the paper suggested for background reading.[1] Convertibility has become a slogan for many in Central and Eastern Europe. However, it is more important to determine exactly what external liberalization contributes to the process of reform than simply to repeat the slogan. First, external liberalization of trade and trade-related services contributes to internal reform: it corrects relative prices, for which world prices provide the best guide, and promotes competition, especially in countries where extensive domestic monopolies prevail. Second, liberalization of foreign direct investment and related transactions, such as the repatriation of capital and profits, is important to the promotion of growth. Although opinions here differ, to me these are the areas in which early liberalization is important; it is less urgent in other areas.

The Role of the Exchange Rate in Planned and Transition Economies

The exchange rate played a very small role in planned economies. The reason is simple: the exchange rate is a price, and prices did not matter, or, if they did, their effect in influencing behavior was typically blunted by the absence of hard budget constraints. It is not possible to affect the consumption of a particular item by raising its price tenfold and then compensating consumers after the fact for the increased cost. Various studies of the influence of the exchange rate on Hungarian exports make this fact clear. No statistical evidence that the exchange rate had had a positive influence on exports was found until the availability of "soft money" (subsidies, credit, and ruble exports) was considered concurrently. After this factor was taken into account, the exchange rate was found to have had the expected positive influence on exports. Exchange rate policy, therefore, plays a crucial role in the reforming or transition economies, because in these economies, prices matter.

Exchange Regimes in Central and Eastern Europe

An important difference among the stabilization and reform programs adopted by the Central and Eastern European countries lay in

---

[1] Joshua E. Greene and Peter Isard, *Currency Convertibility and the Transformation of Centrally Planned Economies*, IMF Occasional Paper 81 (Washington, D.C.: International Monetary Fund, 1991).

exchange rate policy. In Czechoslovakia, as in Poland, the exchange rate was fixed after large initial devaluation. Bulgaria and Romania chose floating regimes. After a relatively small initial devaluation, Hungary followed a policy of adjusting the rate flexibly in light of balance of payments developments.

This eclectic collection of pragmatic approaches reflects the considerations particular to each case. From a macroeconomic perspective, a fixed rate can be particularly helpful as a nominal anchor when other policy tools are hard to use or interpret, as monetary policy is in the economies in transition. A fixed exchange rate can provide a simple yardstick for measuring the stance of financial policies and setting interest rates. Most of the economies in transition are still some way from being able to conduct monetary policy efficiently with indirect instruments and continue to rely on direct credit limits and interest rate guidelines. Even with these, however, monetary policy remains a much less satisfactory tool than it is in more developed market economies. Changes in velocity as these economies undergo transformation make reliance on monetary targeting as the sole or primary policy tool difficult. The financial sector reforms under way mean that money demand will likely remain unstable for some time. In these circumstances, policy must be judged in light of developments in the variables that it is seeking to control—inflation and the balance of payments or pressures on the exchange rate—as well as by the intermediate tools of credit and money growth.

From a microeconomic perspective, the fixed exchange rates in Poland and Czechoslovakia provided a more stable bridge for the importation of world prices, the realignment of relative prices, and the stabilization of inflationary expectations. But the commitment to the fixed rate had to be credible, requiring an adequate level of reserves—or at least a level of reserves perceived as adequate. While reserves were quite low in Czechoslovakia, the early commitment of financial assistance from the IMF, the European Community, and the Group of 24 probably bolstered perceptions of the authorities' ability to defend the rate.

However, fixing the exchange rate was not considered a feasible option in Bulgaria and Romania, given the lack of reserves, or in Hungary, given the vulnerability of the balance of payments to fluctuations in the capital account. In both Bulgaria and Romania, the acute shortage of foreign exchange contributed to sharper-than-expected depreciations and increased inflation. Although exchange rate fluctuations have often been held responsible for exacerbating economic instability, I hold that these variations were less causes than symptoms of continuing perceptions of political and economic instability and of prolonged delays in mobilizing the targeted financial assistance. In these circumstances, flexible rates made possible a program of external liberalization—which might have had to be abandoned or which might have occasioned a more severe drop in output had other objectives been subjugated to a firm commitment to a fixed rate.

Finally, the adjustable peg regime worked well in Hungary, which chose to manage the exchange rate flexibly during the initial stages of its more gradual reform in order to safeguard an external position vulnerable to shifts in private capital flows. With limited endogenous responses of capital to movements in interest rates, the country would have had to offset a large negative external shock primarily through the current account. In such a case, adjusting the exchange rate is likely to elicit a faster response than tightening financial policies would. As its balance of payments position has strengthened and prices have stabilized, Hungary has gradually moved to harden its exchange rate policy in order to reinforce the gains against inflation.

The Hungarian policy of gradually adjusting the exchange rate has not, however, been without cost. Gradual price liberalization and exchange rate adjustment have contributed to the entrenchment of inflationary expectations. None of the economic agents—including those that watched economic developments closely—believed that the country's accelerating inflation would be reversed. Although the inflation rate fell to about 15 percent annually during the second half of 1991, inflationary expectations remained much higher for an extended period, together with corresponding expectations of further exchange rate depreciations. The result was continuing high nominal interest rates and rapidly rising real interest rates that depressed economic activity for at least a year after inflation rates started falling. Interest rates are only now dropping—and rather slowly, especially on the credit side.

Thus, initial conditions were an important consideration in the choice of exchange regimes in the reform and stabilization programs introduced by the various countries of Central and Eastern Europe. Subsequently—as is the case everywhere else—the sustainability of fixed rate regimes and the stability of flexible rates have reflected, to a significant extent, the degree to which underlying financial policies are consistent with maintaining a stable exchange rate. In Poland, slippages of financial policies that eroded the country's competitiveness eventually led the authorities to abandon their fixed exchange rate policy and implement a crawling peg system. In contrast, despite its initial and surprising volatility, the Bulgarian lev subsequently achieved a significant measure of stability for an extended period.

Interpreting Real Exchange Rate Movements

Real exchange rate indexes are well known. They measure relative inflation performance adjusted for exchange rate changes and are used to indicate whether a country's competitiveness is improving or lagging. However, these indexes must be very carefully interpreted for economies in transition.

As subsidies are reduced during the reform process and the share of labor remuneration paid in the form of wages increases, we can expect a significant appreciation of the usual indexes of real effective exchange rates that is consistent with maintaining or improving both competitiveness and profitability. This change will perhaps be most immediately obvious in indexes of the real effective exchange rate based on the consumer price index, because eliminating consumer subsidies (or, as part of tax reforms, introducing a value-added tax) will significantly raise inflation measured on the basis of consumer prices, without affecting external competitiveness or profitability. Producer price-based or unit labor cost-based indexes will also be affected, although to a lesser extent, as the reform process can be expected to lead to an increase in the share of wages in total labor remuneration. Simultaneously, reducing taxes on enterprises or other costs that had previously financed the nonwage component of labor remuneration, such as subsidies, services, and vacation houses, would maintain competitiveness or after-tax profitability despite rising wage costs. These shifts simply reflect a narrowing of the well-known difference between "market" and purchasing power parity-based exchange rates.

This process of reform and stabilization is far from over in the transition economies of Central and Eastern Europe, as illustrated by data comparing prices for various consumer goods in individual countries.[2] While price and external liberalization, introduced by all countries at the outset of their reform programs, resulted in the expected broad convergence of the prices of tradable goods, substantial differences still remain in the prices of nontradable goods, in particular housing and utilities. As these prices are also adjusted over time, higher inflation rates and wage increases than in partner countries will cause real appreciation of the usual indexes of real exchange rates—without, however, implying losses of competitiveness or profitability, provided that other enterprise costs, including taxes, are reduced accordingly.

Also, over a longer period, gains in productivity (probably larger for tradables due to the central role of external liberalization in the reform process) should permit a further real appreciation without impairing the performance of the balance of payments. Judging when this should happen requires going well beyond the usual in dicators of real effective exchange rates and looking carefully, in particular, at after-tax profitability and the balance of payments.

[2]See "Cost of Living in Eastern Europe" (table), *Business Eastern Europe*, April 13, 1992, pp. 172–73.

Martin J. Fetherston

Considerable attention is being paid at the moment to the transition in Eastern Europe and the states of the former Soviet Union. Those of us working in the Asian region need to speak up from time to time and remind our colleagues that Asian transition economies also offer useful and interesting economic lessons. I would like to touch on the exchange rate experiences of four of those economies: China, Viet Nam, Laos, and Mongolia.

What exactly is the meaning of the phrase "transition economies"? This question is important because there are several dimensions to the transition issue. Each of these dimensions may apply in some countries more than in others, and considering them should help to counteract the tendency to have a particular kind of situation in mind when addressing the policy issues that arise in a transition economy. For example, Rüdiger Dornbusch emphasized the problems faced by countries that are establishing new currencies, have not had the experience of managing their own monetary policies, and therefore must start from scratch. When making that point, Mr. Dornbusch is obviously thinking of some of the former Soviet republics. But there are plenty of economies undergoing transition that do not find themselves in this same situation—that, for example, already have their own currencies.

In trying to define a transition economy, I would identify five dimensions that vary considerably from one country to another.

- The first is the severity of the initial macroeconomic imbalances the economy faces, including high inflation rates and balance of payments problems. Of the four Asian economies mentioned, initial imbalances were particularly severe in Mongolia, Viet Nam, and Laos, but considerably less so in China.

- The second dimension is the length of time that the economy has been centrally planned—or, to put it the other way around, how long it has been since the country's last experience as a market economy. And, again, in Asia, there is a range of experience: obviously, substantial parts of Viet Nam and Laos were market economies not that long ago—up until the mid-1970s, or about the same length of time as the states of the former Soviet Union.

- The third is the extent to which the economy was integrated into the Council of Mutual Economic Assistance (CMEA) trading system, because the extent of that integration determined the severity of the problems the economy faced when the CMEA trading arrangements broke down. And, once again, there is a spectrum among the four Asian economies. Mongolia was the most highly integrated into the CMEA system; Viet Nam and

Laos were considerably less so; and China was not a member of the CMEA system at all.

- The fourth dimension involves the political conditions and, more specifically, whether the country is undergoing a political as well as an economic transition. In China, there have been considerable economic reforms, but the political system has remained basically unchanged. At the other end of the spectrum, Mongolia underwent substantial political change beginning in 1990 and adopted a new Constitution incorporating a parliamentary democracy.

- The fifth and final dimension of the transition process involves the country's prospects for attracting external financial support for its transition efforts. Once again, there is a broad range of experience among these countries. China has been able to attract significant support, primarily in the form of project assistance (rather than as balance of payments financing). Mongolia had considerable success in mobilizing support from the international community, including the IMF, which has also supported policies in Laos under the structural adjustment facility. An exception is Viet Nam, which has been making its transition without external financial support.

What are the exchange rate policy issues that have come up in these four economies during their transition processes? Like Gérard Bélanger, I will emphasize eclecticism and pragmatism. Despite the strong arguments put forward by Rüdiger Dornbusch and others for some kind of rules-based arrangement, I think that in very broad terms the experience of these four Asian economies supports the desirability of having some degree of flexibility. It certainly does not indicate that a nominal anchor approach is the only one that can be a success.

Both Laos and Viet Nam had rather complicated exchange rate systems until the mid- to late 1980s, with a proliferation of official exchange rates for various purposes. Of course, this type of setup has characterized many of the centrally planned economies. Flexible, unified exchange rate systems were established in Laos in 1987 and in Viet Nam a year or two later. In both countries, the official exchange rate was adjusted frequently, based on movements in the parallel market. A key issue in choosing a flexible approach—particularly for Viet Nam—was the absence of reserves that could be used to defend a fixed rate. In addition, as Thomas Wolf just emphasized, there was great uncertainty about the level at which such a fixed rate should be set.

Some interesting contrasts have emerged between the experiences of Laos and Viet Nam since the new systems were adopted, mainly in the area of inflation. In Laos, the inflation rate was brought down to a fairly low level, and the market exchange rate over the two years or so has been stable, largely because the authorities have adopted a policy of using exchange rate developments to calibrate their financial policies. Thus, if the market exchange rate begins to show signs of depreciation, the decrease is taken as a signal that monetary policies need to be tightened. Until recently, Viet Nam's experience with inflation was less favorable, and the inflation rate—which had been reduced in 1989—jumped back to around 70 percent in 1991 before it was brought under control. The key factor in these fluctuations was that Viet Nam's monetary authorities were less successful in maintaining the tight financial policies needed to preserve a reasonable degree of stability in their exchange rate while keeping inflation low. But in terms of economic growth, in fairness it must be said that both countries—particularly Viet Nam—have enjoyed some success. Viet Nam, for example, has recently been growing at a rate close to 8 percent. A very interesting issue for further research would be the reasons why transition economies in some parts of the world—particularly Europe, the former Soviet Union, and Mongolia—have suffered very large declines in output at the start of their transition process, whereas some of the Asian economies—such as Laos, Viet Nam, and China—experienced no output declines at all and in fact have enjoyed rather rapid growth rates.

Mongolia was one country that initially established a fixed exchange rate. The rate was devalued substantially in mid-1991 but almost immediately became unrealistic because of the very low level of international reserves and lack of supporting domestic financial policies. The Mongolian authorities have recently announced that they intend to establish a floating exchange rate system in the next few months.[1]

Of these four countries, China has the exchange rate system that conforms most closely to the crawling peg approach. During the 1980s, China implemented a number of exchange rate adjustments, making some moderately large discrete adjustments at some points but also using periods of successive mini-devaluations. Since 1986, China has had a dual exchange market that differs from the kind of dual exchange market Mr. Dornbusch was describing, with different rates for current and capital account transactions. China's second market is for enterprises wanting to trade their quotas for retained foreign exchange, while other transactions—both current and capital—still take place at the official rate.[2] One important aspect of

[1]A floating rate was established on May 27, 1993.
[2]China unified its dual exchange rate system in January 1994.

the Chinese experience is that the overall results have been impressive. Chinese exports, for example, have increased sevenfold since China initiated its reforms in the late 1970s. Exchange rate policy has played a role in that, but many other factors were also involved.

One concluding observation about the role of supporting policies is in order. If there is one common thread among the diverse experiences in Asia and other transition economies, it is that even if a new exchange rate regime is put in place, it will not work in the end if it is not supported by good financial policies. These policies will always be essential.

Summary of Discussion

Most of the discussion took the form of questions to Rüdiger Dornbusch on his presentation, in particular on his recommendation that the transition economies adopt a payments system similar to the European Payments Union (EPU), which combined multilateral clearing and a credit mechanism with well-defined rules. Mr. Dornbusch indicated that the parallel between the current situation in the transition economies was strikingly similar to the situation in Western Europe after World War II, when countries attempted to engage in U.S. dollar trade at the expense of inter-European trade. He urged the transition economies to consider trade among themselves instead of focusing almost exclusively on trade with the West. And he strongly recommended a payments union that would allow the transition economies to cultivate the interregional trade that he felt ought to be taking place, not only among the very complementary republics of the former Soviet Union (FSU), but also among the East European countries. Moreover, a system similar to the EPU would force countries to settle their growing deficits with other members of the system in U.S. dollars, forcing hard currency discipline on countries that habitually run deficits. In addition to encouraging trade, such an arrangement would create a strong incentive to adjust.

On the question of whether FSU countries should set up currency boards, Mr. Dornbusch stated that although currency boards would work in principle, they would not be long lived. Because they would eventually be asked to raise the ratio of domestic currency issue to foreign exchange receipts, inflation would accelerate, and soon a multiple rate system would develop. Only if the fiscal situation was resolved and the government no longer had to print money to cover budget deficits could a currency board system work. Finally, on the issue of national currencies for each of the countries of the FSU, Mr. Dornbusch was highly skeptical about the possibility of moving to a system of convertible national monies, since an orderly transition did not seem possible.

Case Study of Czechoslovakia

Leslie J. Lipschitz

Recently, Czechoslovakia has embarked on a pegged, fixed-rate exchange rate policy. My talk concerns the choice of this regime and the results of that choice. I will start with some basic, relevant facts, touch on the fears many felt when the Czechoslovak authorities decided on a nominal exchange rate peg, and finish up with how the scenario has played out. It is a story with what looks to be a happy ending.

I. Background

In Czechoslovakia, 1990 was a year of preparing for the transition to a market economy. For exchange rate policy, preparation involved unifying a number of different rates and then devaluing the rate several times. In January, certain rates were unified and the koruna was devalued; it was devalued again (to Kčs 24 per $1) in mid-October. On December 28, the tourist rate was unified with the principal rate (at about Kčs 28 to the dollar), and the exchange rate was fixed in terms of a basket of five trading partner currencies. Three days later, 85 percent of prices were freed, and most quantitative restrictions on trade were abolished.

Why did the Government choose a peg rather than a float or crawl? Besides the obvious aspect—that a fixed rate involves less foreign exchange risk in trade—there was quite clearly a desire for a transparent nominal anchor in Czechoslovakia. The authorities accepted the idea that a liberal trade regime with a fixed exchange rate would stabilize the prices of traded goods, providing a reference point around which wages and the prices of nontraded goods would organize themselves and price expectations would cohere.

How was the rate chosen? Probably the choice was less an intellectual than a practical decision. In September, with reserves falling, the Government was considering two scenarios. One envisaged an exchange rate of Kčs 24 to the dollar, the other a rate of Kčs 28 to the dollar. Shortly thereafter, the rate was set at Kčs 24 per dollar. After a

Note: This presentation was made before the division of the Czech Republic and Slovakia and reflects arrangements made before the formal separation.

262

very short respite, the koruna weakened further in the parallel market. But reserves continued to fall (from a level that was already problematically low), so the rate was adjusted in December. The December devaluation was part of a broader package involving tight credit, a restrictive incomes policy, an austere fiscal stance, and a substantial commitment of funds from the IMF and the Group of 24 (G-24). That package was seen as substantive and credible; the exchange rate held, and it has held ever since.

II. The Risks Involved

There were four major risks involved in setting this rate: (1) getting the rate wrong; (2) finding that domestic imbalances were inconsistent with maintaining the rate; (3) putting an excessive financial squeeze on the economy; and (4) being unable to defend the rate against short-term pressures because of low reserves and, consequently, suffering a loss of credibility.

Getting the rate wrong

It is not necessary to know the long-run equilibrium rate to embark on a fixed-rate policy. With some price flexibility, there is a reasonable continuum of nominal rates that can be considered consistent with an appropriate real rate.

Conventional purchasing power parity (PPP) calculations are irrelevant here, because it takes some time for prices to reflect flow costs (rather than inventories and other past influences). Price indexes also are not terribly meaningful; internationally competitive, cheap final goods are no comfort to unemployed workers priced out of the market by an exchange rate that leaves their wage costs uncompetitive.

Also, the short-run exchange rate consistent with stabilization objectives bears no relationship not only to the PPP but to the long-run equilibrium exchange rate. This, I think, is a fundamental theoretical issue that warrants elaboration. If the long-run (equilibrium) real exchange rate is known with certainty, should an immediate move to this rate be proposed? The answer, obviously, is no. In all the transition economies, there is a huge stock of capital, a whole industrial structure, that has been accumulated under arbitrary relative prices. Knowing that comparative advantage is different from what exists and moving immediately to a new real exchange rate that would be in line with comparative advantage in five years' time would almost certainly render a large proportion of the existing capital stock and the industrial structure obsolete. The objective of stabilization policy has to be a more gradual structural change.

Thus, in East Germany, where real exchange rates were set to be consistent with a rapid move toward a West German capital structure, it has been necessary effectively to write off much of the starting capital stock and related jobs. This situation is not ideal. The transitional exchange rate cannot be impervious to its influence in the labor market. Rather, what policymakers should aim at is a set of relative prices that put the most egregiously uneconomic enterprises (or branches of enterprises) out of business and encourage new businesses without obliterating much of the industrial base.

In Czechoslovakia, the real exchange rate has been consistent with a relatively gradual transformation. Large enterprises are closing down their weakest operations and shedding labor, while new, small private enterprises are springing up, encouraged by a good competitive position. Vacancies and new private sector jobs, at least in the Czech lands,[1] have kept pace with the elimination of old positions.

If the initial devaluation had been excessive, wage settlements in the ensuing year would probably have strained the limits set by incomes policy; in fact, as wages easily stayed below these limits, the prima facie evidence does not appear to support the idea that the devaluation was too large. Of course, real wage increases can be expected over time, consistent with a changing and more productive capital stock. And an endogenous and equilibrating real appreciation over time to an exchange rate more in line with the long-term structure of the economy would not be at all problematic and should not be resisted.

Maintaining the rate

Obviously, a large budget deficit, especially if financed by money creation, can undermine a peg. In the case of Czechoslovakia, however, conditions were propitious. There were no large initial imbalances, and both domestic and foreign debt levels were low. The Government, moreover, was committed to a budget that was close to balance. (In fact the deficit amounted to 2 percent of GDP, excluding proceeds from privatization; including these proceeds, it was balanced.)

"Squeezing" the economy

There was real concern that the combination of a fixed exchange rate and inflation inertia would put too much pressure on the

---

[1] The Czech Republic of the Czech and Slovak Federal Republic before separation.

economy. Inflation during 1990 had been 18½ percent, and the devaluations of late 1990 would feed into 1991 prices. The simultaneous terms of trade losses would also raise prices. In addition, there was also some fear that, with price liberalization, monopolistic enterprises would raise their prices sharply (and perhaps repeatedly) to increase profit margins.

Three aspects of policy were seen as guarding against continued high inflation. First, relatively tight credit policies were set. Second, the opening up of trade was seen as curtailing monopoly power. Third, a strict tax-based incomes policy was put in place; it envisaged a fall of some 10 percent in real wages from the end-1990 level.

Keeping up reserves

The danger that reserves would be insufficient to sustain the exchange rate and that a forced devaluation would undermine the credibility of the whole program was of particular concern to then Finance Minister Vaclav Klaus. Reserves were indeed low—below $1 billion, or equivalent to only three weeks of imports. IMF and G-24 financing was seen as a way to alleviate this problem. The IMF provided about $1.5 billion under its stand-by arrangement and compensatory and contingency financing facility; the G-24 pledged an additional $1 billion. The plan was to build reserves to some $2.5 billion by the end of 1991.

III. The Strategy's Success

The strategy was successful in terms of its objectives. Prices jumped by 50 percent in the first half of 1991 and then stabilized.[2] There was no inflation in the third quarter and very little in the fourth. There is evidence that some large enterprises raised their

[2]Enterprises used to a monopolistic structure quickly learned to respect the constraints of the marketplace, especially in terms of tradables. The first thing that happens when trade is opened is that new price relativities are established. A bicycle produced in Germany, for example, will be made of lightweight aluminum and titanium, with many high-tech features. The equilibrium relative price with a Czechoslovak bicycle may be 2:1, but it might take some time to establish this relative price in the marketplace. Very few German bicycles will be imported at double the price of a local one at current Czechoslovak salaries. But it is quite likely that local producers will raise prices closer to German levels for a time. They will probably not be able to sell much at that price—people prefer to save longer for the German product or just to withhold consumption. In Czechoslovakia, this is what happened: people postponed consumption of those kinds of durables, inventories built up, and prices fell back to something closer to a sustainable level.

prices disproportionately in the first few months of the year, perhaps basing their behavior on the monopolistic price determination and automatic credit of the old system. But owing to nonaccommodating macroeconomic policies, these prices produced a buildup in inventories of finished goods that was difficult to finance. Prices therefore had to be lowered quickly. The balance of payments proved stronger than projected, and by the end of 1991 reserves had risen to $3.3 billion.

Real GDP dropped, but the reduction was unavoidable, given the huge terms of trade loss and the demise of the Council for Mutual Economic Assistance (CMEA) market. Output bottomed out at the turn of the year. There is likely to be some real overall growth in 1992, although the uncertain political circumstances related to the dissolution of the country may well influence the outcome. There is a burgeoning private sector made up mainly of small companies, especially in the Czech lands. At present, both unemployment and job vacancies in the Czech lands stand at 2.5 percent. Inflation in 1992 should be about 10 percent, and the current account will probably show a surplus of about $500 million.

The future is somewhat obscured by the division of the Czech Republic and Slovakia, which is scheduled for January 1, 1993. In the Czech lands, there is no question about the course of exchange rate policy. I would expect a gradual real appreciation as wage increases are facilitated by a shift in the structure of industry. The appreciation will, of course, hasten the demise of the old industries. In Slovakia, the whole macroeconomic strategy is being reconsidered. Most likely, there will not be a fundamental shift in strategy there, but it is too early to say exactly how the authorities will use the various instruments under their control.

Comment

Jiří Pospíšil

Czechoslovakia's economy has successfully undergone the first phase of the transformation to a market economy with a stable exchange rate. The country's external position has improved and is now broadly in equilibrium. The 1991 current account ended in a surplus of $360 million—much better than anticipated—and 1992 is also likely to close with a surplus. Despite the breakup of the Council for Mutual Economic Assistance (CMEA) and an overall decline in foreign trade in 1991, Czechoslovak firms have proved to be very flexible, and exports to convertible currency markets have continued to expand in 1992. A significant decline in imports in 1991 contributed to an acceptable trade balance deficit of $450 million, although the deficit worsened in 1992.

These results were facilitated by several devaluations of the koruna in 1990, which totaled more than 100 percent and allowed the economy to begin benefiting from a stable exchange rate. The last of these devaluations, carried out shortly before the liberalization of most domestic prices on January 1, 1991, contributed to a significant jump in prices that was quickly arrested by strict monetary and fiscal policies. By midyear, monthly inflation was less than 1 percent. The money supply declined overall in real terms in 1991, and the state budget recorded an acceptable deficit of 1.8 percent of GDP at year's end.

As prices stabilized, costs as a share of wages fell because real average wages declined markedly in 1991. GDP showed a sharp drop of 16 percent for 1991, but only a small part of this decline may have been caused by the exchange rate devaluation; most of it was due to the breakup of Czechoslovakia's traditional export market, the CMEA. The decline in GDP has slowed, and a recovery could begin in 1993.

Czechoslovakia's experience shows that a single strong devaluation, followed by medium-term exchange rate stabilization, can be successful. But our experience raises a question: for which economies and situations is our technique suitable? Rüdiger Dornbusch pointed out that Czechoslovakia was the only country among the successor states of Austria-Hungary that was able to avoid hyperinflation after World War I—something it accomplished with a very restrictive monetary and fiscal policy. The tradition of price stability continued in the following years, so that there has always been a tendency in

Czechoslovakia to favor external and internal stability and a readiness to make sacrifices to this end.

Because of this tradition, Czechoslovakia was in a better position than most other countries to launch economic reform in 1991, in part because our external and internal debts were relatively small. External debt in convertible currencies stood at $9.4 billion and the Government's domestic debt at 5.2 percent of GDP in 1991 (domestic debt now stands at 9 percent). A tradition of price stability, a smaller financial burden, a less severe dislocation of capital, and internal political stabilization have worked together in Czechoslovakia to support exchange rate stability. The massive initial devaluation and strict monetary and fiscal policy, supplemented by wage regulation, were the immediate means to this end. Now, we are able to see some benefits—although, since we have had only two years of experience with economic reform, it can be argued that a positive assessment is somewhat premature.

On another topic, Mr. Dornbusch suggested in his talk that the former CMEA countries might want to imitate the system of payments used in Western Europe after World War II. I agree with Gérard Bélanger that substantial differences exist between the present situation in Central Europe and that of postwar Western Europe. While the West European payments model would be very attractive to us, I am not sure that it would be effective. To date, our trade with a number of countries, particularly in the former Soviet Union, has led to growth in nonusable assets, even with the system of government clearing that was in place in 1991. To some extent, then, the resources that we paid for in convertible currencies have been transferred to the former Soviet Union. The current system of trade means not only a loss of resources, but also support for the old structure of production, which is not a viable one in the long run.

Why not provide direct assistance to the states of the former Soviet Union, supporting the development of trade among former CMEA countries? In fact, some banks in the region are already making efforts to establish a small clearing system based on new principles that could (at least in part) help renew mutually advantageous trade. However, returning to a government-led clearing system would be very difficult. Czechoslovakia, a small, open economy, is ready to trade with any business partner able to pay. Recent developments point to the potential for expanding Czechoslovakia's trade, first with industrial countries and then with some developing economies.

Despite significant success in containing inflation, our consumer price index increased by about 56 percent in 1991, and a 12 percent increase is anticipated in 1992. Reform of the tax system means that relatively high inflation is expected again in 1993. Accordingly, the koruna has appreciated substantially in real effective terms since

1990, and the issue of Czechoslovakia's export competitiveness is coming to the fore.

While some firms may see profits from exports decline in 1992 compared with 1991, exports are still more profitable overall than domestic sales.

Wage costs are now growing in real terms, but this growth is not likely to offset the wage decrease recorded in 1991. The 1991 devaluation stimulated exports of products with low value added and of commodities that trading partners view as "sensitive." A further attempt to stimulate exports by devaluing would only exacerbate the problem of protectionism all economies undergoing transformation currently face.

In any case, a devaluation does not seem to be necessary, since the adjustment of the pattern of production and trade to the 1991 devaluation is still far from complete. In addition, there is room for cuts in production costs, as illustrated by the low overall rate of unemployment in Czechoslovakia.

An expected increase in imports of investment goods will likely lead to a slight deficit in the trade balance, but this kind of disequilibrium means rapid export growth in the near future. In any event, it seems that a growing surplus in the services account (i.e., transport and tourism) will finance most of the trade deficit and that the remainder will be more than sufficiently covered by direct inflows of foreign investment, so that some increase in reserves can be expected. This optimistic view has been tempered somewhat in the second half of 1992 by expanding imports and signs of capital flight, which are causing a decline in foreign exchange reserves. Unfavorable expectations have arisen because of the imminent division of Czechoslovakia into two independent states and the upcoming tax reform (including the implementation of a value-added tax). However, when this difficult period ends, we will have good prospects for maintaining our stable nominal exchange rate and benefiting from the advantages it provides.

Case Study of Poland (1990–91)

Liam Ebrill

In some important respects, Poland's experience differed from Czechoslovakia's; nonetheless, there were a number of common elements.

I. Reforms before 1990

It is important to remember that Poland had made several attempts at reforming its economy before 1990. In fact, as far back as 1957, there had been attempts to introduce some reforms into the Polish economy. (One of the most famous postwar economists, Oscar Lange, was a Pole celebrated for showing that, in principle, it was possible to find a set of prices within a planned economy that would function like the price system in a competitive market environment.) These early reform efforts, however, were if anything counterproductive and in part explain why Poland faced some particularly serious problems in the years leading up to 1990.

The aim of the reforms—particularly in the 1980s, when things started to go wrong—was to give enterprises greater autonomy. Because it was believed that decentralizing decision making would enable them to react more flexibly to economic changes, enterprises were allowed a certain degree of independence in their own management and finances. But the attitude toward the degree of decentralization that should take place was ambiguous: the authorities really saw the market as facilitating a more efficient realization of the planners' dreams and did not intend to unleash unchecked free-market forces. As the authorities decentralized, giving enterprises a greater degree of autonomy, one of the side effects was a weakening of existing control mechanisms, because it was no longer possible to order state enterprises to do whatever the Government wished. In other words, corporate governance started to break down.

It is important to emphasize that the enterprises were not being irrational in the way they behaved but were operating according to the rules then in force. They were not facing appropriate market incentives—specifically, no one was looking after the interests of capital, and the Workers' Councils were exercising considerable influence.

The year leading up to the "big bang," 1989, was a year of economic crisis in Poland. The authorities lost control of the budget and banking system, and the balance of payments started to deteriorate dramatically. The authorities continued to take steps toward reform. Private citizens were granted access to the parallel foreign exchange market, and as a result, the "black" market became in essence a "white" market. One of the side effects of this development was a gradually accelerating shift out of zlotys into dollar-denominated assets—hardly surprising in the circumstances. In April 1989, as a result of round-table talks between Solidarity and the Government, formal wage indexation was introduced. By August, real wages were up 73 percent from their January level. In August 1989, food prices were liberalized, and the impact was immediate: the monthly inflation rate climbed to 39 percent.

At this point, the Government was having increasing difficulty controlling the fiscal deficit. State enterprises faced soft budget constraints, to which powerful labor interests reacted by increasing wage demands. Against the background of these developments, the ratio of the parallel to the official exchange rate rose in August to 7.4, a very large difference. In late August, the Government took additional steps, introducing a measure of fiscal restraint in an attempt to regain control of the budget. The indexation coefficient on wages was cut in order to break the wage-inflation cycle, and measures were introduced to tighten credit. While inflation remained high, the measures had some beneficial impact: even before the reform program came into effect on January 1, 1990, the ratio of the parallel to the official exchange rate had declined significantly, so that the flight out of zloty-denominated deposits into dollar-denominated deposits slowed. Real wages were adjusted down because of the change in the indexation formulae, but they rose again in December. It was clear something further had to be done.

II. The 1990 Reforms

It is important to evaluate the 1990 reforms as a package—that is, as a broad range of measures covering a variety of issues—and not to focus solely on the exchange rate. An exchange rate rule on its own would not have achieved much; what had to be addressed were the underlying macroeconomic imbalances and structural flaws in the system. The 1990 program had that objective. It was meant to curtail sharply the fiscal deficit and, by introducing a tax-based incomes policy, to control the behavior of wages. The issue of corporate governance was addressed by initiatives concerning ownership transformation. Of these initiatives, mass privatization received the greatest public attention, but it must be emphasized (particularly since mass privatization has yet to occur in Poland) that many Polish enterprises followed more individual routes to privatization—and that these enterprises have been responsible for many of the changes since 1990.

When the 1990 program came into effect, it had immediate effects. What happened in that first year? Instead of the planned fiscal deficit of about zero in 1990, Poland ended up with a fiscal surplus equivalent to 4 percent of GDP. This fiscal adjustment was far greater than anticipated. Moreover, the balance of payments in 1990 was far stronger than anyone had expected: net international reserves increased by about $4.4 billion. Real wages plunged initially, because the tax-based incomes policy allowed for a predetermined increase in nominal wages in January and February, based on an inflation projection that turned out to be a serious underestimate. Accordingly, the wage increases that were granted in no way compensated for the large burst of inflation, which reached 78.6 percent in January alone. The change in the price level occurred primarily in the first two weeks of January and took many people by surprise.

The strength of the balance of payments, the surprising fiscal surplus, and the decline in real wages were, of course, interrelated. Maintaining a fixed exchange rate and damping down demand relative to supply—even if output is falling—is likely to result in a strong balance of payments. One of the reasons for the fiscal surplus that has continued to cause trouble was the enormous increase in the nominal value of inventories, which were taxed for the first time in 1990. As a result, revenue from the enterprise sector showed a large transitory increase that did not reflect real values. Rather, it reflected the impact of inflation and contributed to the long-term weakening of the enterprises's balance sheets. One of Poland's problems even now is that the economy is doing well in many areas, but the tax system continues to rely to a significant degree on the shrinking financial base of the state enterprise system. It has been very difficult to effectively extend the tax base, although important steps have been taken, including approval of legislation mandating a value-added tax (VAT).

On the other hand, there has been added pressure on expenditures, albeit for very legitimate reasons—to support the social safety net, for example, because unemployment has increased rapidly. The result has been something like a dual economy, in that the public sector is struggling to make ends meet as it adjusts (although it is adjusting rapidly) and the private sector is growing rapidly but managing to escape most of the tax net. In Poland's economy, an estimated 58 percent of total employment is now in the private sector—a remarkable transformation, despite the fact that agriculture, which was always considered to be in the private sector, employed a large proportion of the population. Even in the industrial sector, where state enterprises were once pre-eminent, close to 30 percent of enterprises are now considered to be private.

As is well known, there was a sharp decline in output in 1990 and another drop in 1991, when Poland felt the impact of the breakup of the Council for Mutual Economic Assistance (CMEA). But since about November 1991, output has begun to turn around, and the Polish economy has had a fairly positive growth rate for a number of months—one of the best pieces of news from any of the Central European economies. In year-on-year terms, Poland is now looking at positive growth rates.

III. The Exchange Rate

Even before pegging occurred on January 1, 1990, the authorities had already started devaluing the official rate. Nonetheless, the January zloty rate of 9,500 per dollar represented a large devaluation. Some felt the rate was overly depreciated, but others argued for a strong initial devaluation. The comments Leslie Lipschitz was making earlier apply here, too: there certainly was the sense that if the authorities didn't go far enough, there would be trouble. If the authorities had introduced the peg—which was intended to be a cornerstone of the new program—without devaluing sufficiently and had run into balance of payments problems shortly afterward, the credibility of both the peg and the program would have been seriously damaged. It was important to give the peg a chance to work, and it would do no harm to give the export industries an initial stimulus to get them going, considering the changes to which the economy was being subjected.

Prices did increase sharply in January 1990, and discussion continues on what might have been the cause. One explanation that has been suggested in the context of other transforming economies is that a monetary overhang existed at the outset. According to this argument, such overhangs existed because of repressed inflation under the former centrally planned regimes, with individuals accumulating large liquid balances in the absence of anything to spend money on. In Poland's case, this theory may not hold, for two reasons. First, Poland had significant inflation before January 1, 1990, so that any large monetary overhang would have been reduced in value in the months leading up to that date. Second, "dollarization" had occurred before 1990—that is, money was moving out of zlotys into dollar-denominated assets. Accordingly, to the extent that there was an overhang, it may not have been in zloty-denominated assets. Although people could not purchase all the goods and services they wanted in the marketplace, dollar-denominated assets provided an alternative outlet that was used quite extensively.

Now, with liberalization, people with money to spend have tended to switch from dollar-denominated assets into goods. In fact there is some evidence to suggest that this shift occurred in Poland in 1990, strengthening the zloty. In the first three months of 1990, deposits denominated in foreign currency began declining again. This behavior is a fairly accurate bellwether of the sort of confidence the population at large had in the program the Polish Government was implementing. In fact, the steady drift out of dollar-denominated assets into zloty-denominated assets has continued to this day, so that the Polish economy is now really a zloty economy.

There may be no totally adequate explanation for the burst of inflation at the beginning of 1990. Probably it was spurred in part by money coming back into the country from dollar-denominated assets, and in part by the initial overdevaluation of the exchange rate. As for the fixed exchange rate itself, the choice was relatively clear. The earlier discussion concerned Czechoslovakia's potential to break inflationary expectations—something that was, if anything, a higher priority in Poland. The view was that a fixed exchange rate would help achieve this and, in the absence of better ways to implement corporate governance, would also discipline state enterprises. And the exchange rate was not the only nominal anchor in the system: the wage policy, carried out through tax-based incomes policy, served the same function. This second anchor worked, by some accounts, extremely well at the outset of the program, as real wages declined. In fact, it worked too well, and a correction took place in the middle of 1990 to compensate for the unexpected plunge in real wages earlier in the year.

The basic rationale for the fixed exchange rate has not changed. Initially, the fixed rate was expected to last about three months, but it survived from January 1, 1990 until May 1991. By May 1991, the real effective exchange rate had more or less converged with the real effective rate that had existed prior to the January 1990 program. Subsequently, the zloty was devalued twice. A preannounced crawling peg of about 1.8 percent per month has replaced the fixed exchange rate (this crawl is also fixed, with one time derivative). For many months in 1990, inflation remained high, averaging about 5 percent per month. It has been coming down since but has proved to be relatively obstinate, so the tactic that has been selected to combat it is the crawling peg. Presumably the rate of crawl will be adjusted in the future as the anti-inflation program improves, and eventually the economy will tend toward a fixed exchange rate. But the crawling peg still acts as an anchor for the system. Some may claim that it provides a floor for inflation, but at least it encourages some inflationary discipline.

Comment

Krzysztof Barburski

The task for monetary and exchange rate policy in Poland's stabilization program was to create a stable monetary environment for decision making and to reduce deep-seated inflationary expectations. Meeting these objectives was not easy. In 1988 and 1989, the zloty began falling into disuse as foreign currency became the favored means of transaction and people sought to hold their wealth in either goods or foreign exchange. By the end of 1989, the inflation rate had soared to 260 percent. After several years of high and accelerating inflation, inflationary expectations were deeply ingrained, and the credibility of both official institutions and government commitments was low.

Under these circumstances, the authorities decided that the short-term goal for monetary policy would be to establish convertibility for the zloty at a fixed nominal exchange rate in order to anchor price expectations. Compensation for phasing out the remaining indirect and direct measures for export promotion and the margin necessary to maintain export competitiveness were the basic considerations in determining the new rate. On January 1, 1990, the official and parallel exchange rates were unified and the new rate fixed at Zl 9,500 per dollar (at the end of 1989, it had been Zl 6,500). Inflation remained high in the first quarter of 1990.

The fixed exchange rate was regarded as a significant factor in Poland's macroeconomic stabilization. Initially, it was decided to fix the zloty against the dollar on a weekly basis according to movements in cross rates, allowing for fluctuations against other currencies (the exchange rate has been determined daily since the beginning of 1991). The peg against the dollar was considered the best way to discount the psychological effects of the stable exchange rate, since about 50 percent of Polish exports and imports in convertible currencies were denominated in dollars. The U.S. currency was also the one most commonly used in convertible currency settlements between individuals.

The Government originally intended to maintain the stable exchange rate only during the early months of 1990, but actual market pressure on the zloty was substantially weaker than had been feared. The $1 billion Polish stabilization fund that Western countries—notably the United States and Germany—had established to support convertibility was not needed, but it did allow for the possibility of

275

stabilizing the center rate within a narrow band of the official rate, and official reserves grew throughout 1990. Under these conditions, it was possible to keep the zloty fixed much longer than had been planned—17 months, in fact. The initial exchange rate, which appeared to be undervalued, helped to soften the effects on enterprises of the decreased domestic demand that resulted from the stabilization measures. The foreign exchange reserves accumulated in 1990 (gross official reserves increased by $2.4 billion) helped to absorb the shock of the collapse of the Council for Mutual Economic Assistance (CMEA) and the transition to convertible currency settlements among the former members. The pressure on foreign exchange reserves associated with the real appreciation of the zloty became visible in the last quarter of 1990, increasing in the first months of 1991 as convertible currency settlements became more common among the former CMEA countries and the U.S. dollar appreciated.

On May 17, 1991, the zloty was devalued to Zl 11,199 per dollar. In order to prevent the fluctuation characteristic of currencies pegged to a single currency when international foreign exchange markets are unstable, it was decided to return to the pre-1990 policy of setting the value of the zloty against a weighted basket of currencies. The five currencies used most widely in Polish foreign trade are represented in this basket: the dollar (45 percent), the deutsche mark (35 percent), the pound sterling (10 percent), the French franc (5 percent), and the Swiss franc (5 percent).

The inflation differentials among Poland and its main trading partners, which were still significant in 1991–92, weakened the competitiveness of Polish products. These differentials were the main reason for the change of exchange rate regime that took place on October 14, 1991, when the weighted basket was introduced and the crawling peg adopted. The value of the basket was increased by 9 zlotys per business day, or the equivalent of a monthly depreciation of around 1.8 percent. Because this pace of devaluation did not compensate for the growth in domestic prices, the exchange rate still functioned as an instrument of stabilization.

A higher-than-expected real appreciation of the zloty between October 1991 and February 1992 resulted in a drop in the competitiveness of Polish goods, both at home and abroad, causing foreign exchange reserves to fall. Against this background, a step devaluation was made on February 26, 1992, amounting to 12 percent against the basket. Since then, the "crawling" devaluation has continued at the monthly rate of about 1.8 percent (now 12 zlotys per day).[1]

---

[1]On August 27, 1993, the authorities devalued the zloty by 8 percent against the basket (7.4 percent in foreign currency terms) and reduced the rate of crawl from 1.8 percent to 1.6 percent per month.

The growth in exports in 1992 was in part the result of a more active exchange rate policy. In the first six months of 1992, Poland accumulated a trade surplus of $946 million. Foreign exchange reserves reached $4.1 billion at the end of June, covering more than four months of average monthly imports, and reserves increased further in the summer months. In addition, the inflation rate did not exceed the expected level.

Polish residents must channel foreign transactions of more than the equivalent of $10,000 through licensed foreign exchange banks. All export proceeds in foreign exchange must be immediately surrendered to these banks in exchange for zlotys. Initially, when the so-called internal convertibility of the zloty was introduced, foreign exchange banks had to resell foreign exchange to the National Bank of Poland (NBP), which manages external reserves. The NBP provided the necessary foreign currency for the settlement of liabilities due foreigners for all imports, property rights, and attendant services, as well as other services and capital transactions under general or individual permits.

The Foreign Exchange Act of February 15, 1989, which introduced the internal convertibility of the zloty on January 1, 1990, directly involved the NBP in this system of obligatory purchases and sales of foreign exchange. In order to improve the efficiency of interbank settlements in foreign currencies (as defined by the President of the NBP), foreign exchange banks have been authorized since May 1992 to effect within one business day bilateral transactions (including cash transactions) of amounts derived from obligatory resales of foreign currencies by domestic enterprises. Such transactions are conditional, however; the NBP sets limits on how much foreign exchange these banks can hold, and at the end of each business day the banks must sell everything above those limits back to the NBP. Banks that are allowed to handle foreign exchange for domestic and foreign entities may also conclude domestic transactions in foreign currencies among themselves, using resources available from other of their activities—for instance, the foreign currency accounts of individuals and other banks, and banks' foreign exchange deposits.

Foreign exchange banks have also been given the right to establish the exchange rate they use, except in transactions with the NBP, within a range of ± 2 percent of the average daily rate set by the NBP. Resident native persons may make transactions freely on the parallel foreign exchange market. In 1991–92, the parallel exchange rate did not differ significantly from the NBP's average rate (in 1992, the differences were usually not more than ± 1 percent).

In the near future, the NBP plans to work out new rules that will authorize foreign exchange banks to establish foreign exchange open position limits. These limits should, on the one hand, reduce the level of exchange rate risk and, on the other, accelerate the operations of the interbank foreign exchange market. According to the NBP's scheme, foreign exchange banks will be obligated to report whether their foreign exchange positions are short or long and to offset positions that exceed the limits on the interbank foreign exchange market. The limits should not be more than 15 percent of the banks' own funds.

Summary of Discussion

Participants discussed the exchange rate component of Czechoslovakia's 1990 economic program. In particular, there were questions as to why a country with such a low level of reserves would adopt a fixed exchange rate system. The point was made that while the exchange rate was the most worrisome element of the program, the Czechoslovak authorities had believed the overall package would be strong and credible enough to deflect speculative runs on the currency, particularly in the event of an unforeseen shock. Moreover, the country's reserves nearly doubled as soon as the agreement with the IMF was signed, as IMF and other resources quickly became available. In the end, the current account balance was much better than expected.

Although Poland's official exchange rate was pegged at a somewhat less depreciated level than the parallel market rate, the new rate was low enough to represent a clear break with the previous policy of incremental devaluations (around six in a few months). While an initial burst of inflation just after the new devaluation of the zloty caused a sharp decline in real wages, labor was relatively restrained in view of the rising unemployment rate and a 12 percent decline in output for 1990. In the first few months of Poland's program, labor adopted a wait-and-see attitude, despite the growing economic insecurity. Interest rates increased dramatically under the program, moving from negative to positive in real terms.

Finally, participants were in broad agreement that the success of the Polish and Czechoslovak programs was attributable largely to the comprehensive package of reforms undertaken by both governments. But to some extent, these successes masked other urgent needs, especially for banking system reforms and accelerated privatization.

PART V

Round Table: Key Issues in Policy Today

Remarks

C. Fred Bergsten

My remarks, which will reflect the perspective of the global monetary system, will focus primarily on the industrial countries and the exchange rate relationships among them. As Anthony Lanyi said, those relationships are absolutely crucial for developing countries—in fact, they may be more important for developing than for industrial countries. Industrial and developing countries are obviously linked through monetary stability itself, but to me, the most critical link is through trade.

All of you, I am sure, would take the view that open world markets—particularly open markets in the industrial countries—are extremely important to the development of poorer countries—and indeed, to the development and growth of virtually all countries. To my mind, maintaining equilibrium exchange rates, or exchange rates that sustain more or less balanced current account positions among the major industrial countries, is absolutely essential to maintaining open trade markets. What, for example, has been the single most important determinant of American trade policy, particularly in the postwar period? The answer is not the unemployment rate or the growth rate—in fact, it is none of the domestic economic variables.

It is the exchange rate. When the dollar exchange rate has been substantially overvalued, as it was toward the end of the Bretton Woods period in the late 1960s and during the first half of the 1980s under fully flexible exchange rates, American trade policy has been at its most protectionist. The first Reagan Administration—to take the latest case in point—talked a free-trade, open-market game. Yet the Reagan Administration, according to its own Secretary of the Treasury, Jim Baker, applied more import controls than any American administration in the twentieth century. The reason was that the Administration's policy mix, which produced the hugely overvalued dollar, combined with the absence of any domestic or international monetary arrangements to constrain the overvalued dollar, pushed the United States, despite the best of intentions to the contrary, to put import quotas on autos, steel, textiles, machine tools—a whole list of products.

When the exchange rate gets too far out of line, political pressures become overwhelming. Even the most competitive industries are unable to compete; they lose market share and join others seeking protection. In such a situation, no administration can resist protectionist trends, not even Ronald Reagan's. And that, I think, is why it is so important for all countries—including developing countries, and certainly including the newly emerging market economies—that we have a global monetary regime that maintains some semblance of equilibrium.

How has the world addressed this problem? During the postwar period, there have been two broad systemic attempts to address the issue of exchange rate equilibrium. One was the effort to maintain rigidly fixed exchange rates—first, during the Bretton Woods period, on a global scale under the original IMF Articles of Agreement, and then, after 1987, through the European Monetary System (EMS). (Only during the last five years has the EMS tried to avoid currency realignments with a system of fixed exchange rates.) Both these systems failed because they were too rigid and did not provide an exchange rate tool that permitted flexibility in the adjustment process. I would never suggest that the exchange rate tool should be the centerpiece of the adjustment process, but without it, the record shows that adjustment fails and that trade protection, economic imbalances, distorted investment patterns, and the like all come into play.

Likewise, there was a long experiment with unmanaged flexibility of exchange rates between roughly 1973 and 1985—with purity from 1981 to 1985—and it, too, failed miserably. Exchange rates, which were determined solely by market forces, responded to "bandwagon" psychology in the markets (including interest rate differentials that may or may not have had much to do with underlying economic relationships). In such circumstances, exchange rates can be driven far out of line. In the first half of the 1980s, for instance, the dollar became so overvalued that U.S. trade policy was driven into protectionism, placing serious strains on the entire monetary and trade system until the trend was arrested in the mid-1980s. Likewise, the earlier period of floating rates—which were not quite so purely maintained, as some sporadic attempts at management were made in 1975–76 and again in 1978–79—resulted in significant disequilibria: yen and deutsche mark undervaluation, dollar and sterling overvaluation, and a consistent pattern of repeated currency misalignments that led to economic problems.

Note that I use the word "misalignments" rather than "volatility." I have very little concern about volatility causing real economic problems. The issue is *misalignments*, which occur when rates are persistently out of kilter with the underlying economic relationships among nations. Zero current account balances may not be the only acceptable positions, however. It is possible to make a clear case for some countries to run modest structural surpluses and for others to run modest structural deficits, at least for some time. Current account balances must meet certain tests. For purposes of my analysis, purchasing power parity (PPP) is totally irrelevant. A PPP exchange rate between the yen and the dollar, for example, would probably be somewhere between Y 180–200 to the dollar, compared with the November 1992 rate of about Y 120 per dollar. With such a rate, the Japanese current account surplus would probably hit $300–400 billion a year, and the world economic system would collapse because other countries simply would not accept such a rate. So PPP rates, while valuable for many analytical purposes, such as comparing real incomes across countries, in my view have nothing to do with exchange rates in the real world. In that world—our world—as I have said, market rates should maintain some rough equilibrium among the competitive positions of countries, using as approximate measures current account balances, but also taking into account internal balances or the absence of them.

If the fixed rate system breaks down because it is too rigid, and the freely flexible rate system results in massive misalignments, what is left? The conclusion I reach is that we need to find some synthesis of the two extremes, extracting the best features of both fixed and flexible rate systems and avoiding the worst. When the Bretton Woods system collapsed in the late 1960s and early 1970s, there was extensive discussion about the possibility of this kind of intermediate system. In those days, it was talked about in terms of wider bands around parities, crawling pegs—which of course would mean modest variations in central parities—or some combination of the two, such as widening the band around parities and letting the parities slide, glide, or crawl. Those systems were actively considered but rejected in the face of subsequent events: first, the oil shocks, then the failure of the Committee of Twenty to work out systemic reform in an explicit way. And so the world went to unmanaged flexibility.

Another variant that has been tried is a truly adjustable peg system, which keeps exchange rates fixed but allows them to be adjusted from time to time. This type of peg was used to some extent in the earlier stages of the Bretton Woods system and in fact kept the system afloat for at least the first decade or so. But then, as large imbalances began to develop toward the end of the 1960s, the rigidity that I mentioned before set in, and the system did not contribute to the adjustment process.

Likewise, the EMS had an adjustable peg system during its first seven or eight years. There were frequent parity realignments within the EMS—on average, at least one a year—between 1979 and 1987, and they clearly worked. The EMS countries were extremely good at anticipating the onset of disequilibria, adjusting their parities frequently and by small amounts. These changes did not reward speculators, because most of the alterations remained within the margins of the existing bands, and the step gains of the recent EMS crisis (which are still going on) were not a factor. This adjustable peg variant of a fixed rate system continued to work until the EMS countries got ahead of themselves. In 1987 they rejected the notion of adjusting the pegs and tried to fix the rates permanently. In my judgment, they made the move toward economic and monetary union too quickly, before underlying policies and conformity of economic performance would permit. In the end, the system fell apart, resulting in the enormous number of floats, unregulated parity changes, and the like that have taken place since September 1992. The lesson is that some limited, intermediate variable—an adjustable peg—does in fact work.

A third method of approaching the issue of intermediate exchange rate options involves limited flexibility. Earlier, I mentioned wider bands, crawling pegs, or some combination of the two. This sort of system is what my colleague John Williamson and I came up with at the Institute for International Economics about ten years ago: a system of target zones, with rates maintained within fairly wide real exchange rate ranges (not nominal ranges). The ranges would change with inflation differentials, but in addition, they would need to be changed from time to time in response to real shocks and differences in underlying competitive positions.

Interestingly, the world seemed to be moving toward such a system in the mid-1980s. When the Group of Five finance ministers launched the famous Plaza Agreement to bring down the dollar in September 1985, they changed the system. They prefaced their intervention policy with the observation that the effort to maintain equilibrium exchange rates without government intervention had failed. They had thought everything would converge, but when convergence did not take place, they elected to involve themselves in the active management of the exchange rate system.

Although their first action was the effort to bring down the dollar, the change was systemic. A second and more important systemic change occurred with the Louvre Accord in early 1987, when the Group of Seven industrial countries (there were actually six at the time) adopted so-called reference ranges around the currencies in a weaker version of the target zones that Mr. Williamson and I had developed earlier. Unfortunately, from a systemic standpoint, those reference ranges were adopted prematurely—before the currency adjustments had gone far enough in repairing the huge disequilibria that had existed prior to 1985, and so the ranges could not hold. The yen-dollar range had to be re-based within a few months, and there were crises in the fall of 1987 that led up to Black Monday. But the Louvre Accord was evidence of the desire of the industrial countries' monetary authorities to find an intermediate alternative to total flexibility without going back to completely fixed rates.

One other important development emerged from the 1986 summit of the Group of Seven countries: the adoption of the so-called Tokyo indicators. This series of indicators was intended to guide the coordination of the adjustment process, and it laid the foundation for what occurred a few months later—the decision to limit exchange rate flexibility. In practice, however, the Tokyo indicators may never have meant much, and they were not widely used. There was very little linkage between the indicators on the real side and the reference ranges on the monetary side; finally, the whole experiment collapsed before it had really been tried.

Yet some remnants of that "reference range" thinking of five years ago remain, and in fact the current exchange rate levels are not too far from the levels of five years ago, when the Louvre Accord was modified (roughly the end of 1987). Many people, including outgoing U.S. Undersecretary of the Treasury David Mulford, assert that the reference ranges not only worked but are still in place. This claim is probably too ambitious, because there have been enormous oscillations since then, as well as continued disequilibria of exchange rates. Nevertheless, an effort was made to find a synthesis between the excessive rigidity of fixed rates and the excessive movements and misalignments of freely flexible rates. This "third way," to use the currently popular political jargon, would draw on the best of both.

Where do we go from here? With the breakdown of the EMS, I think the officials of the Group of Five and Group of Seven countries will be very cautious about trying to move to any new regime soon. On the other hand, it is clear that significant problems remain—for example, the imbalance of the yen. According to my analysis, which of course is based on the need for some kind of current account equilibrium, the yen in 1992 was undervalued in real terms by at least 20–25 percent. In nominal terms, it was weaker against the dollar in 1992 than it was at the end of 1987, at which time, even with the appropriate lags, there were a huge Japanese surplus and an enormous American deficit. But during the five years after 1987, cumulative Japanese inflation remained around 12 percent lower than American inflation, and Japanese productivity grew 10–12 percent faster than American productivity, further improving Japan's competitiveness. In real terms, just to keep the real yen-dollar rate at the 1987 level would have required an appreciation of approximately 20 percent of the nominal yen rate against the dollar—i.e., from 120–25 to the dollar to about 100 against the dollar.

There are also yen imbalances vis-à-vis European currencies. I am suggesting that there has been currently a generalized yen undervaluation, the result of which, of course, is the largest Japanese trade surplus ever. The bulk—if not all—of Japan's present economic growth is the result of its expanding trade surplus, not of growth in domestic demand. This scenario puts huge negative pressure on other countries and once again stimulates the kind of protectionist responses that have emerged in earlier, similar periods. For example, the U.S. auto industry and auto workers have demanded tight, comprehensive new quotas on auto imports—also covering the Japanese transplants here in the United States—based on the argument that three quarters of the U.S.-Japanese trade imbalance, which is again soaring, is in the automobile industry. This argument is obviously fallacious; I oppose it and hope President Clinton will oppose it. But it is also a reminder of the trade problems caused in part by currency relationships that are allowed to get out of hand.

In sum, I would say that we are in a period during which the major industrial countries—the Groups of Five and Seven—are trying to find a more effective international monetary system somewhere between pure fixity and unfettered flexibility. Some more or less successful experiments have already been launched: the Plaza Agreement, which certainly succeeded in realigning rates for a time, and the Louvre Accord, which had limited success but was premature and did not really get a fair trial. It remains to be seen whether we can find a more balanced and effective global monetary system in the 1990s. Finding such a system is very important for all countries, including developing countries and emerging market economies, because of the effect the system will have on world trade policy and growth, and especially on the future of an open global economy.

Michael Mussa

In terms of the general issue of exchange rate policy, the most important principle to understand is that it is not a separate dimension of economic policy. Rather, it is part of the constellation of economic policies—monetary policy in particular, but also to some extent fiscal and trade policy. It is impossible to maintain an exchange rate policy independent of the other key elements of economic policy. Fred Bergsten, I think, adopts the same point of view. He believes that policy commitments on exchange rates constrain the way a government conducts other economic policies. But there is also in Mr. Bergsten's view the idea that it is possible to have a meeting in the Hotel Okura and magically to appreciate the Japanese yen by 20–25 percent, without really doing anything else to any other element of U.S. or Japanese economic policy. There may in fact be times when a clear, forceful statement backed by a modest amount of intervention can move an exchange rate back toward the underlying economic fundamentals, as happened in the correction of the overvaluation of the dollar in the mid-1980s. There are also circumstances in which a tightening of monetary policy can take a big bubble out of asset prices, as the Japanese authorities have recently shown. But in general, to believe that there will be many opportunities to influence important economic variables without changing something fundamental and important about the main controls of economic policy is, in my view, a mistake.

In terms of exchange rate policies for different countries, the second important principle is "one size does not fit all." A constellation of monetary, fiscal, and exchange rate policies appropriate for one country or one group of countries is not necessarily appropriate for others. In this regard, several important differences between the economic circumstances of different countries influence the nature of exchange rate policies. The major industrial countries have open capital markets capable of mobilizing huge flows of resources when persuaded that what the authorities think may be the right exchange rate is not sustainable. The markets in these countries are thus able to place a very important constraint on the conduct of economic policies directed at influencing exchange rates. On the other hand, the degree of capital mobility relevant to many—though not all—developing countries is not nearly as great as it is for major industrial countries. The capacity to conduct an exchange rate policy that will not be disrupted by capital flows is somewhat different in countries whose capital markets are relatively insulated.

Another important distinction is that many developing countries do not have the same capacity as industrial countries to separate fiscal and monetary policy. For example, in the 1991 fiscal year, the United States was easily able to finance a $300 billion fiscal deficit, despite the fact that the M-2 grew at a very sluggish pace. In contrast, in many developing countries, the capacity to finance deficits domestically is closely connected to the conduct of monetary policy. Thus, a developing country that has a problem controlling its fiscal deficit will have a problem controlling credit and monetary aggregates, and that limitation can be an important constraint on domestic exchange rate policy. In this context, it is also worth noting the linkages that generally exist between structural policies and fiscal, monetary, and exchange rate policies in formerly centrally planned economies. The inability to harden the budget constraints of state enterprises that still dominate most of the formerly centrally planned economies has severely affected these countries' ability to maintain fiscal and monetary discipline, a weakness that is inevitably reflected in exchange rate policy. Again, I emphasize the second fundamental rule of exchange rate policy, "one size does not fit all." Exchange rate policy depends on both the nature of a country's economy and the constraints on domestic economic policy.

With that in mind, let me turn to some of Mr. Bergsten's remarks, which relate primarily to exchange rate policies for industrial countries. These remarks also apply to several developing countries whose internal financial markets are beginning to resemble those of the industrial countries.

First, Mr. Bergsten has emphasized the key link between exchange rate policy and trade policy—the desire to have an exchange rate system that will help maintain an open trading system. This objective, of course, is a fundamental principle embodied in the IMF Articles of Agreement. The idea behind this principle derives from the unfortunate experience of the interwar period. Competitive depreciations and other actions to stimulate employment, together with restrictive policies aimed at defending unrealistic exchange rates, contributed to a monumental collapse of world trade and economic activity. The objective of the Bretton Woods system was to move away from an exchange rate system that impeded the free movement of goods and resources toward an exchange rate system that supported the growth of world trade and, in turn, the prosperity of the world economy.

Mr. Bergsten maintains that efforts to fix exchange rates under the Bretton Woods system—and, more recently, under the exchange rate mechanism (ERM) of the European Monetary System—have proved injurious to trade and that in the end, both systems failed. But in fact, the Bretton Woods system functioned fairly successfully for at least 15 years, during a period when world trade and economic activity expanded very rapidly. The primary reason the Bretton Woods system collapsed was that beginning in the late 1960s, the anchor country (the United States) pursued monetary and fiscal policies inconsistent with the desires of some of the system's key participants. A similar problem has recently afflicted the ERM. Although the recent difficulties in the ERM have a variety of causes, and although many countries share responsibility within the system, the central problem (which has produced most of the tension within the system) has been the divergence between the policy mix pursued by the anchor country, Germany, and the domestic policy needs of some other members. For example, the United Kingdom experienced a two-year recession prior to the summer of 1992, and when an economy that has been in recession for two years is forced to raise its interest rates substantially to defend the exchange rate peg, the policy is not credible.

However, it should not be concluded from this experience that fixed exchange rates and adjustable peg systems always give rise to major policy tensions. For most of the period since its inception in 1979, the ERM has functioned reasonably well, reducing exchange rate turbulence among participants and facilitating convergence toward low inflation rates. The lesson from recent experience is that when major divergences do arise among the domestic policy needs of different participants in a pegged exchange rate system, it is important to recognize this fact and to make appropriate and timely adjustments.

On the other side of the coin, Mr. Bergsten suggests that the system of floating exchange rates among the world's major currencies has also failed to some extent. We certainly saw an extraordinary appreciation of the dollar in the early 1980s, particularly in 1984–85, as the dollar's value became detached from any credible notion of underlying economic fundamentals. However, I think it is a misreading of the economic history of the early 1980s not to recognize that an important part of this substantial appreciation was in fact desirable from the standpoint of the world economy. In the first two years of the U.S. economy's expansion after the 1980–82 recession, real domestic demand grew in the United States by 15 percent. Some 3.5 percentage points of that growth was pushed out through the deterioration of the U.S. trade balance and helped to propel a recovery from the recession in the rest of the world. This spur to global growth was not a bad thing in the early 1980s, although the dollar did appreciate excessively in 1983–84.

We need to ask, though, what else the United States could have done in the way of a policy response to the dollar appreciation in 1984, aside from having a meeting, making pronouncements, and doing a bit of intervention. It is useful to recall that during 1984, the Federal Reserve retightened U.S. monetary policy because of fears of a resurgence of inflationary pressures. That action clearly contributed to the dollar's further appreciation. In my judgment, however, it would have been a mistake for the Federal Reserve to continue with an expansionary policy that could only have increased worries about inflation and perhaps even fueled the resurgence the monetary authorities feared.

Further, Mr. Bergsten suggests that he and John Williamson invented target zones ten years ago. In fact, among the IMF documents from the initial period of floating in 1974 is an extensive memorandum from J. Marcus Fleming, then Deputy Director of the Research Department, describing a proposal to establish target zones for exchange rates among the major industrial countries. The idea was that the industrial countries, by adopting target zones for exchange rates, would simultaneously commit themselves to adjusting their underlying economic policies in order to keep exchange rates within those zones. At that time, the major industrial countries were not prepared to undertake such a commitment, and hence the target zone proposal died. However, I think the essential idea of Mr. Fleming's notion of target zones remains relevant. If these zones are to be meaningful, effective, and credible in the market, they need to be backed by a willingness to adjust underlying economic policies. The real issue is whether it is appropriate to divert economic policies from other objectives in order to use them to keep exchange rates within prescribed target zones.

Finally, Mr. Bergsten has observed that the yen is currently 20–25 percent undervalued. I think, however, that at its present level vis-à-vis the dollar, the yen is probably appropriately valued, given the savings and investment situations in the United States and Japan and the relative cyclical positions of the two economies. The United States is now beginning to rebound from the recession, but it is not yet apparent that the Japanese economy is beginning to recover convincingly from its slowdown in growth. It is natural in such circumstances for both the U.S. current account deficit and the Japanese current account surplus to enlarge somewhat. This enlargement of payments imbalances may well generate trade policy pressures and tensions in 1993 and beyond, particularly if Japan's current account surplus grows much beyond 3 percent of GNP. But such trade policy tensions are not necessarily—and especially not in this instance—a signal that the exchange rate is diverging far from its appropriate underlying equilibrium value, given both the relative cyclical positions of the two economies and the factors influencing their savings and investment positions over the long term.

Moreover, there is a practical difficulty with the proposal to reduce payments imbalances by inducing an appreciation of the yen. As the old proverb says, "No matter how much you wave your hands, you won't fly." What is to be done if the pronouncements do not produce the desired appreciation? What policy adjustments would have to be made to effect such an appreciation? Some people think fiscal policy can be manipulated to influence the exchange rate, and it is useful that the Japanese have undertaken a substantial fiscal package to strengthen domestic demand growth over the coming year. Perhaps this action is helping to push up the yen. I am not, however, particularly hopeful that fiscal policy is an easy way to manipulate the exchange rate. Monetary policy is generally the tool most readily at hand for influencing the exchange rate of a currency. It may be possible to appreciate the yen vis-à-vis the dollar through a further significant easing of U.S. policy. But with short-term interest rates in the United States at their lowest level since the mid-1960s and the economy beginning to show some strength in its recovery, I think it is very difficult to argue that it would be economically desirable, from a broader policy perspective, to further ease U.S. monetary policy at this stage. It would also be inappropriate to tighten monetary policy in Japan, lifting the official Japanese discount rate 2–3 percentage points to appreciate the yen. The Japanese stock market is now 50 percent below its peak, and raising Japan's short-term interest rates substantially at this point would probably push the economy into a deep recession that would be good for neither Japan nor the rest of the world.

For these reasons, I am much less assertive than Mr. Bergsten in saying that we ought to have a target zone system and commit underlying policies to the defense of those zones. We need to ask whether such policies might have a more important function than defending someone's idea of what the sustainable equilibrium exchange rate should be.

Summary of Discussion

Participants expressed support for efforts to coordinate economic policy in order to maintain medium-term exchange rate alignment and advocated using monetary policy to reduce short-term exchange rate volatility. Most participants agreed that the exchange rate was an important indicator and felt that when it appeared too far out of line with economic fundamentals, it should influence the conduct of monetary, fiscal, and even intervention policy. Transparency was also seen as key to effective exchange rate policy; among other things, a single exchange rate should be established for all current account transactions. However, participants did not believe that any one system could be the best choice for all countries. A country with a fixed rate system that had some credibility should maintain that regime, as switching to a crawl could create unnecessary problems. On the other hand, countries with high inflation rates that could not be reduced to approximate those of industrial countries might create serious problems for themselves by attempting to establish pegs.

Participants did not see that having the central bank intervene in the forward exchange market served any particular purpose. But in countries where the private sector had not developed such a market, central bank involvement could be justified.

A discussion of exchange rate policy in developing countries with economic characteristics similar to those in industrial countries touched on specific examples. Participants noted that if Mexico adopted a fixed exchange rate and kept it in place for a period of time, the rate would acquire some credibility and be able to withstand a terms of trade shock. However, a better way for Mexico to move to a fixed rate vis-à-vis the U.S. dollar might be to slow the rate of crawl to zero temporarily, but not to commit to a peg until credibility was established. On the other hand, because Chile's trade was much more diversified than Mexico's, it was less obvious that pegging the Chilean currency to the U.S. dollar would be appropriate at all.

The discussion then turned to the question of whether a country's exchange rate should be determined by a targeted current account balance. Participants were skeptical of this practice, since setting the exchange rate by this method would require information on variables—including price elasticities and the exchange rate link to the inflation rate—about which not enough was known. It was agreed that despite this shortage of information, target ranges could be set. Further, while participants agreed that identifying the correct exchange rate was impossible, they felt that a rate far from equilibrium could be identified, allowing authorities to recognize those times when corrective action might be needed.

The final point concerned the problem industrial countries' quota restrictions posed for developing countries. While quotas on products such as textiles and steel were viewed as a serious concern, participants were impressed by the success a number of East Asian countries had made despite these barriers. The view was expressed that while quotas (or similar trade barriers) were not an absolute impediment to successful development through a more open domestic trade strategy, they remained a problem. The consensus was that since many developing countries had unilaterally liberalized their trade regimes in the last several years, these countries in particular should be more vociferous in criticizing the industrial countries for their perceived backward movement on trade policy issues.

List of Participants*

Moderator

Chorng-Huey Wong
Assistant Director, IMF Institute
Washington

Authors

Anupam Basu
Senior Advisor, IMF Policy Development and Review Department
Washington

Guillermo Calvo
Senior Advisor, IMF Research Department
Washington

W. Max Corden
Professor, Johns Hopkins University School of Advanced
International Studies
Washington

Rüdiger Dornbusch
Professor, Massachusetts Institute of Technology
Cambridge, Massachusetts

Sebastian Edwards
Chief Economist, World Bank
Washington

Manuel Guitián
Associate Director, IMF Monetary and Exchange
Affairs Department
Washington

Steven B. Kamin
Staff Economist, Federal Reserve Board
Washington

Paul R. Masson
Assistant Director, IMF European I Department
Washington

---

*The titles and affiliations listed are those that were in effect at the time of the
seminar (December 1992).

294

Peter J. Quirk
Division Chief, IMF Monetary and Exchange Affairs Department
Washington

Carlos A. Végh
Economist, IMF Research Department
Washington

Commentators

C. Fred Bergsten
Institute for International Economics
Washington

Liam Patrick Ebrill
Division Chief, IMF European I Department
Washington

Leslie J. Lipschitz
Assistant Director, IMF African Department
Washington

Michael Mussa
Director, IMF Research Department
Washington

Saleh M. Nsouli
Assistant Director, IMF Middle Eastern Department
Washington

Lorenzo L. Perez
Assistant Director, Western Hemisphere Department
Washington

Thomas M. Reichmann
Assistant Director, IMF European I Department
Washington

Reinold H. van Til
Division Chief, IMF African Department
Washington

Discussants

Krzysztof Barburski
National Bank of Poland
Warsaw

Gérard Bélanger
Senior Advisor, IMF European I Department
Washington

John R. Dodsworth
Division Chief, IMF Central Asia Department
Washington

Mohamed A. El-Erian
Division Chief, IMF Middle Eastern Department
Washington

Martin J. Fetherston
Division Chief, IMF European I Department
Washington

Hans M. Flickenschild
Advisor, IMF Policy Development and Review Department
Washington

Anthony Lanyi
Deputy Director, IMF Institute
Washington

Claudio M. Loser
Deputy Director, IMF Western Hemisphere Department
Washington

Carlos Noriega
Secretariat of Finance and Public Credit of Mexico
Mexico City

John Odling-Smee
Director, IMF European II Department
Washington

Jiři Pospišil
Chief Executive Director, Czech National Bank
Prague

Peter Wickham
Division Chief, IMF Research Department
Washington

Thomas A. Wolf
Assistant Director, IMF European II Department
Washington

Participants

Imtiaz Ahmed
Director, State Bank of Pakistan
Karachi

Johnny Akerholm
Director, Bank of Finland
Helsinki

Samuel Kye Apea
Deputy Secretary, Ministry of Finance and Economic Planning
Accra

Daumantas Bernatonis
Assistant Governor, Bank of Lithuania
Vilnius
Charles Sydney Rodney Chuka
Director, Reserve Bank of Malawi
Lilongwe

Daniel Daco
Advisor, National Bank of Belgium
Brussels

Wolf-Dieter Donecker
Division Chief, Deutsche Bundesbank
Frankfurt

Guzman Nicolas Eyzaguirre
Director of Research, Central Bank of Chile
Santiago

Carlos Eduardo de Freitas
Head, Central Bank of Brazil
Brasilia

Yoshiya Gou
Deputy Director, Ministry of Finance
Tokyo

Kheuangkham Inthavong
Deputy Director, Bank of the Lao People's Democratic Republic
Vientiane

Maurice John Pette Kanga
Director, Central Bank of Kenya
Nairobi

P. B. Kulkarni
Executive Director, Reserve Bank of India
Bombay

Keun Yung Lee
Deputy Director, Bank of Korea
Seoul

Nikolay Vladimirovich Luzgin
Head, National Bank of Belarus
Minsk

Nadia Mohamed Hussein
Deputy General Manager, Central Bank of Egypt
Cairo

Ahmad Hasan Mustafa
Head, Central Bank of Jordan
Amman

Rezsö Nyers
Director, National Bank of Hungary
Budapest

Brian O'Reilly
Deputy Chief, Bank of Canada
Ontario

Abdelmalek Ouenniche
Central Director, Bank Al-Maghrib
Rabat

Gary Potts
First Assistant Secretary, Department of the Treasury
Australian Capital Territory

Pedro Pou
Second Vice President, Central Bank of the Republic of Argentina
Buenos Aires

Victor V. Rakov
Deputy Managing Director, Central Bank of the Russian Federation
Moscow

Alhaji M. R. Rasheed
Director, Central Bank of Nigeria
Lagos

Syahril Sabirin
Managing Director, Bank Indonesia
Jakarta

Galaye Seck
Director of Money and Credit, Ministry of Economy, Finance
and Planning
Dakar

Alexander N. Sharov
Deputy Chairman of the Board, National Bank of Ukraine
Kiev

Ebrahim Sheibani
  Vice Governor, Central Bank of the Islamic Republic of Iran
    Teheran

Ralph W. Smith, Jr.,
  Assistant Director, Board of Governors of the Federal
    Reserve System
    New York

B. Sh. Tadzhiyakov
  First Deputy Chairman, National Bank of Kazakhstan
    Alma-Ata

Germán Utreras
  Manager, Central Bank of Venezuela
    Caracas

Eugène Yai
  Director, Ministry of Economy, Finance, and Planning
    Abidjan